Eighteen Layers of Hell

Eighteen Layers of Hell

Stories from the Chinese Gulag

Kate Saunders

CASSELL

Cassell
Wellington House
125 Strand
London WC2R 0BB

127 West 24th Street
New York, NY 10011

First published 1996

British Library Cataloguing-in-Publication Data
A catalogue record for this book is available from the British Library.

Cover photographs taken from Harry Wu's video footage of the camps.
© Yorkshire Television. Courtesy of Harry Wu, Roger Finnegan and Tim Tate.

ISBN   0-304-33294-1 (hardback)
          0-304-33297-6 (paperback)

Typeset by Ben Cracknell Studios

Printed and bound in Great Britain by Biddles Ltd, Guildford and King's Lynn

Contents

CONTENTS

Foreword

No totalitarian rule can exist without a machinery of suppression to maintain its order. In addition to an elaborate judicial and administrative system, it needs a political theory to justify the operations of such a system. Nazi Germany, based on its *Herrenvolk* theory and National Socialism, established its immense concentration camp system. Likewise, Lenin and Stalin, on the theory of exterminating the exploiter classes and establishing the Communist revolution, organized a gulag system.

The Chinese Communist Party's labour-reform camp system is no different from that of the communist power in the former Soviet Union, in its political theory, brutality, violation of principles of humanism or the scale of its forced labour. Nevertheless, it does eclipse the Soviet gulag in the following two areas.

Firstly, production and economic results are highly stressed. Forced labour in the *laogai* camps plays an important role in China's national economy. It places great emphasis on effectiveness, profits and economic results that are standard norms in average enterprises. To strive for greater profits, the *laogai* camp system does all in its power to escalate from a primitive form of labour to that seen in modern enterprises.

Secondly, greater emphasis is placed on destroying the *laogai* inmates mentally and ideologically. The *laogai* camp system possesses a set of measures and methods of brainwashing, i.e. "thought reform". For the Chinese Communists, the aim is not to destroy a hostile element physically through violence, but to destroy him mentally and ideologically, while threatening him with violence. Thus, the "reformed" prisoners, deprived of freedom and dignity, but grateful for being allowed to exist, contribute their sweat and blood to their rulers, while those who "reformed" them are crowned with laurels of "socialist revolutionary humanism".

Some *laogai* survivors have written accounts of their experiences, but only a few. There are memoirs, like Jean Pasqualini's *Prisoner of Mao*, Nien Cheng's *Life and Death in Shanghai* and my own *Bitter Winds*. A few are academic research works on *laogai* camps, such as Jean-Luc Domenach's *China's Archipelago* and my *Laogai: The Chinese Gulag*. Kate Saunders views the *laogai* camps from a Western journalist's viewpoint. It is the first time that a Western journalist has so emotionally described the experiences of *laogai* survivors. The reader sees vividly the students in Tiananmen Square, Tibetan monks, counter-revolutionaries of early years and religious believers, as well as intellectuals. She gives a clear, complete picture which helps the Western reader comprehend the *laogai* and the Chinese Communist regime.

Memoirs of survivors portray only a small part of the thousands upon thousands of indescribable nightmares that have occurred in the People's Republic of China. They are so difficult to comprehend not only for Western journalists and readers, but for Chinese readers and writers as well, unless they experienced them body and soul. As the Chinese proverb says: "All bamboo on South Hill made into writing brushes, the crimes are too numerous to record; all squalls in East Sea drained, the evils are too rooted to eradicate."

It is my wish that Kate Saunders' book will provide the Western reader with a true understanding of the *laogai*. I believe that *Eighteen Layers of Hell: Stories from the Chinese Gulag* will be an important step on the road leading China towards democracy and freedom.

HARRY WU

Preface

Except for some familiar names such as Chiang Kai-Shek, the pinyin system for romanizing Chinese has been used throughout this book. This system has its origins in a system of romanization developed in south east Asia in the early 1930s and used later in parts of China. Pinyin itself was introduced by the Chinese in the 1950s, supplanting the older Wade-Giles system (in which 'Beijing' was known as 'Peking' for instance.) Generally the pinyin system is pronounced as it looks, with some exceptions: the 'q' is pronounced like 'ch', and the pinyin 'c' is pronounced like 'ts'. The pinyin system has been adopted by most international agencies and in journalism and academic texts.

Generally, metric Western systems of measurement and currency have been used. There are currently 15 *yuan* to a pound, although this value fluctuates according to the economic climate. A *mu* is a Chinese term representing 0.0667 hectares (or 0.16 of an acre).

Publishers and dates for books mentioned in the notes are given in the Bibliography.

I am indebted first of all to Harry Wu for inspiring this book and for blazing such a steady trail through frightening and tangled territory when he could have just bought a caravan in Wyoming and listened to Mozart. My thanks also go to Harry for his generosity in sharing his story with me. I am also indebted to the other former prisoners whose stories make up this book: Fung Je Mo, Liu Xinfu, Liu Shanqing, David Chou, Zhu Xiaodan, Liu Qing, Tang Boqiao, Zhang Xianliang, Palden Gyatso, Bagdro, and Han Dongfang. I would like to thank them all for their generosity, and for bringing their nightmares into the daylight once more for the sake of this book. Some of the former prisoners who helped me cannot be named in full owing to the precarious nature of their situation in Hong Kong. Suffice to say that I am grateful to Miss Zhang and also to the writer Mr Hu for their help, ideas and contacts. Thank you also to Ting Huang in Los Angeles for his able interpretation and his great help with follow-up phone calls and queries. Ugyen Norbu in London gave a vivid interpretation of my interview with Palden Gyatso (his mischievous grin always indicated that Palden had said something quite rude which he was too embarrassed to translate). I am particularly grateful to Mark Baber, who spent hours over many pints of lager telling me his story, even though he has a book of his own to write. Mark's courage, resourcefulness and good humour were inspiring and provided an invaluable contribution to this book.

I would also like to thank the following people: Katherine Baber and Isobel Kelly at Amnesty International; Philip Baker and Bing Sum Lau; Robbie Barnett, for his astute judgements; Sue Byrne; Chen Ching-lee; Anthony Chiu; Jeff Fieldler; Robert Ford; Paul Foreman; Louise Fournier, for her sterling work on chain-hoists and thoughtful support; Leslie Gardner; Lia Genovese; Jane Greenwood, my editor; Jie Quan Sue; Annie Knibbs; Maysoon Pachachi; the Medical Foundation for Victims of Torture; Keith Morris, for his practical and abstract help; Robin Munro; Tsering Shakya; Jimmy Wang; Max Wooldridge; Xiao Qiang of Human Rights in China; and the Society of Authors, for enabling me to complete important research in Hong Kong.

Acknowledgements

The author and publisher wish to thank the following for permission to reprint copyright material. Although every effort has been made to contact the owners of the copyright material reproduced in this book, it has not been possible to trace all of them. If such owners contact the publisher, the appropriate acknowledgements will appear in any future editions.

Jack Bevan, for a line from 'Winter night' by Salvatore Quasimodo, published in *Modern European Poets* (Penguin, 1965), p.74. Reprinted by permission of the translator.

Brian Keenan, from *An Evil Cradling*, published by Vintage, 1992. Reprinted by permission of the author.

Introduction

There is no written language in the Archipelago and oral communication is broken off when people die . . . Only random particles of that struggle have occasionally come down to us, illuminated by moonlight that is indirect and indistinct.[1]

It is the nightmare of prisoners that no one will believe them. This nightmare is the reason why a frail, elderly monk struggled across the Himalayas from Tibet to safety, carrying a small monk's pouch full of smuggled handcuffs, electric batons and knives.[2] It is the reason why a former prisoner risked his life, freedom and happiness to return again and again to the country he had escaped years before. And it is one of this reasons why the experiences of imprisonment featured in the following pages are so compelling.

This book is about former prisoners of the Chinese *laogai*, or 'reform through labour' system. Since the foundation of the People's Republic of China in 1949, more than thirty million people have disappeared within the bamboo gulag.

Perhaps the most shocking aspect of the Chinese *laogai*, which is the world's biggest system of forced labour, is that it is still in existence. Six to eight million people in China today are forced to carry out hard labour in camps across the country, while millions more are held for years without trial in detention centres and prisons, or for re-education through labour institutions. Torture is routine within the camps, and administered as punishment for those who do not meet work quotas. The execution rate is double that of the rest of the world put together.

New evidence shows that since Mao Zedong founded the People's Republic of China, he was in some way responsible for at least forty million deaths and perhaps eighty million or more. This includes deaths he was directly responsible for and deaths resulting from disastrous policies he refused to change. This figure includes the deaths of those held in forced labour camps.[3] In comparison, Hitler is blamed for twelve million concentration camp deaths and at least thirty million other deaths associated with World War II, while Stalin is believed to be responsible for between thirty million and forty million 'unnatural deaths' following purges and a famine created by collectivization.

In their immensity these statistics seem almost incomprehensible in human terms. Perhaps the only way that we can encompass the tragedy and the horror is through the stories of individuals rather than statistical abstractions.

The voices of Anne Frank, Primo Levi and Alexander Solzhenitsyn have opened up our concepts of suffering, life and death in this century. Until recently, however, there have been few corresponding voices from China. Until only ten or fifteen years ago, intellectuals, writers and others in China remained silent about the scale of their suffering in labour camps and political purges. This dearth of personal testimony does not indicate a lack of evidence for the existence of the *laogai* and fallout from Mao's political campaigns. On the contrary, it means the evidence is even stronger – as the silence points to the efficiency of a system which suppresses criticism from within by laying claim to every corner of the human mind, from the unconscious to self-consciousness.

Some of these voices speak through this book. Through their stories, it is possible to gain an insight into the emotional pain of imprisonment and torture behind the statistics. It is one thing to know how many died of famine during the 'three lean years' in 1959-62. It is quite another to know that when a starving man eats twenty ears of not fully ripened corn, he dies of 'bloating up', and his shirt and trousers look like the skin of a toad that has been burst open by a swollen belly, as novelist Zhang Xianliang graphically describes in his semi-autobiographical book *Grass Soup*.[4] Similarly, it is one thing to digest the statistics of the number of men who died in labour camps from hunger and exhaustion, and quite another to know exactly *how* a man dies of hunger and exhaustion. Sometimes he literally forgets to breathe and dies by a slow atrophying which finally exhibits itself in a kind of 'death mask'. (His skin turns a dull, dark colour, the mucus of his eyes increases, and his preternaturally bright eyes gaze on the world with the so-called 'thousand-mile stare'.)

All of the Chinese interviewed for this book now live in exile – with one exception, the writer Zhang Xianliang. Sometimes their pain is focused in anger: against the Communist Party, or against the world for acknowledging the full horror of the Holocaust and the Stalinist gulag, but not caring about the Chinese *laogai*. Often they experience a profound sense of separation and isolation from others who have not shared a similar ordeal.

Despite the dehumanizing structure and regime of the labour camps, all the prisoners who passed through the system describe the humanity of men and women who refused to be crushed and destroyed. This humanity is often present in small, seemingly insignificant incidents. One prisoner said:

> Once when I was in the Transit Centre folding book leaves – and I was one of the slowest – a guy behind me, a poor, ordinary, worker, saw a louse on my shoulder and took the time from his folding to crush it for me. He didn't have to do that. He knew my background, but he didn't hold it against me. I was so grateful to him I could have cried.[5]

To survive at all brings its own pain. As Holocaust survivor Elie Wiesel once said, 'I live and therefore I am guilty. I am still here because a friend, a comrade, an unknown died in my place.' An awareness of those who were lost gnaws at the hearts of those who survived the Chinese camps.

We often forget that the statistics of those held in labour camps today can be multiplied by at least two or three to take into account the suffering of their families. For some mothers, fathers, husbands, wives or sisters the moment of arrest is just as real, just as raw as it was to their loved one. And, even after years have passed, they still remember it with complete clarity. Tears still well up in Jie Quansue's eyes when she recalls the day her father was taken away. As a child, Jie used to wait beside the door for her father to come home for work every day. He would always arrive at 7.30 p.m., in time for supper. One day he didn't return. Jie waited for three hours beside the door, refusing to eat and sleep. Her father didn't come home for more than twenty years (see Plate 1). Today Jie and her family live in a pleasant suburb of Los Angeles, in a house cluttered with children's toys and the raw materials for Jie's jewellery business. After his release from the *laogai*, her father was given permission to join them in the USA. He is now a treasured grandfather, who never tires of being with his daughter's young children.

Solzhenitsyn referred to 'the first unfamiliar letter home' of a man who had been 'plowed over by interrogation', reporting that he hadn't been shot. 'At home, they continued to remember him as he had been, but he would never be that person again.'[6] Imprisonment in the *laogai* changes a person entirely. To survive entails playing the game; and the individual is inevitably changed by the game.

Today in China millions of prisoners carry out back-breaking work from sunrise until sunset to fuel the country's economic miracle. Although camp authorities claim that labour camp products are not exported, investigations by the Laogai Research Foundation run by Harry Wu, a former *laogai* prisoner, and human rights groups prove otherwise. Some prisoners work waist-deep in vats of stinking toxic chemicals; others carry out dangerous work on nuclear sites or underground excavating coal. Still others create artificial flowers for export or make Christmas tree lights and toys which are sold in British shops. It is indefensible that, among the gold rush of investment in mainland China at present, a blind eye is turned to the lives of those entrapped within the money-making machine. Within the context of the global market and resulting social and cultural involvement, our lives in the West are now entangled with the fate of these prisoners.

Milan Kundera once wrote, 'The struggle of man against power is the struggle of memory against forgetting'. The awareness that those in the outside world might one day listen to their stories gave many of the former prisoners interviewed in this book a purpose in living, when death was often preferable. For years they endured a terrible silence: a lack of contact with the outside world and their families, or even long periods in solitary confinement. Today their voices should be heard above the clamour of China, the awakening giant.

Notes

1. Alexander Solzhenitsyn, *The Gulag Archipelago*, vol. 1, p. 461.

2. Palden Gyatso's story is told in Chapter 13.

3. The figure of eighty million 'unnatural deaths' – most of them in the famine following the Great Leap Forward – was given by the Tigaisuo (System Reform Institute), led by Zhao Ziyang, the deposed Communist Party chief, in the 1980s (source: Valerie Strauss and Dan Sutherland, *Washington Post*, 17 July 1994).

4. Zhang Xianliang, *Grass Soup*, p. 200.

5. Jean Pasqualini, *Prisoners of Mao*, p. 214.

6. Solzhenitsyn, *The Gulag Archipelago*, vol. 2, p. 549.

EIGHTEEN LAYERS OF HELL: STORIES FROM THE CHINESE GULAG IS DEDICATED TO MY FAMILY: PETER, SHEILA, ANNA AND PATRICK SAUNDERS, AND TO THE MEMORY OF JOE MCEVOY.

CHAPTER 1

Beneath the Iron Crust
China's *Laogai* System

> *Dawn, and our train will soon arrive;*
> *The deadly silence of the prison cars arrests all noise.*
> *All but the fearful, restless clanking of the wheels . . .*
> *From the windows, glimpsed in the dark night,*
> *Black snowflakes flutter over the wilderness.*

Tang Qi[1]

Millions of Chinese have made a similar dark journey. They have been forced to travel to the great deserts past the Demon Gate Pass, where breath freezes into ice in winter and snowstorms smother the body; to the northern desert of Takelamagan, which means in Uygur 'those who go in don't come out'; and to nuclear installations in the wastelands of Qinghai and Xinjiang. Others have endured torture and the unceasing grind of production lines in prisons and detention centres in towns and cities. From the moment they are taken, these prisoners' lives are no longer their own.

When someone in China disappears, their family says they have gone for *laogai*, reform through labour.[2] The *laogai* consists of a vast network of prisons and labour camps stretching across the length and breadth of the People's Republic – from Manchuria in the north to Hainan in the south, from Shanghai in the east to Tibet in the west. It is the largest system of its kind in the world, and the number of prisoners who have disappeared within it may be as high as forty to fifty million.

The Chinese government has admitted to the existence of 684 'reform through labour' centres, 155 prisons, 492 rehabilitation centres (including both administrative 'labour re-education camps' and 'women's re-education' centres) and 37 social reintegration centres for juvenile offenders. And that includes only the facilities for sentenced criminals administered by the Ministry of Justice. Pre-trial detention centres of all

1

types, including jails (*kanshousuo*), 'shelter for investigation centres' (*shourong shencha suo*) and police lock-ups at county, district and neighbourhood levels number several thousand. The People's Liberation Army also administers a separate network of several dozen large prison camps in the far north-western region of Xinjiang.[3] Labour camps are not just confined to one region; they are situated throughout the entire land mass. Prison camps and detention centres are sited in every major city as well as all Chinese provinces, and new camps are still being built to carry out vast industrial and agricultural projects in remote wasteland areas of 'China's Siberia', Xinxiang and Qinghai (Plates 2a, 2b).

Since the foundation of the People's Republic of China in 1949, an estimated thirty to fifty million prisoners have died from starvation, exhaustion, disease or torture in the *laogai*. Others have been beaten to death or 'suicided' (Chinese legal jargon for murder that implies responsibility on the part of the victim), and buried in mass unmarked graves. An estimated ten to sixteen million prisoners still work on the grim production lines of farms, factories and prison camps, or are held for years without trial in detention or shelter centres. Some six to eight million are forced to carry out hard labour.[4]

In the 1950s, 90 per cent of the prisoners in labour reform camps were counter-revolutionaries (*fangeming fenzi*). According to a Public Security Bureau document issued in 1985, the number of counter-revolutionaries in the *laogai* today is 10 per cent of the total population.[5] This total includes historic counter-revolutionaries: those who served in the Guomindang regime at any level before the Communist defeat of the Nationalists in 1949.[6] Although China has consistently denied the existence of political prisoners, it does admit the presence of 'counter-revolutionaries' in its jails, and is currently the only country in the world that has specific counter-revolutionary crime provisions written into its legal system.

One of the most chilling aspects of the system is the retention of prisoners at the camp after their sentences have ended (*juiye*). This practice bears some similarity to the Soviet practice of internal exile for prisoners who have completed their sentences, but, if anything, the Chinese version is even more harsh. Ex-prisoners in the Soviet Union are generally required to settle in the administrative district in which their camp is located. In China, however, 'forced job placement' prisoners are simply assigned to another work team, under the same military authority as before, and often in the same camp.[7] One of the only differences is that they are now paid a small wage. In return, a prisoner is expected to continue to 'acknowledge your crimes, reform your way of thinking, and labour hard for your own good and for the good of all the state'.

Forced job placement is, in effect, an unofficial life sentence. Harry Wu claims that the number of such prisoners has increased to the point that certain labour camps are composed entirely of FJP personnel. For example, before 1970 Wangya coal mine in Huoxian county, Shanxi province, accommodated convicted labour reform personnel; after 1970 it was composed entirely of forced job placement personnel. Shanghai's Xinsheng Construction Company is a similar example.

The forced job placement camps have a dual purpose. They prevent the people most likely to be against the regime after experiencing the labour camps from returning to society. They also provide a valuable pool of cheap labour to develop agricultural and industrial sites, to reclaim wasteland and to maintain productivity in factories.

The labour reform system in China is divided into three distinct categories: convicted labour reform (*laogai*), re-education through labour (*laojiao*) and forced job placement (*juiye*). Organizational units include prisons (*jianyu*), which are usually located near large and medium-sized cities, juvenile facilities and detention centres.

Relocation to a labour camp is often an attractive option for prisoners who are flung into detention centres following their arrest. 'One month in a detention centre,' said one, 'is equal to a year of labour reform.'[8] Former inmates describe cramped, squalid cells crawling with giant cockroaches which swarm over the body at night, and lice which burrow deep into one's clothing. The main purpose of the detention centres is to house criminals who have not yet been sentenced; criminals who have sentences of under two years may also serve their full term in detention centres. All prisoners, whether sentenced or not, are required by law to engage in forced labour.[9] The population of detention centres in China fluctuates according to various political movements promoted by the government, which may not always meet with the support of the people.

Many inmates of detention centres have been imprisoned under the 'shelter and investigation' scheme, which allows local authorities to make arbitrary arrests and imprisonment sometimes for up to ten years.[10] The police employed 'shelter and investigation' to detain many of the people who had participated in the Tiananmen Square demonstrations in 1989 and the 5th April Movement of 1976.

Conditions in a typical detention centre (in Huangpu district, Shanghai) were described by a Hong Kong businessman who was imprisoned in 1986:

The first horror of the Huangpu detention centre was sleeping. Thirteen or fourteen prisoners were crowded into a cell about three square metres in area. In the daytime there was room to sit with our legs drawn up, bodies touching. But at night we would be squeezed into two rows of straight bodies, with the rows head to head so as to fit more tightly together, like a row of frozen yellow fish. Even then there might not be room for everybody. In that case guards would beat the prisoners with bamboo truncheons and trample them with their boots to squeeze them into the line of sleepers. They called this 'bamboo grill'.

In the winter, the prisoners could hardly breathe. In the summer it was worse. Each man wore only a pair of pants, but he was soaked with sweat. When we got up in the morning, the cement floor was covered with a pool of sweat half a centimetre deep and the prisoners' backsides were covered with swollen bedsores which hurt and formed scabs that bonded their pants to their bodies. As soon as you stood up to use the toilet the scabs would tear and your pants would be covered with blood.[11]

Every detention centre has its own rules, some of which are set by wardens. In the Huangpu district detention centre, the local rules are that inmates are forbidden to talk to each other, are not allowed to close their eyes for more than three seconds during the day, are not allowed to move or change from sitting or standing without permission and are forbidden to make any noise.[12]

One of the primary functions of the detention centres is to force prisoners to confess to their crimes, and for this reason interrogation is more severe than in either prisons or labour reform camps. Even after confessions are made, however, prisoners can still remain in detention centres. Prisoners whose fate is still undecided by authority can remain there for years.

Juvenile offenders who are under 18 are kept in juvenile detention centres organized on military lines throughout China, and are forced to labour like other prisoners. The minimum age for execution in China is 18; however, if the state wishes to execute a boy of 16, it will give him a suspended death sentence for two years, and then shoot him when he reaches 18. The failings of the parents are often emphasized by policy-makers pontificating on the causes of juvenile crime and keen to absolve the state and society from any responsibility in the development of the criminal. In their confessions, juveniles often conform to this convention – encouraged by their interrogators – by interpreting their crimes in this way too. One 19-year-old criminal who was sentenced to death apparently wrote the following letter to his parents:

I have committed murder. I have disappointed and brought suffering to those still living. My only regret is that ever since I was born, you have pestered me so much that I developed a wild nature, which has brought about my downfall. I hope that after my death, you will be stricter with my younger brothers and sisters, so as to forestall a further tragedy.[13]

High-profile criminals and dissidents are often held in prisons because of the tighter security. A secret network of prisons throughout the country, for instance the infamous Q1 near Beijing – described as the 'twentieth-century Bastille' by Wei Jingsheng – houses 13 per cent of the country's criminals according to internal Chinese Communist Party documents. A document states:

> *Prisons will house criminals sentenced to death with a two-year reprieve; counter-revolutionaries sentenced to life terms or terms of over five years; common criminals sentenced to terms of over ten years; and special cases such as spies, foreign criminals, criminals with knowledge of classified material, and female criminals.*[14]

According to these internal documents collected by Harry Wu, 87 per cent of criminals are confined to labour reform disciplinary production camps.[15] They are organized along military lines, with prisoners divided into squadrons, companies, battalions, detachments and general brigades.

The rationale behind re-education through labour (*laojiao*) is

> *to create a level between peace-keeping management and legal sentencing . . . to bridge the gap between light and serious offences by creating a closely-knit, reasonable three-layered system . . . Reform through labour will allow us to avoid complicated judicial procedures . . . and serve a useful function in allowing a swift response to societal threats.*[16]

In reality prisoners being 're-educated through labour' are organized on the same military lines as other labour reform prisoners; the styles and methods of labour production are also exactly the same.

Torture is routine in all sections of the *laogai* system, and is used against both political and common criminal prisoners. The ones most likely to be ill-treated are the less educated or less privileged such as the unemployed, vagrants, workers or peasants. They do not have the social status, economic means or political connections to protect them. There are fewer reports of torture and ill-treatment in detention of people of high social standing, such as Communist Party officials or prominent intellectuals whose names are known in the West.[17]

Throughout Chinese history, individual rights have always been sacrificed to the 'greater good': harmony and order as opposed to chaos. Harry Wu points out that the Rodney King case, in which a black man with a bad criminal record was beaten up after speeding by Los Angeles police and awarded millions of dollars in compensation, could never have happened in China: 'People would say, "Why, the police are not stupid, the judges are not stupid – this is a bad guy! Why would taxpayers pay three million to him?" And I would say: you have to know that he is an individual, he is alone, and hence the government should not violate his human rights.'

This fear of *luan*, or chaos, lies at the heart of the institution of the labour camps. In order to preserve harmony, society must be rid of 'bad elements', from criminals to counter-revolutionaries, and from mentally handicapped people to murderers. Under Mao, locking up these unsavoury elements was not enough. Inmates of the *laogai* also had to be changed from within, thus ensuring ultimate obedience to the state. Political power does not only grow from the barrel of a gun. It begins with the capture of the mind and the crushing of the human spirit.

While the scale and cruelty of the Soviet gulag and the Chinese *laogai* are similar, the main difference between the two is the concept of 'thought reform' refined by the Chinese Communist Party. The defining idea behind the *laogai* was the possibility of personal transformation in the interests of the ruling party. The idea was originally taken from Soviet Russia, which wanted to produce a new kind of person through labour and discipline. The Soviet labour camps had been founded in the period from 1917 to 1921; Russian regulations mirrored the overblown and overbearing legal jargon and approach used by Chinese policy-makers, for instance in their 1961 'Decrees for Strengthening the Struggle with Social Parasites Who Avoid Beneficial Labour and lead Anti-Social Lives'. But the Chinese took the concept of struggle with 'social parasites' further and more seriously.

When Mao took over in 1949, he had the advantage of a feeling of goodwill from 'the masses' for having united the country after years of civil war. He exploited this advantage to the full, gathering more support by emphasizing the revolutionary character of the Chinese as a whole. He believed that years of poverty and backwardness were an advantage for a new revolutionary republic. He said:

> China's 600 million people have two remarkable peculiarities; they are, first of all, poor, and secondly, blank. That may seem like a bad thing, but it is really a good thing. Poor people want change, want to do things, want revolution. A clean sheet of paper has no blotches, and so the newest and most beautiful words can be written on it, the newest and most beautiful pictures can be painted on it.[18]

The Party, of course, was the poet and the artist, filling the blank sheets of the people.

While life in Siberia was inhumane, ultimately prisoners still had the freedom to think and exchange ideas. In China, this freedom has been denied, leading to an even greater isolation and loneliness for the individual prisoner. In his novel *Getting Used to Dying*, about the psychological effects of this remoulding in labour camps (particularly during the Cultural Revolution), Zhang Xianliang wrote:

[This kind of investigation] is something excruciating: we who were investigated had to link our lives together, conversation by conversation, sentence by sentence. And we had to remember each sentence as though it had been given a serial number. Otherwise we would soon be attending our own funerals, or at the very least being viciously beaten. This training drilled into me the ability to write. The person who is investigating is responsible for drawing out the life story of the person being investigated. The one being investigated must therefore continually try to concoct his own life. He must relate, for example, what his conversation was with such and such a person and at such and such a time . . . The process is like both reading and writing a novel. This strict exercise has given China many modern Shakespeares.

In China, thought reform became the basis for the consolidation of the Communist dictatorship. 'Our *laogaidui* system constitutes an important part of our public security system,' an internal Chinese Communist Party document declared in 1985.[19] 'It is one of the tools of the dictatorship of the proletariat; it serves to punish and reform all counter-revolutionaries and other criminals.'

In 1989, the Party used similar language in justifying its arrest of thousands of students, workers and citizens who had taken part in the Tiananmen Square democracy movement both in Beijing and across the country. On 17 October of that year, the Ministry of Justice publicly praised 'National Ministry of Justice collectives outstanding in preventing chaos and controlling violence'. The announced list contained 52 work units, 30 of which were labour reform camps, including Hainan Island's Qionghai prison and Xinjiang Uygur Autonomous Region's Number One prison – indicating that arrests were not confined to Beijing. In May 1989, weeks before the bloody crackdown in the square, the media had reported that many prisons in the Beijing area were transferring prisoners out of the region in order to be able to accommodate students and protesters.

The Communist regime has established a thought reform system on a national scale that reaches into every area of society, from nursery schools to the higher echelons of industry and business. It is a system which uses secrecy, isolation from the outside world, spreading of superstition, repetition of lies, distortion of truth and other similar methods not just to obtain the populace's blind obedience but to inspire in them a willingness to follow the Communist Party and believe in socialism.[20]

In China today, thought reform is a less effective weapon for ensuring the submission of prisoners and the population to the state. This is because of the breakdown of the people's belief and faith in Communism, which is partly a natural historical progression and partly a result of the economic opening up of China and influx of Western ideas and ideals. The 'lost generation' – those who are now in their thirties and forties and who were most affected by the Cultural Revolution and its aftermath – has suffered intense disillusionment with the Party. Millions of them served long sentences in labour camps, or had to endure years of back-breaking work and constant self-criticism after being 'sent down' to the countryside. They witnessed, and participated in, purges against families and friends, and the replacement of trust with suspicion.

Many of those from the 'lost generation' are now filling prison cells once more. Increasingly in today's China the disempowered and the disenfranchised have turned to crime; money has become the replacement for ideology, and the lack of personal morals fostered by the upheaval of the Cultural Revolution is a perfect breeding ground for corruption.

An anti-crime drive which began in Auust 1983,[21] led to a doubling of the population in the labour camps. A report issued by the Central Commission on Politics and Law stated that, in the first five months of the campaign, 1,027,000 criminals had been arrested on charges of homicide, arson, robbery, rape and hooliganism; 975,000 had been prosecuted, 861,000 sentenced, including 24,000 sentenced to death. (This figure probably includes those sentenced to death with a two-year reprieve.) According to the same report, 687,000 new prisoners entered labour reform, and 169,000 labour re-education.[22] This was said to be the largest sweep of criminal offenders since the 1950 campaign against counter-revolutionaries.

Many of these offenders received harsh sentences for comparatively minor crimes. Women in particular were often convicted for dubious 'sexual offences'. Mark Baber, a 33-year-old Oxford graduate who was imprisoned in Shanghai Number One municipal jail for nearly four years, was told of a woman held in the same prison complex who was serving a four-year sentence for having sexual relations with two men and telling each of them that she loved him.

A secret directive issued on 25 August 1983 by the Central Committee of the Chinese Communist Party revealed how counter-revolutionaries were still an important enemy in the crackdown against crime.

Previously, the campaign was thought to have been aimed at criminals such as murderers, arsonists and rapists. But the confidential document, obtained by Asia Watch[23] lists a 'seventh category' of those to be included in the campaign, namely 'active counter-revolutionary elements who write counter-revolutionary slogans, fliers, liaison messages and anonymous letters'. The Party document explains: 'The seven types of criminal elements should be dealt resolute blows and given severe and prompt punishment . . . Those requiring severe punishment must be sentenced heavily, and those who deserve to die must be executed.'[24]

The *laogai* system has always been a mirror of social conditions in China beyond the barbed war. During the three-year famine from 1959 to 1961, prisoners and citizens alike died of starvation; sometimes peasants even broke into the labour camps for food, convinced that the supply would at least be more regular. The intensity of thought reform and purges within the camps reflected the political campaigns outside during the Cultural Revolution. And during the 1989 democracy movement at Tiananmen, controls within some prisons were relaxed as both guards and prisoners shared an optimism about the future.

Today, the increasing levels of violence and lack of effectiveness of 'ideological remoulding' in the camps reflect the disorder and changing values in the world outside. The transformation of the *laogai* into money-making operations run without state subsidy is another reflection of the economic fervour that now grips China in the wake of Deng Xiaoping's 'socialist modernization'.

China's system of labour reform is rooted in Communist tradition: prisoners like the French-Chinese Jean Pasqualini grew the rice that Mao ate;[25] others were responsible for reclaiming and transforming the vast Manchurian wastelands. Other convicts began China's plastic industry, run its great chemical and agricultural installations, and have developed the country's nuclear industry.

However, the gulag system has become an increasingly important part of the country's developing economy. Deng Xiaoping justifies the increased emphasis on production in the *laogai* in political terms:

> *Under the present conditions, using the suppressive force of our nation to attack and disintegrate all types of counter-revolutionary bad elements, anti-party anti-socialist elements and serious criminal offenders in order to preserve public security is entirely in accord with the demands of the people and with the demands of socialist modernisation construction.*[26]

The multi-million-dollar rush to invest in mainland China by companies across the world has marginalized concern for the abuses of human rights in China's *laogai* system. As trade increases, so does the demand for products made with a stable supply of labour; better still, at 'zero labour cost'. The *China Labour Bulletin* reports that the cost of producing a ton of coal in state-owned mines was US$37, while in a labour camp the same amount could be mined for $2.5. Labour costs in forced labour camps are at least ten to twenty per cent lower than in other factories.[27]

The lack of general knowledge about the *laogai* system has contributed to the unwillingness of investors to face what is hidden beneath the 'iron crust'[28] of the Chinese archipelago. Although the miseries of the Soviet gulag are well known and have been documented by such conscientious witnesses as Alexander Solzhenitsyn, Irina Ratushinskaya and Anatoly Marchenko, the existence of the Chinese gulags has not yet been entirely accepted in the West. The reason is a combination of factors including the conspiracy of the *ancien régime* in Beijing and the complicity. of the West.

The conspiracy of silence in China begins with a classification of all documents about the *laogai* as state secrets (much of the material in this book would be classified as such). It continues with a careful monitoring of published material. Over the past forty years, no national or local newspaper, magazine or government document in mainland China has reported on the total number of prisoners and the relationship between production in the *laogai* and trade with the West, except as isolated examples featuring individual camps or provinces.[29] Any Chinese journalist or writer who attempted to uncover the truth about the camps and their involvement in trade with the West would be forced to spend time in one of them.

Another explanation for our ignorance of the 'bamboo gulag' is the silence of Chinese intellectuals on the subject. Part of this disinclination is caused by a desire for their country not to 'lose face'. When Mao's doctor Li Zhusui revealed the secrets of the Chairman's sex life and his fondness for several concubines at a time, even some tough-minded dissidents were embarrassed. And since the foundation of the People's Republic, writers and artists have adopted a stringent self-censorship to save themselves from imprisonment, torture and execution. This tendency still runs deep in the bones of Chinese intelligentsia. Zhang Xianliang, Zhang Jie, Wu Ningkun, Wang Ruowang, Gu Hua and notably Harry Hongda Wu, who has dedicated his life to exploring the theme, are some of the few intellectuals whose writings and memoirs are infused with their experiences in the *laogai* camps.

So, if the West is not yet ready to accept the reality of the *laogai*, then perhaps neither are the Chinese themselves. Perhaps it is only a question of time. Harry Hongda Wu, who spent nineteen years in the *laogai*, says:

'After Stalin died in 1953, Solzhenitsyn wrote a book on the Gulag Archipelago. The first copies were smuggled out to Paris around 1960. Eventually, in 1974, 21 years after Stalin's death, he won the Nobel Prize for a story mainly focusing on the 1930s and some of the 1940s.'[30] Similarly, although 'black books' were being smuggled out of the Nazi concentration camps, many people did not confront the truth until the camps were liberated and the archives opened in 1945.

Notes

1. Tang Qi, *Dawn in the Great Northern Wilderness*, extracts in Geremie Barmie and John Minford (eds), *Seeds of Fire: Chinese Prisoners of Conscience* p. 68.

2. *Laogaidui* is a political term invented by the Chinese Communist Party when they first came to power. It means, literally, 'labour reform team' in Chinese, and refers to a labour reform camp or prison under the control of the CCP Public Security Ministry. Harry Wu notes that during the Cultural Revolution the meaning of the term was broader: it also meant 'cowsheds', 'May 7 cadre schools' and 'bases for the sent-down' founded by all levels of party organizations, Red Guards and rebels (Harry Wu, *Laogai*, p. 6). Except during this period, the term *laogaidui* refers to labour reform camps under the auspices of Public Security and the judiciary. The term *laogai*, meaning simply 'reform through labour', is used throughout this book.

3. The Chinese 1993 reply to the UN Committee Against Torture, quoted in the Asia Watch report, *Detained in China and Tibet* (1994), p. xxiv. The People's Liberation Army, the official fighting force of China, began as the Red Army, which was famous for its guerilla warfare during the years of struggle before the Communist 'Liberation' of China in 1949. Today it is a modern military organization of more than three million soldiers.

4. These statistics are estimates by Harry Wu, Director of the Laogai Research Foundation and former *laogai* prisoner (see Chapter 7), based on information contained in internal Chinese documents, testimony from former prisoners and an inside knowledge of the system. A full explanation of how he arrives at these statistics is given in his book *Laogai: The Chinese Gulag*. He reaches the total number of those who have disappeared in the *laogai* camps since 1949, for instance, by adding up the numbers of those imprisoned during various purges and political campaigns. Most of these figures are available in official Chinese documents, although they tend to be an underestimatation to say the least. Wu reaches the figure of ten to sixteen million prisoners in the camps today by adding the known prison populations of detention centres, juvenile offender centres, labour re-education camps and so on in each province of China. He also makes estimates of prison population and numbers of penal institutions where documentation is unavailable. Wu's statistics have been disputed as too high by some. However, his research on the system, including details of more than a thousand labour camps, is the most thorough and wide-ranging currently available.

5. Wu, *Laogai*, p. 51.

6. In the 1950s, 50 to 60 per cent of the prisoners in the *laogai* belonged to this category, totalling about ten million in all (*ibid.*, p. 24).

7. Steven W. Mosher, *Made in the Chinese Laogai: China's Use of Prisoners to Produce Goods for Export.*

8. Anne Thurston, *A Chinese Odyssey.*

9. *PSB Regulations of the People's Republic of China, 1950-1979* (Beijing: Legal Press, 1980), article 8, quoted in Wu, *Laogai.*

10. The journal *People's Public Security* (*Renmin Gong'an*), no. 7 (1989), p. 18, reported that the number of 'sheltered' people was 1.5 million in 1988.

11. Amnesty International.

12. *Human Rights in China, Detained at Official Pleasure: Arbitrary Detention in the People's Republic of China*, 4 June 1993.

13. Shao Daosheng, *A Preliminary Study of China's Juvenile Delinquency*, p. 110. The author is director of the Criminal Remoulding Psychological Professional committee of the Chinese Law of Reform Through Labour Society. It is difficult to establish whether the letter is genuine, as no further details are given.

14. Wu, *Laogai*, p. 5, note 16.

15. *Ibid.*, p. 8.

16. 'Re-education Through Labour Is Our National Unique Public Security System', *Legal Quarterly*, Southwest Political Science and Law Institute (April 1983), pp. 29-30, quoted in Wu, *Laogai*, p. 10.

17. Amnesty International, *Torture in China*, ASA 17/55/92, p. 4.

18. S. Schram (ed.), *The Political Thought of Mao Tse-Tung*, p. 253.

19. *Laodong gaizao gongzuo* (*Labour Reform Work*), Beijing, quoted in Wu, *Laogai*, p. 19.

20. Harry Wu.

21. Some rumours say that this was put into action by the Party after an attack on Deng Xiaoping's motorcade by a gang of youths.

22. *The Chinese Communist Party's Forty Years in Power, 1949-89*, quoted in Harold Tanner, 'The Theoretical Bases of Labour Reform'.

23. Asia Watch, *Prison Labour in China*, 19 April 1991.

24. Decision of the Central Committee of the Chinese Communist Party to Strike Severe Blows Against Criminal Activities, dated 25 August 1983.

25. Jean Pasqualini, *Prisoner of Mao*.

26. *Selected Works of Deng Xiaoping*, p. 155.

27. Asia Watch, *Prison Labour in China*, 19 April 1991.

28. Alexander Solzhenitsyn, *The Gulag Archipelago*.

29. Wu, *Laogai*.

30. Interview with Harry Wu, 'To Destroy Hell: Harry Hongda Wu's Crusade Against the Chinese Gulag' by Kees Kuiken.

CHAPTER 2

The Death of the Father
George and John

Since then, at an uncertain hour,
That agony returns,
And till my ghastly tale is told
The heart within me burns.

Samuel Taylor Coleridge, *The Ancient Mariner*, II, lines 582–585

It is nearly 2 in the morning in the Oasis Motel, Los Angeles, and Mo Fengjie and Liu Xinfu are demonstrating how execution was carried out in China during the Cultural Revolution. First, they push aside the yellow leather armchair and the bowl of cored apples on the table. Then Mo Fengjie takes Liu Xinfu's shoulder, turns it sideways and thrusts his arm behind his back. He says: 'Often the shoulder bone would be broken when the arms were forced behind the back like this. The executioners would also dislocate the jawbone or cut the throat to stop the prisoner shouting slogans.' Liu Xinfu collapses on to his knees. 'Then, the gun is fired into the back of the head[1] from a distance of about a foot.' The family of the executed man or woman would be forced to meet the cost of the bullet. For identification, a steel wire would be drawn through the bullet hole of the corpse, and an identity tag attached to the wire.

Liu Xinfu, a slight, small man with a dark shock of hair, rehearsed his own execution over and over in his mind during twenty-four and a half years in a labour camp. 'Every time I was taken out of my solitary confinement cell I had to prepare myself mentally for being shot against a wall,' he says. Fear still lurks in his eyes, and when he first entered the room, he was noiseless as a ghost. But when he talks his voice is clear and his eyes burn.

Mo Fengjie is big and formidable, with a belly that bulges over the top of his gun-belt. Pimps, hookers and drug-pushers who hang around the downtown motel where he works as a security guard have a healthy respect for 'Big George'. 'Today, I'm too fat,' he says with a grin. 'When I was in the camps, my legs were so thin you could circle them with a hand and my shit was like hard stones.' (Plates 3 and 4.)

While he is talking, there is a sudden burst of gunfire from outside the room. He dons his holster and his bullet-proof combat waistcoat and politely excuses himself from the room. There is another burst of gunshot and then silence from the courtyard outside. Fengjie, who prefers to be known as George, reappears, calmly pours a fresh cup of green tea from an immense thermos flask he has brought for the purpose, and continues the discussion.

George and Liu Xinfu, who also likes to be known by his Christian name of John, are good friends. 'He is very brave,' says John about George. 'John is very kind,' says George. 'He always helps other people; he shelters many exiles from China, feeds them and gives them somewhere quiet in his house to sleep. He gives money to people. Just recently, he contributed to a flood relief fund in the Midwest.'

George and John both now have wives and children in the USA, but they have an understanding which perhaps even their families cannot share. Both of them were imprisoned in the *laogai* because of the 'sins' of their fathers. And although each of them suffered more than twenty years of physical and psychological torture, the most painful memory for each is the persecution and death of his father.

Paul Louis Mo, George's father, was a kind, compassionate and deeply religious man. He was born in 1912 in Guangdong province, and studied medicine at the Aurora University of Shanghai. In 1949, he was sent to America for advanced studies at a Catholic hospital in San Diego, California. And in 1950, Mo brought his family back to China via Hong Kong. Optimistic about a brighter future in China after the takeover of the Communist Party in 1949, the entire family finally settled in Beijing, where George's father became a doctor in the church-sponsored Sea Star hospital.

Paul Louis Mo was a devout Catholic, and ultimately this was to seal his fate. Every night he led George and his other children to kneel before a crucifix to pray for 'world peace' and the 'fraternity of human beings'.

In 1950, the Party instigated a campaign to 'reform' the church. Premier Zhou Enlai met Protestant leaders and encouraged them to distance the Chinese church from Western imperialism. All economic aid from the West to the church was cut off, and missionaries began to be expelled. The Party strongly pressured the churches to follow the 'Three Self' campaign (self-governing, self-supporting and self-propagating).

This campaign was aimed at 'encouraging' the mainland church to break away from the papacy. The Three Self campaign, however, merely replaced dominance by Western missions with dominance by the Chinese Communist Party.

The Communists asked George's father to quit his job in the Sea Star Hospital and work for the Communist Police Hospital at a higher salary. Mo refused. Then they asked him to spy for them when he was treating many of his regular patients, who were diplomats stationed in Beijing. The political commissar of the Police Hospital even visited the family home in an attempt to persuade him. 'When he left, he offered his hand, but my father ignored it purposely,' says George. 'Afterwards he explained to us, "I don't shake the Communist's dirty hand."'

When the chargé d'affaires of the Dutch embassy was ill and had to return to his country, he asked George's father to accompany him. Mo went as far as Canton with him, but was not allowed to leave the country. On 22 April 1954, when George was 10 years old, his father was arrested on the train whilst returning to Beijing. No one told the family where he was. George's mother, Cao Dezhen, made repeated visits to the local police substation, the Beijing Police Department, even the National Police Headquarters. She used all her diplomatic contacts in an attempt to establish the whereabouts of her husband. Still they were told nothing. Cao Dezhen's refusal to accept the absence of her husband was noted by the Party, and her stubbornness was the reason why she was branded a Rightist three years later.

During this period, Paul Louis Mo was being held at Number Thirteen Grass Heights of Beijing – a detention centre for pre-trial political prisoners. Because he pleaded not guilty to the charges against him, he was tortured by guards, who also ordered prisoners to beat him. George says: 'One of them, named Wong Mingdao, scratched his eyes, stabbed his nostrils with a pen, and used a bamboo pin to pierce the flesh right under his fingernails.'

In 1956, two years after his arrest, Paul Louis Mo was charged on six counts. 'At the time I was rather young,' says George, 'and I was crying when looking at a letter he had smuggled out of jail to my mother. I wanted to remember all that. We wrote down all the six charges they created against him.'

Mo was charged with involvement in 'illegal religious and counter-revolutionary' activities, and for being a 'US spy'. He was criticized for his involvement with a church-sponsored foundling hospital, where the Communists claimed nuns were ill-treating and killing the children. 'No matter how absurd and illogical the story stayed, they did not care, now they forced my father to "expose" it,' says George. 'The last charge was more confusing than anything I could imagine.' It read: 'He disclosed the information in French about the Chinese economy when he was eating at the Bosco Academy [a Catholic orphanage].'

George says: 'Everyone can see that the other charges were made up to frame him – only this one seemed like truth. When I was visiting him in prison, I asked him in a low voice, "Disclosing information about the economy in French at Bosco, what was that?" He laughed and said, "I don't understand myself. Maybe I mentioned the market price of cucumber, do you really think that's information of the economy?"'

George's mother decided that they should not appeal against the verdict, because, according to the Communists, to appeal meant pleading not guilty. A not guilty plea would attract a much heavier penalty. Paul Louis Mo pleaded guilty, and was sentenced to fifteen years.

The family's life became increasingly difficult in the absence of George's father. The Communists confiscated their property, including the few milk cows on which they had depended for their livelihood. Cao Dezhen, who was also a doctor, had to support her family of eight children and two grandparents by herself. When her husband was taken, her youngest child was scarcely a year old. In 1957, she was classified as a Rightist for her resistance to the regime. And because she refused to divorce her husband, she was forced to give up her job and become a cleaning janitor, with a subsequent decrease in pay.

Occasionally their uncle in Hong Kong sent money. But Cao Dezhen was determined that her children's education should not suffer. George remembers: 'Every month we all used to change from our ragged clothes and dress in our Sunday best to see our dear dad in Beijing Number One prison. We taught my younger brothers to sing some Cantonese folk songs to please our dad. Every time he saw us, he wanted to hug us. My younger brothers and sisters were so tiny and skinny, he could embrace two or even three of them at the same time. We took our scholarship records to show him, and Dad was always proud when we did well at school.'

Sometimes the prison guards would not let the family in to see their father. It was only after his father's death that George found out why. Former prisoners told him that at those times his father had been locked into a 'confinement cage'. Some of them said he had spent nearly half his time in the confinement cage. This treatment was used to punish his continued resistance to the Party. Prison guards didn't kill him immediately because they valued his skills as a doctor in the prison clinic.

George and his brothers and sisters added one more prayer to their evening routine: '"Oh dear God and Holy Mother, please let our father come back home soon." I never cried at daytime, but late at night when

I was kneeling all alone in front of Madonna, I always cried and prayed,' says George. 'At the age of 15, I swore to turn grief into strength, to cry no more, and to take action against the Communists.'

One of George's classmates, Sung Kwanghwi, shared his hatred for the Party. They pooled their money to buy an old mimeograph machine and planned to print fliers of what they heard on Free China's 'Central Broadcasting Station', the Voice of America and the Fighter of Freedom – Voice of the United Nations. George lent his classmates pictorial magazines his father had brought back from America, in order to disprove the Communists' lies about the evils of the West.

In August 1961, at the age of 17, George joined a student organization called the China People's Socialist Party. Their resentment against the government increased owing to the famine: 'the population of some villages was reduced to half, with the other half dying from hunger,' remembers George. 'All this resulted in the uprising of the farmers, who were suppressed by the Party.' The situation in China at the time was described by J. F. Kennedy: 'There are storms on the horizon and there are black currents under the surface of the sea.'

When one of the members of George's organization changed his mind and gave himself up to the police, George knew it was only a matter of time before he was taken. It was almost time for dinner when they arrived. George had just cycled home from high school in Beijing one autumn afternoon after classes when the Public Security Bureau entered his house, handcuffed him and took him in a jeep to Beijing Number Two prison, the pre-trial detention centre for political prisoners. Later he heard that the police had confiscated his old printing machine and $5 activity fund. 'Please don't laugh,' he says. 'This was all we could afford for our political work at that time.'

In his cell at Number Two prison, there was nothing except for bare boards: no bed, blankets or toilet. A small wooden bucket was placed outside, which George was allowed to use for urination twice a day. 'I didn't have to work at first; instead I sat on the bed and read newspapers, waiting to be called to court,' he says. On the prison grapevine, he heard news about his father, who was being held within the same prison system. He was told that prison guards had chained his handcuffs to a fixed piece of metal in an attempt to break his will. George felt even more isolated and alone, knowing of the suffering of his father, and unable to see him.

When his interrogation began, George realized that officials knew everything about his group's activities. The student who confessed had seen to this. 'Still I had to pretend to confess more, and to admit more mistakes,' says George. 'This wasn't so bad. The worst thing was the starvation. That caused constant suffering.' The lack of food was used as a punishment for those who would not confess. It was an easy punishment for the authorities to enforce during the 'three lean years' of 1959 to 1962.

The famine was a result of Mao Zedong's obsessive attempt to heighten economic productivity in China through mass organization and the inspiration of revolutionary fervour among the people. Millions of people were made to devote every spare minute to producing steel in an immense decentralization of industrial production, and there was a radical collectivisation of peasants into 'people's communes'. The exaggerated reports which claimed dramatic increases in production masked the human disaster of famine brought on by the so-called Great Leap Forward.[2]

There was so little food that some of the prisoners needed to go to the toilet only once in 27 days to excrete faeces. They passed urine about every eleven days. 'My shit was as hard as a rock,' says George.

All of the teenagers who had been involved with George's underground organization were sentenced at the same time, two years after their imprisonment in the detention centre. George's official verdict stated: 'Mo Fengjie possessed extremely reactionary thoughts and deeply engrained hatred toward the Party and the People's Republic because his father was sentenced to be reformed by the government. He swore to revenge and overthrow the Communist Party leadership. [He also] set up a reactionary organization, listened to an enemy-sponsored radio station [Voice of America] and attempted to distribute reactionary propaganda materials.'

Finally his sentence was announced: five years. George was sent to a metal-working factory, the Beijing Tung County Hardware Factory on the outskirts of the city. He was soon transferred to a farm in Heilongjiang, Yinghe farm, for hard labour. 'On the farm I was building irrigation systems, moving the earth by hand, digging ditches and building highways,' says George. 'In the summer we had to do metalwork, making machine tools and lathes. Every day we worked for at least ten hours, and in the evening were forced to take part in political study for two hours.'

George, still weakened by two years of virtual starvation in Beijing, was constantly exhausted. He survived because rations were increased to ensure that prisoners could meet labour targets. And some of the older prisoners, who weren't able to stomach too much food, shared their meals with George. But he was facing problems with his political 'attitude'. 'I was constantly the object of struggle sessions because I always used to say that I had freedom of thought,' says George. 'I refused to remould my thinking.'

In the camps, George was punished for his political attitude by being tied to a lamp-post naked during the summer months. A black cloud of mosquitoes would feast on his skin. Sometimes he was forced to wear a 'peace jacket' strapped on to the body. Air was then pumped into the 'jacket' so that breathing was almost impossible. George once even had his face pushed inside the vast, hot oven which provided heating for the prison farm in the winter, when temperatures in the vast province of Heilongjiang, bordering Siberia, would plunge to minus 40 degrees. Other tortures George suffered included whippings that tore his flesh, solitary confinement, and being ordered to work in icy cold water while he was suffering from a fever.

During the Cultural Revolution, John, the youngest prisoner in the labour camp where he was assigned, was also the focus of endless struggle sessions and enforced self-criticisms. He was beaten up by other prisoners every two days for three years to punish him for his 'attitude'. 'We were under pressure to say exactly what the cadres wanted,' he says. 'Everyone knew how to lie. But I never lied.'

John was born in Sichuan in 1945. When he was 4 years old, his family moved to Shanghai, where his father was an official in the Treasury Department of the Guomindang government which had previously been located in Chungking. In that same year, Chiang Kaishek, leader of the Nationalist Guomindang, fled to Taiwan and Mao Zedong declared China a Communist state. Chiang Kaishek, who died in 1975, became the military and political leader of the Guomindang after the death of Sun Yat-Sen, who struggled against warlords in an attempt to unite China throughout the 1910s and early 1920s. Chiang Kai-shek set up a nationalist, Guomindang government in 1928 and continued Sun Yat-Sen's fight against warlords and the Japanese. He finally lost the struggle to control and unify China to the Communists.

Colleagues of John's father urged him to follow other members of the Guomindang and take his family to Taiwan, where he would be safe. But he insisted that the bank needed him, so he was going to stay. Years later, John's father came to regret his decision.

John still remembers the exact date of his father's arrest; 4 February 1958. He was detained at the bank for several days before his family were informed, and was then, abruptly, sentenced to seventeen years, which he spent in a labour camp in Anhui province. For the first ten years he wasn't allowed to see his wife, three daughters and three sons.

The absence of his father had a profound effect on John, who was the oldest boy in the family. He built up an idealized image of the father he scarcely knew, attributing to him the qualities John felt he lacked himself. His ability to endure suffering in the *laogai*, however, indicates that he possessed the very qualities of strength and determination he admired so much in his father.

At the age of thirteen and a half, John was a normal, boisterous schoolboy who was often involved in fights at school. Life at home was hard without his father. His mother, who became a laundrywoman, sold most of their furniture and clothes to pay for food, and his sister scavenged through rubbish for scraps. In addition to the precariousness of life on the breadline, John's mother was constantly anxious about the family's security. Arrests were frequent: the Public Security Bureau had quotas to meet for detainees, and for each person above the quota they received a reward of 8 yuan. 'They would stop buses and trains, and just grab people,' remembers John.

Because of his family background, John was discriminated against in school by his teachers and classmates. He was regarded as belonging to one of the 'five black family categories', meaning that he and his family were perceived to be disloyal to the Communist system. The categories of 'black families' included landlord, rich capitalist, counter-revolutionary, bad element and Rightist. They were particularly vulnerable to attack from the system, which controlled basic necessities such as jobs and housing. Even medical care was granted according to 'class origin'. John's sister died at the age of 25 from tuberculosis due to lack of medical care.

One day John had a fight with some of his classmates. 'When I got home the police grabbed me. They told me they were taking me to the police station because I'd been fighting at school. My mother and sister were allowed to come with me. When we arrived the police asked me if I had anything to say, and when I said no, they put me in a cage.'

The cage measured 2.5 metres by 1 metre, and held twenty people. It was so packed that John, despite his thin, small build, could not even sit down. For several long and frightening months John was held in the cage with twenty adult men including criminals, 'Rightists' and others who had been plucked from the streets and imprisoned. At night there was scarcely room to sleep, and the cage was noisy with the moans and cries of its inmates. Several times a day, prisoners would be dragged from the cell for interrogation. John was interrogated twice, and after about three months – his memory of the length of time he was imprisoned there is hazy – he was sent to a prison farm. There were no charges against him. When he arrived at the farm, the prison warden told the policemen, 'We don't want this little kid.' It made no difference. John was 'accepted' for reform through labour, and assigned to a group of about twenty other, older, teenagers. Their job was to build roads and houses around the wasteland areas beside the farm. They worked for more than ten hours a day, six days a week. Even if it was snowing, all the prisoners worked barefoot. Food was either noodles or rice, occasionally with a small portion of vegetables, and 50 grams of oil each a month. Some prisoners supplemented their diet with raw wheat filched while they were working in the fields, or with food from the farm pigs' trough. Stealing this food was a punishable offence. Prisoners were given 'pocket money' of half a yuan a month. 'It was never enough, and the food was scarcely adequate,' says John. 'We were always on the brink of starvation.'

John couldn't keep up with the older, stronger men, and often fell behind with his work. 'We had to carry poles with buckets of earth suspended in the middle, and the load was too heavy for me,' he says. 'So an older prisoner would shoulder more of my load. In return, I gave him half my food.'

Every night inmates had to attend two-hour study sessions. 'We were told that if we showed the correct attitude, we would be released early,' says John. The teenagers were treated more leniently than the older inmates, but they were still brutalized by the violence they witnessed daily. 'If one of the men said they were innocent and didn't want to be in the camps, they were beaten,' says John. 'But we weren't beaten at that time. Many of the older people committed suicide or went crazy. I was very homesick.' (Plates 5 and 6.)

John's mother, brothers and sisters were allowed to visit him every three months, and they were also permitted to bring food – although they could scarcely afford to feed themselves. All of his family were still suffering persecution due to their Nationalist background. 'My two brothers went to Beijing to hide, and my mother scraped together enough money to bake them some buns to eat on their journey,' recalls John. His two sisters became doctors, and were sent to poor rural areas in Anhui and Hunan provinces.

When John was 20, he was being held in the same camp complex as his father, Baimaoling farm in Anhui province. Today, this camp includes industrial, tea, livestock, tool, construction and commercial companies. It also boasts six tea and livestock farms and two transportation teams, and twelve major factories including the Laodong Valve Works, Number Two Valve Works, construction material work, marble works, a brick yard, a mineral water factory and a print house among other factories. Prisoners like John were instrumental in developing the immense 260,000-square-metre site.

'My father was separated from me by 60 kilometres,' says John. 'But he came to see me twice, after applying for a day off and a transit period. The first time we met, my father told me he was glad I had grown up. My reaction was, what's so good about it? He preached to me about the correct attitude and told me to follow Mao Zedong's thought. Since my early childhood, I had always been a bit afraid of my father, and I wanted to be close to him. We discovered that feeling when we met in the camps.'

The second time they met, four years later, John's father told him all about their family history, going right back to the Ming Dynasty. He warned him not to tell anyone else. John was proud to have learnt the history of his ancestors. He says: 'My father also said he regretted not going to Taiwan when we had the chance. He explained he had felt a sense of duty as the supervisor of the bank. He mentioned my cousins in Taiwan, who were all college graduates. "I only wish it were the same for you," he said. "I want you to study for a degree when you are released."'

Like so many Chinese, John's father believed that what had happened to the family was fate: it was fixed and irrevocable. Maybe this gave him the strength to keep going, and to endure what might otherwise have been a crushing sense of guilt. 'While he was in the camp, my father had never admitted that he had committed any crime, so they went out of their way to persecute him,' says John. 'He was constantly beaten and abused.'

At the height of the Cultural Revolution, John underwent a similar fate. Every morning before going to work, all the prisoners gathered together to pledge their loyalty to Chairman Mao. Because of his obstinate refusal to confess his 'guilt', John was made to kneel before the group, his legs bound with rope. Then he would be beaten by his fellow prisoners. 'It was always the same four people, the other prisoners would just pretend,' he says. 'For three years, every two or three days, they beat me until they were tired. They beat me until I was numb and could scarcely see with my eyes.'

The physical abuse didn't work. John still refused to show repentance. Even the threat of execution couldn't persuade him to change his attitude; he had already mentally prepared himself for death and had no fear of it. There was only one other weapon in their armoury to break down this difficult prisoner: solitary confinement. John was locked into a dark cell empty of everything but a toilet bucket, emptied once a week, a thin blanket and an oil-lamp. A window high in the wall without glass let in air and some light. If John attempted to block the window to protect himself from the cold, he was punished and told he was 'escaping the supervision of the masses'. Under the door was a small trough, and John's meals were slipped into it each day, thus ensuring no human contact with the guards. The only book he was allowed in his cell was Chairman Mao's *Little Red Book*; occasionally his friends managed to slip notes under the door with information about what was going on in the rest of the prison.

John spent three years in the dark cell. The only release he had from the four walls was during struggle sessions, when he would be taken outside, a dunce hat placed on his head indicating his 'counter-revolutionary' status, and beaten. 'I was already extremely ill and weak from virtual starvation,' he says. 'And when I returned to the cell from these sessions I couldn't even open my eyes, and I could scarcely walk. I still think it is a miracle that I wasn't beaten to death.'

On 7 March 1973, John received an order to report to the camp supervisor. He says: 'I can remember that day very clearly. It was raining hard and nobody had gone to work. I was expecting another beating, but when I reached the office the supervisor told me I had to go to my father's prison camp. I knew that something bad had happened when they immediately gave me a permit pass.'

When John reported to the cadres at his father's prison farm, they asked him to sit down. 'Normally a prisoner would never be asked to sit down,' he says. 'So then I knew my father was dead. They told me he had hanged himself. I said I wanted to see him.'

Two of his father's co-workers were called into the office. They told John that they had last seen his father washing his rice bowl after breakfast. Because it was raining, none of the prisoners had gone to work that morning. When John's father didn't report for the afternoon study session, inmates were sent to search for him. He was found in the small shed near a field where he lived. When they opened the bamboo door they saw him there, hanging from the roof of thick plant roots he had woven together himself.

John was taken to see his father's corpse. It was covered in a white sheet, and lay beside the body of another prisoner who had hanged himself that day. 'I wanted to see my father's face, but I was told not to look, as it was too horrible,' says John. 'Then I told the authorities I wanted to watch over the body for the night. It is a tradition in China for the eldest son to watch over his dead father on the night of his death. But I was told that I would not be allowed to do so. The person giving the orders thought I would be afraid.'

The next day, one of John's brothers came to the camp, and they put a new set of clothes on their father's body ready for the cremation. They asked the group leaders to hold the ceremony the next day, when they would be able to accompany the body to the crematorium. But when they arrived back at the camp the morning afterwards, they were presented with their father's ashes. 'They told us we hadn't given a formal order delaying cremation,' says John. 'A higher-level authority had given the order to carry it out straight away.' The ashes are now kept in John's childhood home in Shanghai, where his 80-year-old mother still lives.

The only thing John has left of his father is a worn grey jacket covered in neatly sewn patches.

During the Cultural Revolution, George's family suffered even more than before. His mother, sisters and brothers were criticized and denounced. His mother and two teenage brothers were called 'monsters and demons' because they had returned to their mother's countryside home to live with her relatives. George's eldest brother, Feng-chia, was denounced as a counter-revolutionary by his work unit, and denounced and beaten in 1970. His elder sister and her husband were accused of being 'suspected spies'. Their house was searched and their property confiscated.

At Yinghe province farm, George continued to struggle against the system. 'I never gave up fighting,' he says. One day he asked for a paper and pen and wrote solemnly, 'I have freedom of thoughts and I refuse the reform of thoughts.'

In September 1966, George's five-year sentence officially came to an end. But because he was still regarded as an active counter-revolutionary who had refused to reform, he was kept at the camp for two years. The only difference from before was that he received a small amount of pay each week. A prisoner was assigned to guard him, 24 hours a day. If he went to the toilet, the prisoner would wait outside. When he slept, his guard would sleep beside him. Cadres told the prisoner to beat him up frequently. In November 1968, he was moved to a remote people's commune in Tai-lai county of Heilongjiang province. 'This action was called "accepting lower class farmer's supervision and transformation",' says George. 'Actually, it is a lifelong exile.'

Life was still miserable, and some of the young people who had been 'sent down' to the countryside with him committed suicide by jumping into the village well. Several of them managed to escape. 'At least I was strong, and my work satisfied the peasants,' says George. 'I realized how poor the people in rural China were at that time, and how hard they had to work to feed themselves. I created a theory about it. Basically I said that the Communist Party exploited the ordinary peasants and that taxes were too high. There were taxes such as a "road rolling fee", "patriotism grain tax" and even "giving preferential treatment to families of revolutionary army men and martyrs". Although the peasants could easily sell their products at the market, cost of fertiliser and other essentials were high, and so it was difficult to scrape a living from the land.' George also said that the peasants' burden had been increased even more by the need to share the cost of barefoot doctors, veterinarians and rural teachers, who were previously paid solely by the government.

To the Party, these were heretical opinions. When George's theories were discovered, he had to submit a self-criticism. 'As a punishment, I was chained up, and whipped on my bare skin with one of the whips they use on cattle,' he says. 'I had deep cuts on my face, and my scalp was bleeding.'[3]

George thought about suicide, but he didn't want to cause pain to his mother, and it would have been against his Catholic faith. In 1969, he was given another reason for living – to avenge the death of his father. Paul Louis Mo had been beaten to death seventeen days before the end of his fifteen-year sentence. 'As a doctor with religious belief, love and excellent medical skills, my father in his last thirty years had helped thousands of people, including the children he loved so much,' says George. 'But when he left this world, he had nothing but bruises all over his body.'

Gradually the story of his father's last months began to emerge. In August 1966, all of the prisoners in Beijing Number One prison, including Paul Louis Mo, had been transferred to the Da Qing Yao colliery at Da Tong city of Shanxi province. George's father had to care for those wounded in frequent accidents due to the dangerous conditions. He had to perform surgery without anaesthetic because the cadres said they should save money on medical supplies.

Several dozen prisoners, headed by Xu Guanzeng and Wang Ruqing, formed a clandestine organization in order to rebel against prison conditions. Paul Louis Mo became the focus of the group: as the prison doctor, he could meet prisoners separated from the rest in different work units. Wang Ruqing and Mo would inspire other friends with sayings about freedom by Lincoln, Kennedy and Eisenhower. Mo would also try to obtain as much medicine as he could for other inmates.

These subversive activities did not attract the loyalty of all the prisoners who found out about them. Finally, they were informed upon, and flung into solitary confinement. They were tortured in an attempt to make them confess to their 'crime' and the involvement of others in the group. George says: 'They forced my father to bow his head very low and bend over for hours, hung him up and whipped him, pulled his hair and ears, and hung a heavy basket full of stone and coal with iron wire as its handle around his neck as he was bending over.'

Xu Guanzeng, Wang Ruqing and eleven others endured similar torture: they were whipped, beaten and made to stand in the yard in freezing temperatures, with bucket after bucket of cold water poured over them. In March 1970, they were shot. 'The policemen trussed them up like ducks, then paraded them through the streets to expose them in front of the public before execution,' says George. 'The policemen had already dislocated their jaws to keep them from shouting anything against Communism.[4] Every one of them had a "death tag", a narrow, flat piece of wood with his name on it, pierced into the flesh of the neck. Blood dripped to the ground as they walked to the site of their executions.'

Paul Louis Mo did not even leave the prison for the execution ground. He was beaten and tortured so badly that he died of internal injuries.

Three years after the death of his father, George joined an illegal group of private contractors building houses and carrying out tree-felling in the Greater Xing'an mountains. He escaped from the village, and with his comrades roamed the vast forests on the Russian border. 'It was like a guerrilla underground,' he says. In 1976, he set up a farm within the Chang Bar Twin people's commune in Hubei province. Together with a colleague, he built an electromagnetic mixing machine which brought more than $10,000 to the brigade.

After the Cultural Revolution, he had high hopes of rehabilitation from the government. 'I appealed to the Communist court against my criminal record,' he says. 'But my appeal was rejected. This means that, under the Communists, I will always be regarded as a counter-revolutionary.' George was still an outsider. He had been an exile in his own country since his release from the camps five years before. In 1976, he became an exile from China when he escaped to West Africa.

George's uncle facilitated George's departure from China by sending him a visa passbook for Togo in West Africa in 1981. It was at a time when China had broadened its entrance and exit policy. But still George had serious difficulty in leaving: he belonged to the 'appeal-rejected counter-revolutionary' category – considered to be 'problematic' at a high level. George had to use bribery, persuasion and concealment of his past record to obtain a passport. He arrived in West Africa, where he stayed with his uncle for a year and a half before arriving on 3 April 1983 in the USA, where his mother and all his siblings have also settled. George married and settled down in Los Angeles with his wife Linda and their daughter Mary, who is now 14. 'Mary's doing excellently at school and wants to be a doctor,' says George. 'I don't really talk to her about what happened to me in China. She doesn't really want to hear about it.'

America has a special significance for George. 'Here is the place where my father had lived and loved,' he says. Aware of the education he missed out on during his lost years in the camps, George began to study again, between shifts as a security guard in the Oasis Motel. He is influenced by the works of J. F. Kennedy, Eisenhower and the French philosophers Diderot, Montesquieu and Rousseau. 'I tried hard, observing the society and reading lots of books,' he says now. 'My thoughts were elevated from a narrow revenge for my father to a deep belief of searching for freedom.'

George has treasured the memory of his father by bringing out materials from Beijing about his life and death, and about the continued persecution of Catholics in China. Before he finally left his country, he researched the destruction of churches and religious settlements, such as the Yu-San Tabernacle in Shanghai. He took pictures and smuggled out the negatives, and he talked to priests and worshippers about their experiences, in order to collate a historical record. He has gathered these documents together with photographs, carefully photocopied and bound together, of his father and family. One group of pictures was taken at the Tsao Tsun graves for the prisoner of Da Tsen Yao coal mine in Shanxi province in 1975. They show the ragged, decomposing body of George's father before the family cremated his corpse. Other photographs depict headstone number 176, where Paul Louis Mo's remains were buried, and a simple shrine adorned with a cross of flowers. This was taken at Tai Shan, Shan Ton, after George reburied his father's ashes. A devastating sense of loss is tangible in the neatly labelled pages.

It is nearly dawn at the Oasis Motel, and John's pager is bleeping. It's his wife, concerned about his absence. 'Are you still talking?' she says.

John supports his wife and two young children with a successful furniture removal business in Los Angeles. 'My own needs in life are small,' he says. 'And I believe we should all help each other – everyone is in the same boat. So I try to shelter exiles from China when I can; we feed them, and they sleep in my place.'

Like George, it took John several years to finally make it to America; and one attempt ended in his reimprisonment. 'I had escaped from the farm and wanted to leave China for Hong Kong,' he says. 'First I went to Beijing to find my relatives, and to ask them for some money for my passage across. But one day I was caught on a train in the city by police who demanded my identity cards. I didn't have any, so I was sent back to Shanghai, where they discovered I had escaped from the prison farm. So I was sent back.' John made another escape attempt from the camp only months later. This time he was successful, and he roamed the countryside, making a living as a locksmith.

Before he finally left China, the verdict on John's case was reversed, and he was rehabilitated. He had been imprisoned for nearly 25 years without charge. 'My father's name was cleared, and they had also said I was innocent,' he says. 'My family received 600 yuan as compensation for the death of my father. I got nothing. My rehabilitation left a bitter taste in my mouth. We had suffered one death, and I had lost more than 24 years.'

In Chinese culture, the father–son relationship has a significance beyond the personal bond. It is symbolic of transcendence: of the continuance of family. From Confucius onwards, it was the ultimate model for almost all other relationships in Chinese society. As the eldest son, John has a sense of his own place in the line of ancestors, from the Ming Dynasty and beyond, which informs his own experience. The direct link between himself and these ghosts of the past broke on the day his father was found hanging from a rope in his bamboo shack in Baimaoling Farm.

In his Los Angeles home, John keeps his father's jacket folded in a suitcase and stored in his wardrobe. 'I often think about his suicide,' he says. 'For years afterwards, I was happy for him because he had been released: he was free of suffering. Even now, I still dream about being brave like him.'

Notes

1. The prisoner is usually dispatched by one bullet to the occiput, where the neck joins the skull.

2. Communist general Peng Dehui was alone among high-ranking Party officials in criticizing Mao's policies behind the Great Leap Forward at a high-level congress in 1959. He was purged from the Party for expressing the innermost thoughts of many.

3. It is a tragedy for China that men like George were tortured for ideas like these, which could have contributed to the development of the country. Soviet writer Yuri Garushyants believes that the idea of defending human rights was developed in precisely the period in which China was most isolated from the outside world, and when its representative thinkers were living in exile in distant villages or imprisoned in labour camps (Yuri Garushyants in Susan Whitfield (ed.), *After the Event: Human Rights and Their Future in China*).

4. In 1976, a woman counter-revolutionary in Liaoning province, Zhang Zixin, had her larynx cut before being shot to stop her shouting counter-revolutionary slogans (Wu, *Laogai*, p. 69).

CHAPTER 3

No Day or Night
The Experience of Survival

You never in the entire world could understand, unless you were there. There was no day or night. There was no happiness, just fear. There was nothing but the next thirty seconds.

Holocaust survivor Roman Ferber [1]

Remembering things past is like entering another world.

Survivor of a *laogai* camp [2]

Former prisoners of the Chinese *laogai* often experience an intense isolation and separation from their families and friends after their release from the camps, and they regard other inmates – those who have experienced similar pain and suffering – as their 'real' friends. The gulf of experience between former prisoners and their families or old friends is often so great that it swallows these relationships whole, leaving only emptiness in their place.

In his story 'The Homecoming Stranger', the poet Bei Dao gives a moving picture of a man returning to his family after twenty years of hard labour. Before dawn on the morning of his return, Lanlan finds her father in the kitchen: 'Under the light, wearing a black cotton-padded vest, he was crouching over the wastepaper basket with his back towards me, meticulously picking through everything; spread out beside him were such spoils as vegetable leaves, trimmings and fish heads.' Lanlan noticed that he was holding something behind his back; an ordinary cigarette packet. '"Oh Lanlan," beads of sweat started from his balding head, "yesterday I forgot to examine this cigarette packet when I threw it away, just in case I wrote something on it; it would be terrible if the team leader saw it . . . Of course, I know, it's beyond their reach, but better to find it just in case."'[3]

29

Lanlan's heart hardens against the 'wrinkled and mottled' figure of the old man she can no longer accept as her father. His silence seemed to her a mute apology for his life, for her suffering when she was a child without a father, and for when as a 12-year-old she was forced to kneel on broken glass for defending him against the Party. When he breaks down and apologizes for that inability to protect her, and his unworthiness as a father, her own reserve crumbles and images of those twenty years flood into her mind:

> I seemed to smell the pungent scent of tobacco mingling with the smell of mud and sweat. I seemed to see him in the breaks between heavy labour, leaning wearily against the pile of dirt and rolling a cigarette, staring into the distance, through the fork between the guard's legs. He was pulling a cart, struggling forward on the miry road, the cart wheels screeching, churning up black mud sods . . . He was digging the earth shovelful after shovelful, straining himself to fling it towards the pit side . . . He was carrying his bowl, greedily draining the last mouthful of vegetable soup . . . I dared not think any more, I dared not. My powers of imagining suffering were limited after all. But he actually lived in a place beyond the powers of human imagination. Minute after minute, day after day, oh God, a full twenty years.[4]

The initial feelings of distance between former prisoners and their loved ones are often exacerbated by the difference in their physical appearance, whether this is through malnutrition, ill-health, torture or the passage of time. 'The look in a zek's [prisoner's] eyes is impossible to describe, but once encountered, it is never forgotten,' says the Soviet poet Irina Ratushinskaya. 'When you emerge, your friends, embracing you, will exclaim: "Your eyes! Your eyes have changed!"'[5]

For some political prisoners, it is said, prison can be the best experience of their lives, drawing them together in a common cause against a single enemy represented by their torturers.[6] This may have been true in Tsarist Russia, where prison camps were the universities of the revolution, or in Stalinist gulags where comrades were placed together in a cell,[7] but it is rarely true for prisoners in the Chinese labour camps. The techniques of thought reform, in which the prisoner's identity is broken down, prisoner is set against prisoner, and cells are populated by at least one informer, have generally obstructed the development of such close personal alliances.

One of the exceptions to this may be the camaraderie among Tibetan counter-revolutionary prisoners in Chinese labour camps in Tibet (see Chapter 13). Jailed for their pro-independence activities, these 'politicals' frequently express their solidarity with a shared sense of humour and jokes at the expense of officialdom. 'We gave the Chinese prison guards nicknames – one was called Black Death,' says the Tibetan monk Palden Gyatso, who was in prison for 33 years. 'We had a lot of jokes, and most of them were quite rude.'

The yearning for love among many prisoners is often an expression of their frustration with such an existence. Mao talked about the necessity for people to devote themselves to the Party in the language of a Barbara Cartland novel; he made the abandonment of the self and the sacrifice of one's life for the people's ideals sound as romantic as falling in love. However his decree that such emotions between two people were contrary to the needs of the Party led to a unique form of emotional and sexual repression both in the *laogai*, and in Chinese society. 'Falling in love is so powerful that it makes you forget almost everything else, even making revolution,' says Anchee Min, a former Red Guard who was 'sent down' to work in a communal farm before being picked by Madame Mao's associates to become a star of the Chinese propaganda film industry.[8] 'Instead of wanting to struggle and destroy things, you want to find peace and to celebrate living. Because the Party knows that people in love are no longer completely under its control, its leaders have always been deeply fearful of love.'

In her beautifully written autobiography, Anchee Min recalls how Little Green, her best friend on the communal farm during the Cultural Revolution, was once caught with a man. They were discovered making love in the fields near the barracks. Anchee's company leader ordered the men to beat Little Green's lover, to make him understand that 'today's woman was no longer the victim of man's desire'. Little Green underwent four days of 'intensive mind re-brushing', after which she appeared at a public trial. In a high, strained voice, Little Green declared that she had been raped. Her lover was executed for his 'bourgeois' crime, and later Little Green went insane.[9]

Lu Haoqin, an inmate at Qinghe farm and friend of Harry Wu, had a similar fate. Lu's yearning for his lost fiancée, and his memory of their one sexual encounter, led him firstly to constant masturbation, then propositioning of other prisoners before he was taken away in a straitjacket. Eventually he committed suicide.[10]

Other prisoners experience their isolation and sense of separateness from society and others in different ways. In his novel about life in a labour camp, Zhang Xianliang writes of his kinship with lice in the absence of loving human company. When lice don't bite, his character remarks, they can be quite lovable, and they made him feel less destitute. 'I have my little dependants too!'[11]

This same disregard for human feelings is at the heart of numerous Party policies involving separation of the family. Since the political campaigns of the 1950s, millions of young people have been 'sent down' to the countryside; intellectuals and students have been relocated to 'cadre schools' or for re-education and reform through labour, and millions have been forced to stay and labour in the same farm or factory even after their sentence is completed. This has caused a widespread breakdown in the unity of the traditional Chinese extended family.[12]

Jeremy Woodcock, a family therapist and psychologist who works for the London-based Medical Foundation for Torture, uses the example of an Iraqi family to illustrate how the imprisonment of an individual inevitably affects the rest of the family. He told me what happened:

The father was taken away from the family when his son was just 2 years old. When he came back several years later he was broken by the torture he had endured. He was in a terrible state, and a shadow of his former self. His wife hid him away, and whenever anyone knocked on the door she was in paroxysms of terror.

When the family came to see me, the boy was 8, and his behaviour was very defiant. His father was angry about it. He'd had a very hard life; he'd had to grow up quickly and become an adult at the age of 11. He still had nightmares about the torture he'd suffered during his imprisonment, and he was focusing all his anxiety and unresolved issues on to his son. I explained to him that the boy, Akhmed, knows at a certain level what he'd been through. Akhmed was aware that his father was different, and that he wasn't the father he used to be, nor the one he wants.

The turning point came just at the beginning of the Gulf War. Akhmed was doing some plasticine modelling, and he made a figure of a snake with flames coming from its mouth. Then he modelled a figure which he said was Saddam Hussein. The father was literally terrified. But then the boy took the snake and curled it round the plasticine model of Saddam, and the father's fear disappeared. The son was symbolically saying that he knew what had happened.

Although cultures differ, psychological studies show that people recover from trauma in ways which are broadly similar. There has been an increased recognition of the effects of trauma on the psyche, and 'post-traumatic stress syndrome' is the psychological buzzword for them. Symptoms include sleep disturbances, heightened irritability, nightmares and outbursts of anger. Survivors may also find themselves reliving the trauma through a seemingly unrelated experience. Sometimes they cannot remember everything about their ordeal: the brain has mechanisms that block those experiences that cannot consciously be dealt with.

'People who experience trauma are often affected somatically, which means that something emotional is turned into something physical,' says Judith Hassan, a therapist who works with survivors of the Nazi Holocaust.[13] Pain manifests itself in the body in different ways; through a limp in a leg kicked by a prison guard, a stooped back, feelings of claustrophobia after years of being cooped up in a small cell. Hassan believes that as survivors of extreme trauma such as imprisonment and torture approach middle age and redundancy, or old age and family bereavements, their problems become worse. This is because the mind starts to play tricks as one grows older: distant events from long ago can be recalled with great clarity, while the short-term memory begins to suffer.

Similarly, the sense of loss for those who perished scarcely fades, particularly when the survivor has had a chance to develop his or her own skills and career, and to watch their own family grow older – knowing that those they left behind were deprived of the chance to do the same. Harry Wu is reduced to tears when he talks about his stepmother, who killed herself soon after she heard of his imprisonment. He is not only motivated in his human rights work by feelings of pain for other prisoners. He also wants to destroy the system that made his stepmother take her own life.[14]

And what of the guilt of those caught up in the system – of those who were directly involved in violence, even killings, of others? Many of those drawn into the spiral of brutality during the Cultural Revolution simply blame the Gang of Four for inciting their behaviour, so freeing themselves of any personal responsibility. However personal resentment and anger still festers beneath the surface. When reporter Fox Butterfield visited a restaurant in 1977, just after the Cultural Revolution, he made the mistake of asking to 'settle the accounts' instead of simply requesting the bill. The waitress was angry, telling him the phrase was not polite any more owing to the number of personal vendettas between factions and families in China at the time.[15]

Colin Thubron recalls meeting a man who bludgeoned an elderly porter to death during the Cultural Revolution because the old man was reading a Westernized novel:

> Looking back on those years, he seemed not to comprehend the person he had been. Now that society was regulated again and authority telling him how to think and feel, he saw only a nightmare self, a sleep-walker from whom all constraints had been lifted. He did not understand. Nor did I. He said bleakly: 'We thought the porter was a revisionist.'[16]

There has been little attempt in Chinese 'labour camp literature' to analyse the relationship of the oppressor and the victim, and to untangle the responsibility of the individual with that of society and the leaders currently in power. Nien Cheng's is a lone voice: in her prison memoirs, *Life and Death in Shanghai*, she wonders how one single person could have caused the extent of misery that was prevailing in China. 'There must be something lacking in our own character, I thought, that had made it possible for this evil genius to dominate.'

Psychological studies indicate that the answers to the universal questions of how one person can torture or kill another are rarely found in the individual psyche. Psychiatrist Derek Summerfield of the Medical Foundation for Victims of Torture, says: 'The idea that you're going to find the answer by looking inside the brain is a romantic abstraction. The whole business of looking into the psyche of the individual fits in with contemporary Western interest in psychology, which is ultimately only one way of looking at things. What we should really be looking at is the social context of these acts.'

According to these studies, particularly one which investigated torturers who served the Greek dictatorship of 1967-74, it should not be assumed that every torturer or executioner is a sadist. Bruno Bettelheim believed that nine out of ten guards in the concentration camps were 'normal' men with wives, families and hobbies, whereas the other one derived some sadistic pleasure from his treatment of inmates. From the Greek study, Dr Haritos-Fatouros, Professor of Clinical Psychology at the University of Thessalonika, concluded that feelings of shared humanity are often not strong enough to override our obedience to authority. Any of us might torture a stranger, even a friend, she says, if we were told to do so.

This conclusion corresponds with the research of Yale psychologist Stanley Milgram in the early 1960s. Milgram found that the vast majority of his subjects were willing upon instruction from authority and with only minimal persuasion to administer electric shocks to their fellow experimental subjects which they believed to be harmful and even potentially lethal. Even when the subjects (who were actors) appeared to be writhing in pain before the eyes of their tormenters, most of these ordinary Americans complied with the demands of authority and science and continued to increase the voltage.[17] Milgram states that most of his subjects who delivered shocks did so out of a 'sense of obligation', which led him to conclude that directed cruelty does not require a sadistic personality.

Dr Haritos-Fatouros's research showed that regimes seeking the ideal torturer need candidates who are young, educated, with a track record of obedience to authority and an upbringing in a family sympathetic to the political aims of the state. Mao's China during the Cultural Revolution and beyond, with its adherence to ideology rather than humanity, was a perfect breeding ground for such an individual. Military organizations in the West offer a similar breeding ground: the training of a torturer is similar to the training of a US Marine in its demands for obedience, discipline, submission to a higher authority and emphasis on conflict with the enemy.

Derek Summerfield points out that a Western arms dealer who sells a cluster bomb to another country and then returns home to his children, knowing they are not the ones who will be blown to bits, bears a similar responsibility to a torturer in a Chinese jail who applies an electric shock prod to a prisoner's genitals before going home to help his children with their homework. 'The system provides the context for the dehumanization,' he says. 'Individuals should have responsibility – and so should governments.'

Nineteen-year-old US Sergeant Joe Queen's job was to bury Iraqis alive during the Gulf War. Queen had been among one of the first American troops to cross the Saudi border in an armoured bulldozer. After burying the Iraqis alive in their trenches, he had to cover the trenches with sand, clearing a smooth passage for the rest of the First Armoured Mechanized Brigade. Military sources in Baghdad and Washington put the total number of Iraqis buried alive during the war as between one and two thousand. Queen said: 'You're up there in the half-hatch and you know what you got to do. You did it so much you could close your eyes and do it. I feel sorry for them that stayed in the trenches, but they did what they did for their country, just like we would. The military furnished us with this piece of equipment and that's what it's designed to do.'[18]

When Queen returned from the conflict to his home town in Bryson City, he went on tour for a week to local elementary schools, telling the children what he did during the war. It is a chilling example of society's acceptance of brutality – as long as it is against a state-designated enemy.

China is clearly not the only state to use doublespeak and demonization of the enemy to further its aims. The language of warfare is a prime example of propaganda as false naming, in which killing civilians becomes 'collateral damage', an MX missile becomes 'Peacemaker' and poisoning entire areas with Agent Orange becomes 'an environmental adjustment'.

When journalist John Pilger asked arms salesmen what a multi-purpose cluster bomb actually did, he had to deal with an incarnation of Major Major from Joseph Heller's *Catch 22*. 'That's classified,' he was told. When asked why, the latter-day Major Major replied that this was classified too. When asked to describe the working of a 'cluster grenade' by Pilger, another salesmen went into breathless detail: 'This is wonderful. It is state of the art, unique. What it does is discharge copper dust, very very fine dust, so that the particles saturate the objective.' The 'objective', Pilger was told, 'is often people'.[19]

Demonization of the enemy occurred during the Cultural Revolution in China, when the designated foe was deemed to be, variously, 'stinking Rightists', 'bourgeois imperialists', 'capitalist running dogs', 'class enemies' and so on. Western leaders and politicians are just as guilty of dividing the world into 'goodies' and 'baddies', as in tacky Western films. Former US President Richard Nixon once said: 'It may seem melodramatic to say that the United States and Russia represent Good and Evil. But if we think of it that way, it helps to clarify our perspective on the world struggle.' Ronald Reagan, too, identified the Soviet Union as 'the focus of evil in the modern world'.

The use of such emotive language stirs up hatred, thus allying the people to the side of the government, and assuaging the guilt of those who are sent to kill the 'enemy'. The propaganda used by the state to justify war builds up a support system within the society, to lend practical and emotional encouragement to troops in the field carrying out their duties. In this way, the act of murder is transformed into patriotism. This could apply equally to the Gulf War, the two World Wars and the Cultural Revolution.

In her autobiography, *Red Flower of China*, Zhai Zhenhua relates how the Cultural Revolution turned her into a 'devil':

> *We were in a war and there are always casualties on battlefields. I shouldn't be intimidated by the death of one class enemy. The revolution had to succeed, and I had to continue to do my part. When I was assigned new tasks, I tried to be as brave as before.*

Depth psychology has given us the argument that the enemy is constructed from denied aspects of the self. 'From the unconscious residue of our hostility, we create a target; from our private demons, we conjure a public enemy,' writes Sam Keen in *Faces of the Enemy*. 'Perhaps more than anything else, the wars we engage in are compulsive rituals, shadow dramas in which we continually try to kill those parts of ourselves we deny and despise.' (Keen believes that the 'warriors' of the future will be the men and women who attempt to engage and bring into consciousness what Jung called the 'shadow' self, so confronting the 'enemy' within, and dissociating themselves from outer projections.)

Depth psychology aside, individuals such as Pol Pot, Hitler, Mao and others clearly exist and are guilty of perpetrating atrocities against humanity. The fact that we project our vices on to the enemy does not automatically mean that the enemy is innocent of our projections. But it is worth remembering that dictators could not survive without the complicity and support of their followers. The number of 'good', responsible men and women who succumbed to Nazism tells us something about our shared humanity as well as the importance of a social context.

And just as the social context is set by governments interacting with society, so government and society are made up of individuals. People like Han Dongfang, whose story is told in Chapter 17, have shown that it is possible for individuals to defy the demands of their superiors and to retain a personal conscience even within a military structure.

Many individuals turn to cruelty as a last resort through fear. One Chinese, Song Erli, describes how fear of being an outsider socially and culturally precipitated much of the cruelty of the Cultural Revolution:

> People were cruel out of fear. If you weren't cruel towards the class enemies, that meant you'd lost your class stand and were no longer revolutionary. That isn't so dangerous to idlers, but it is danger to those who aspire to power, and at any given time there will be people who aspire to power. Otherwise there would be a vacuum. So it was a combination of ambition and fear that made people so cruel.[20]

Inside the *laogai*, there was an even greater level of social control in place, justifying even more violence than that of the society outside. Violence against the prisoners is intensified by the insistence that prison officials are always right, and prisoners are always wrong. This perceived monopoly of the truth on the part of the authorities sanctions violence as a method of controlling recalcitrant prisoners or those whose work does not come up to scratch. The continual assertion of authority and power by guards weakens the effectiveness of any dissent from the prisoners. 'Even the most seemingly insignificant actions of the guards are designed to assert their authority,' says Mark Baber, who was imprisoned for three years and ten months in Shanghai Number One jail. 'They control every aspect of prison life, from refusing extra blankets in winter to deciding on the size of prisoners' meals.'

Every day, a prisoner's life is in the hands of others. This gives a terrifying amount of power to the opinions of just one resentful cadre, for instance, and is open to the worst forms of abuse. Liu Xinfu (whose story is featured in Chapter 2) discovered only after his rehabilitation that a low-level cadre had proposed putting him to death because of his 'intransigent attitude'.

Prisoners freed from the *laogai* take some time to 'relearn' freedom in themselves. Often they find themselves attempting to come to terms with previously buried emotions, now brought to the surface. One inmate of a Chinese prison waited to die on Death Row for more than a year.[21] Every night, in the early hours, he would wake with a start, waiting to hear the crunch of a truck on gravel and knowing that by dawn he might be shot. Even though he was sitting in a cell a little bigger than a trunk with his hands and feet in irons, he devised a way to kill himself with pieces of cloth torn up to form a noose to hang from a hook fashioned from dried rice noodles. After he had managed to wrap the cloth around his neck, he thought of his mother, and knew that he couldn't commit suicide, for her sake. So he waited another year on Death Row.

Just before Spring Festival, an official came to see the prisoner. He told him that soon it would be the holidays, and that he would be allowed to spend them at home with his family. He didn't have to come back to the prison again. The inmate nodded, and the official repeated, 'Don't you understand that you're free?' The official had told him the news slowly. He was afraid the prisoner would react like another inmate, who had died when the guard blurted out that he was free. But the prisoner didn't say anything. He didn't even smile.

Sometimes the beginning of freedom is as abrupt and frightening as the moment of capture.

Notes

1. Roman Ferber, in Elinor J. Brecher, *Schindler's Legacy*, p. viii.

2. Survivor of a *laogai* camp quoted in CICRC, *The White Book on Forced Labour in the People's Republic of China*, vol. 2, p. 220.

3. 'The Homecoming Stranger' in Bei Dao's collection of stories, *Waves*, p. 164.

4. *Ibid*.

5. Irina Ratushinskaya, *Grey Is the Colour of Hope*, p. 279.

6. Jeremy Woodcock of the London-based Medical Foundation for Victims of Torture says: 'It's a common phenomenon. After being tortured, they return to the cell where their wounds are bandaged by their comrades. Sharing a common cause draws them closer together and enables them to express their inner world.'

7. In *The Gulag Archipelago*, Solzhenitsyn writes: 'But it was not the dirty floor, nor the murky walls, nor the odour of the latrine bucket that you loved – but those fellow prisoners with whom you about-faced at command, and that something which beat between your heart and theirs, and their sometimes astonishing words, and then, too, the birth within you, on that very spot, of free-floating thoughts you had so recently been unable to leap up or rise to . . . Tomorrow I would be telling them my story . . . and they would be telling me their stories too. How interesting tomorrow would be, one of the best days of my life! (Thus, very early and very clearly, I had this consciousness that prison was not an abyss for me, but the most important turning point in my life.)' (vol. 1, pp. 181, 197).

8. Anchee Min, *Red Azalea: Life and Love in China*, p. i.

9. In a disturbing incident revealing a similar attitude in the Party in more recent years, a woman was sent to a labour camp in the early 1980s for talking about sex to a foreigner, reported Fox Butterfield (*Alive in the Bitter Sea*, p. 202). The climate in Chinese society is more liberal today owing to the influx of ideas from the West, but the Party's official attitude towards such things is still deeply disapproving.

10. Harry Wu, *Bitter Winds*, pp. 190–5.

11. Zhang Xianliang, *Mimosa*, p. 15.

12. The night before Anchee Min was 'sent down' to the countryside, she realized how easy it had been before to sing 'I'll go where Chairman Mao's finger points' without understanding its significance. 'I felt like a bare egg laid on a rock. Maybe I would come to a real birth or maybe I would be smashed by the paw of some unfamiliar creature' (*Red Azalea*, p. 42).

13. *The Guardian* (4 January 1995).

14. One Holocaust survivor spent the rest of his life punishing himself for what happened to his family. He didn't eat any meat for forty or fifty years, saying, 'That's the way my children were cooked at Auschwitz.' Brecher, *Schindler's Legacy*, p. 141.

15. Butterfield, *Alive in the Bitter Sea*, p. 478.

16. Colin Thubron, 'Mistakes', in the *Granta* Ten Year anniversary edition.

17. Stanley Milgram, *Obedience to Authority*.

18. *Guardian Weekend*, 16 December 1995, p. 12.

19. John Pilger, 'Death for Sale', *The Guardian*, (12 November 1994).

20 Anne E. Thurston, *Enemies of the People*.

21. This story is told by Bette Bao Lord in *Legacies*, pp. 193–6.

CHAPTER 4

The State as Psychopath
Torture in Chinese Prisons

Torture is forbidden in Chinese prison. The authorities look after prisoners in accordance with laws and treat them with humanitarianism.

Ma Yuzhen, Chinese Ambassador to the UK[1]

Torture is an organized ritual in which the body is marked by the power of the state; it is the state acting as psychopath, sanctioned by the social structure. Ultimately, the state wants the screams of the tortured to penetrate their cells and to paralyse a whole society.

Although torture is prohibited by law in China, police and other state personnel continue to use it to extract confessions or to intimidate or punish prisoners. The 'cell boss' system, in which officials devolve responsibility for discipline within the cell to one of the most hardened prisoners, intensifies the terror.

In October 1988, the People's Republic of China ratified the United Nations (UN) Convention Against Torture and Other Cruel, Inhuman or Degrading Treatment or Punishment. As a State Party to the Convention, China has the obligation to take 'effective legislative, administrative, judicial and other measure to prevent acts of torture in any territory under its jurisdiction' (Article 2 of the Convention). China has not done so. During the eight years since China's ratification of the Convention, the incidence of torture in China's prisons, labour camps and detention centres has, if anything, increased.[2]

Since 'liberation' in 1949, the Chinese have employed a wide variety of ingenious and imaginative tortures, often with lyrical titles drawn from literature or mythology. 'Su Qin carries a sword on his back', for instance, refers to the way warriors traditionally carried a sword on their back (Plate 7). It consists of having one arm reaching back over the shoulder and the other arm twisted behind the back; the two hands are then pulled together at the back and shackled. Often the prisoner is forced to stay in this position for hours or overnight. 'The old ox ploughing the land' refers to a punishment in which two people are handcuffed together back to back and tied with a rope. This happened to two prisoners, including one named Xie Baoquan, in 1989. The guards then made a group of prisoners pull the rope and forced them to run, beating them with sticks and batons until they ran faster and faster, dragging the men behind them. The man in front had to crawl as fast as he could on the ground, dragging Xie along with his back scraping the rough concrete ground. When the torture ended, the concrete was covered with blood. The flesh of Xie's back had been scraped off, and the wounds suppurated through the winter. His back was covered with a cotton blanket which regularly became soaked with pus from his wounds, impregnating the cell with a smell of rotting flesh.[3]

Other common tortures are aimed primarily at degradation of the prisoner. Just after liberation, making prisoners swallow human excrement was widely used to humiliate the victim, who was immobilized with head thrown back and mouth kept open with a wooden pin. The torturer then pushed down the excrement, whether liquid or solid, with big spoons.[4] Today, a performance called 'paying respects to the cell god' (bai lao men), is commonly used by cell bosses to punish and intimidate new arrivals to the prison cells.[5] The new prisoners are ordered to kneel down in front of the 'cassia blossom vase' (prison slang for the toilet bucket) holding several rice straws, and perform prostrations to their mothers, the prison cadres and the cell boss. Finally the prisoners have to suck some of the contents of the toilet bucket up through the rice straw. The cell boss asks, 'Does the cassia blossom taste sweet?' And the prisoners must reply: 'Yes, delicious.' If they falter, the punishment will begin again, or they will be tortured in other ways.

Sophisticated equipment is not needed to cause extreme pain and degradation. A board the size of a door with a hole in the middle serves as an effective 'shackleboard' in Chinese prisons (see page 43). Handcuffs, thumbcuffs, shackles and chains have been used in China to restrain prisoners and as means of inflicting pain as punishment or to assist interrogation since the 1950s. Some are extremely heavy or have tightening devices to compress the flesh. When locked on a prisoner's wrist, handcuffs can be closed more and more tightly, cutting off the circulation, digging into the skin, lacerating the flesh and sometimes even breaking the bones.

If the bones do not break the pain is minimal at first. But after a few minutes, the hands turn black and lose all feeling. Pain runs all the way up the arms and into the head, where it concentrates, sending waves of pain out to every part of the body. Soon the head feels as if it is going to burst, and after another fifteen minutes the prisoner breaks out into a sweat. After twenty minutes, if the prisoner is lucky, they will faint. If not, they will be in agony, writhing on the floor, sobbing, begging and pleading with the tormentors to take off the handcuffs. When they are finally unlocked, the pain does not stop. The prisoner experiences a new type of pain, as if the insides are being pierced by thousands of needles.[6]

Suspension by the hands and feet is also common in the labour camps. The 'hanging aeroplane' involves suspending prisoners by the arms with their hands tied together behind their back so that the arms are contorted when the prisoners are suspended, causing extreme pain. Suspension can severely damage the muscles and nerves of the arms and shoulders if prolonged, or cause dislocation of the arms from the shoulder sockets. On other occasions, the guards might grab the prisoners from behind, force their wrists together at the back, and yank their arms back and up towards the head, so that the prisoners falls down on their knees, as the arms nearly break loose from their sockets. For variation, the wrists could be forced together in front, the arms jerked up over the head and then back, in the torture known as 'chicken claws'.

Different labour camps, prisons and detention centres have their own forms of punishment and discipline. Liu Qing, a small, mild-looking man with hair pulled back in a ponytail, was imprisoned in 1979 for his Democracy Wall activities, mainly for producing and distributing transcripts of the secret trial of dissident Wei Jingsheng. At Weinan Number Two prison in Shanxi, as punishment for smuggling out a manuscript about his experiences, Liu was forced to sit rigid and still every day for four years on a low bench without talking or moving. If he moved even slightly, he would be kicked by guards. When he tried to control his breathing by the Oriental discipline of *qi gong*, he was also beaten. Other prisoners have reported being made to stand on one foot, to lean against walls or the floor in various positions such as with the arms outstretched, and being tied to chairs, beds or pillars in painful positions.[7]

Tang Boqiao, a democracy activist who was imprisoned in Hunan, describes two of these tortures which were common in 'strict regime units' of labour camps in the province. The 'golden chicken standing on one leg' entails the prisoner having one arm handcuffed to the foot on the opposite side and then having the other arm chained high up above head height. In this way, the prisoner is left to stand on only one leg, and, when exhaustion sets in, the leg buckles under the body, wrenching the arm socket. The 'pillar standing feat' involves the prisoner being made to stand atop a pillar of around one metre in height with hands chained behind the back and fixed to the wall. After 24 hours of this ordeal, even the strongest of prisoners become exhausted. When they are unable to prevent themselves from falling asleep, the prisoners fall off the pillar, with their full body weight behind them, and again wrench their arms.[8]

Electric batons are some of the most frequently used torture instruments in Chinese prisons, and they are purchased from trade fairs – sometimes made by European or American companies – in varying shapes and sizes (Plate 8). During the 1980s, Chinese police officers were equipped with them; they are widely used casually to intimidate detainees, and to assist the interrogation process. Like an umbrella, electric shock batons have a button on the handle where the thumb rests. At a touch, a shock of at least 70,000 volts is released through two prongs at the nozzle of the baton, often emitting a crackling blue light. The batons are shaped in such a way that they can be inserted inside the body, and there is evidence that they have been applied to the soles of the feet, inside the mouth, on the genitals or inside the vagina or ears of victims.[9] An electric shock from a baton causes severe pain and affects muscle control; victims often feel nauseous and may have convulsions or faint with the shock.

In many cases the use of these batons can contribute to the deaths of prisoners. In December 1987, a middle school teacher from Henan province, Li Rongcheng, was arrested by the municipal public security officer.[10] His arms and legs were bound so that his body was forced into the shape of a curved bow, his head was stretched toward his back by a leather thong, and then he was subjected to shocks from five electric cattle prods. The public security officer Cui Yuanwu ordered: 'Shock his old buddy [his penis] so he won't be able to use it for twenty years.' Li Rongcheng was dead by the next morning.

Tang Boqiao's former teacher, Professor Peng, was one of the victims of a primitive and horrific form of torture known as the shackleboard, which has been used in several places of detention in Hunan province, including Changsha Number One Detention Centre and Hunan Provincial Number Three prison at Lingling. Peng was a retired professor of Hunan University, then in his seventies, who had been arrested for participating in sit-ins and hunger strikes with students during the pro-democracy movement in 1989. When he was first taken to Changsha Number One jail, he had showed great defiance: every day he would shout loudly from his cell 'Why are you detaining me!' and 'I demand to be released!'

As punishment, Peng was taken from his cell and placed on the shackleboard – a horizontal plank roughly the size of a door, equipped with metal shackles at the four corners and a hole at the lower end. Prisoners are laid upwards on the board, and the hands and feet are secured by the four shackles. The hole allows the prisoner to defecate. Some recalcitrant prisoners are strapped to the board for several months, which often leads to mental disturbances.

Tang used to hear Peng crying out every night from the punishment cell where he was bound to the shackleboard. '"Let me out!" "I need to take a bath" and "We are not afraid!" he would shout. He remained very sensible and coherent, however, and took care never to utter extreme slogans. Sometimes he would even sing the old primary school anthem, "Learn from the Good Example of Lei Feng." At the last line ("Stand firm and never waver!"), his voice would rise to a crescendo, as he bravely sought to give heart and encouragement to the rest of us. We, in turn, would cry out in unison, "Professor Peng! A good example!"'

One day Tang could bear Peng's suffering no longer, and he shouted out a demand that he should be released from the shackleboard immediately. The jail warden argued that the reason why Professor Peng was kept in shackles was because he was 'psychiatrically ill'. When Tang pointed out that, under Chinese criminal law, the mentally ill are meant to be 'exempt from prosecution', the cadre replied that, as there was no concrete proof of his illness, Professor Peng did not qualify for this exemption.

Tang's final image of the old professor remains with him today. 'Professor Peng was taken off the shackleboard after three months,' says Tang. 'He was a shadow of his former self. Some time later, while I was being taken down one of the jail corridors to an interrogation session, I happened to pass by Peng, who was just then being brought back from one himself. All shrivelled and dried up, he was barely conscious and was being carried out on a warden's back. I began to say, "Professor Peng, you've suffered so much . . ." but my voice became choked with sobs and I couldn't go on.

'Somehow, he managed to smile at me – just like before, in May 1989 when we held the sit-in protest together outside the Changsha government offices. "Don't worry, little Tang," he said. "I'll be all right." That was the last time I ever saw him.'

Later, Tang heard that the hospital had given Peng a clear diagnosis of psychiatric illness, and the government allowed him to return home. But immediately after his release, Peng was forcibly committed to a psychiatric institution. Soon afterwards, he was found dead. It was thought either that he committed suicide or that the authorities had taken their own steps to be rid of him.[11]

The idea of the 'Third Degree' originates from Himmler's order authorizing the use of what he specified as the 'Third Degree' in inter-rogation. The traditional 'Third Degree' consists of close confinement, starvation diet, hidden cells, extraordinary exercise or labour, sleep deprivation and beatings. In addition, doctors were to be at hand to prevent prisoners from being killed under torture. Edward Peters and his predecessor, French legalist Alec Mellors, designate this system as the basis for the modern practice of torture.[12] Peters believed he was 'clearly intending by that term to indicate torture'. Combined with thought reform, the Third Degree has been perfected in Chinese detention centres and labour camps in order to extract confessions.

Of these punishments, the combination of isolation and insufficient diet is believed to be the worst. Although Chinese regulations limit punitive solitary confinement to fifteen days, it is often imposed for months and even years. Liu Shanqing, whose story is told in Chapter 5, spent more than six years in solitary. This form of isolation can severely affect a prisoner's mental health. Liu Qing retained his sanity during his brief spell in solitary confinement, but one morning he noticed large patches of tangled hair on the cotton blanket under his body. 'I went on to have a look at the small mirror on the viewing board and discovered that my forehead had extended to the very top of my head,' he writes. The stress of Liu's situation and the damp chilliness of his cell also caused his left foot to swell, and his eyesight to deteriorate. 'I began to talk to myself; sometimes I carried on agitated debates with an imaginary opponent. Also, I recalled some formulae in mathematics, physics and chemistry and tried to deduce and draw many lines on the wall.'

After long periods in such conditions, prisoners suffer from a form of sensory deprivation, so that the merest glimpse beyond the cell wall can send them into a state of rapture and longing. Liu writes:

> In April, through the broken window in the men's room, surrounded by high walls and electric wire fences, I saw a small blade of green leaf of devil's ginger pushing up through the black dirt. Such green colour! It dazzled my eyes. I felt a strong urge, a strong desire to be under the blue sky.[13]

The existence of 'dark cells' has been reported in prisons and labour camps in Tibet, Liaoning and Hunan provinces, among others.[14] Some are known as *xiaohao*, which means literally 'dark number', and others as *heiwu*, 'black cells'. The names speak for themselves: the cells usually have no windows and are completely dark. It is like walking into a coffin: some cells are not big enough for the prisoner to lie down or even stand up.[15] Usually there is no bed, no heating, no sanitation and no ventilation.

Some prisoners who emerge from months or years of solitary confinement have difficulty in talking. Liu Qing recalls one prisoner whose tongue was stiff, and speaking tired him very much. The mental injury was even more apparent. The most dreadful thing, according to him, was that the prison authorities installed in his cell a high-power electronic instrument which could control his thought, induce him to think in the direction of the evidence needed by the authorities and record his thoughts for use the next day in his interrogation. He said that [they were using] this instrument incessantly, trying to induce him to commit suicide. When he was not talking about those things, his thinking was as normal as could be.'[16]

Prisoners who have served sentences in labour reform camps report frequent beatings if they fail to meet work quotas. Chen Poking, a pro-democracy activist held in Guangzhou Number One Re-education Through Labour Centre in Hua county, Guangdong province, reported that inmates who labour slightly more slowly than the rest are brutally beaten and mistreated by supervisors and team leaders, who are prisoners themselves. 'Inmates are often beaten until they are blood-stained all over, collapse or lose consciousness,' Chen wrote in a letter smuggled out of the camp in 1994. Prisoners in the camp are forced to work for as long as fourteen hours a day, in a stone quarry during daylight hours, transporting and loading stones into boats, and at night making artificial flowers which are sold for export.[17]

The conditions of arrest and confinement are another form of torture in China. The bleak, degrading conditions, the ever-present thuggery of 'cell bosses', the boredom of political study and the demands of forced labour are often almost unendurable. Prison guards control every aspect of an individual's life in the laogai; they decide how much food you eat, how you sleep, whether to send you to the punishment block or how to torture you. These conditions, which foster an almost constant state of anxiety, drive many prisoners over the edge, and suicide is common. Or attempted suicide, at least. The authorities hold such a sway over prisoners that they do not only control their lives, they also attempt to control their deaths.

Liang Zhenchang, who was arrested after the 4 June demonstrations at Tiananmen, became so deeply disturbed by the regime at Beijing Number Two prison that he attempted to commit suicide by swallowing three sewing needles inserted into a cigarette filter. However, he was discovered by officials, sent to solitary for two weeks and then returned to his cell. Any remission of sentence for medical treatment was out of the question for Liang. New regulations introduced by the government in 1988 and 1990 rule that prisoners who attempt 'self-injury and mutilation' must not be granted medical parole.[18] Sun Hong, another dissident held in the same prison, attempted suicide by driving a long sewing needle hard into the left side of his chest. He was discovered by guards and rushed to the prison clinic, where the needle was removed. Then he too was sent to the solitary block for ten days.[19]

The new, more severe, regulations on self-maiming are aimed at ending a practice which has been common in the labour camps. Prisoners in labour camps have resorted to this self-mutilation in an attempt to gain a respite from forced labour and, secondly, to be released on bail to seek medical treatment. Tang Boqiao lists several types of self-imposed injury. One way is to inject kerosene (often mixed with rotten food) into the bloodstream, via parts of the body such as the abdomen, legs or head. After a while, the affected part begins to swell and fester, and the authorities, in theory, are forced to allow the prisoner out for treatment. Another method prisoners use is to break their own limbs deliberately. This is done by placing the arm or leg between two heavy slabs of slate and then striking down hard on the slate with either a pickaxe or a sledgehammer. On the basis that labour reform units have only basic medical facilities, prisoners will also swallow small pieces of razor blade or slash open the abdomen in an attempt to be released.[20]

A description of prisoners transferred to Xinjiang in 1983 refers to inmates with steel wire, nails, small spoons, empty toothpaste tubes and pieces of glass in their stomachs.[21] When they were in pain, they didn't have to get up to work:

> They could lie in bed, knitting their brows and moaning, and they'd get a bowl of noodles or some fried eggs. Look at that fellow over there. He's had two operations, and they didn't find a thing in his stomach! He's afraid of pain, so he doesn't dare to swallow glass. He'd just hold his belly and roll around in the sand . . . and the doctor believed he really had swallowed something and cut his stomach open in a hurry to see what was there. They use anaesthetic during the operation, so it doesn't hurt. After one operation, you can rest for at least half a year.

In the 1950s and 1960s, prisoners resorted to similar desperate measures in the camps, and often stood a better chance of success than prisoners today. Ma Wenpiao, a prisoner working on the Chungking to Chengdu railway in the early 1950s, successfully escaped from the forced labour camp by taking poison. He bought some plantain peas with the help of another prisoner, and during the night he secretly ground up some fine grains in a bowl and mixed them with water. He smeared this mixture over his head and scrotum: it was extremely painful. The next morning, the camp chief examined the swellings, and judged them to be serious enough for treatment. Ma managed to flee from the camp on the way to hospital, and, after about ten days on the run, he disguised himself as a commercial traveller and arrived in Hong Kong.[22]

The most gruesome incident of self-maiming Tang came across in prison was that of a prisoner who used a twin-hook device, which he had designed himself for the purpose, to gouge out his own eyes. His attempt to secure release on bail backfired – he was serving a life sentence, and the camp commander strictly adhered to a regulation which lays down that lifers are not eligible for release on bail. The man was forced to continue hard labour despite the loss of his eyes.

Far more people are now being condemned to death and judicially executed each year in China than at any other time since, probably, the early 1950s. According to a top judicial directive in June 1981,

All High People's Courts should report to the Supreme People's Court, on or before the fifth day of each month, the number of death penalties approved and executions carried out by them during the previous months, in order to facilitate the completion of overall (national) statistics for submission to senior levels.[23]

By April 1984 however, following the 'crackdown on crime' campaign, the nationwide wave of executions was so great that the reporting process had broken down.

The conditions in which condemned prisoners are held on Death Row are a torture in themselves. The use of their bodies for organ transplants after execution – and sometimes even before – is a further source of suffering. Chinese doctors who have fled the mainland say that 90 per cent of kidney transplants performed in China involve the use of prisoners' organs. There is no system of voluntary organ donation in China, and tradition demands that a body should be buried intact. 'They say that about two thousand kidney transplants are carried out every year in China, and the number is growing. That is about the same number of judicial executions reported by Amnesty International last year, a number that was a considerable increase over the previous year,' says BBC reporter Sue Lloyd-Roberts, who went undercover in Chinese hospitals with Harry Wu to investigate the trade. 'It would not be fanciful to suggest that the two sets of figures are growing in tandem.' The lucrative trade in human organs, which are sold to patients from Hong Kong, America, Taiwan and Europe, hardly creates an incentive for the authorities to reduce their application of capital punishment. Asia Watch reports that 35 per cent of the two hundred criminal offences in China currently carry the death penalty.

If doctors need the kidneys of an prisoner (they are sold for around $30,000 each), the prisoner is shot in the head to preserve the vital organs. If they need the corneas, they are shot in the heart. Sometimes they may not be shot at all. One Chinese doctor living in the West tells how he and three other doctors were driven to a prison one night and ordered to take both kidneys from four anaesthetized prisoners. His only explanation was that 'the kidneys had to be fresh because they were needed for high-ranking Party officials'. Without kidneys, a person dies in 24 hours. After the kidneys had been taken away by military helicopter, the doctor was told that the prisoners would be executed the next day.[24]

A young woman prisoner, Zhong Haiyun, a former teacher at a middle school, was sentenced to death after writing a number of articles and 'big character posters' that were critical of Hua Guofeng, Mao's successor. At her execution in April 1978, Zhong was shot twice in the head but did not die. Instead of waiting for her death, medical personnel were allowed to take her body into a specially erected operating facility on the prison premises and remove both kidneys while she was still living. One kidney was transplanted into the body of the son of a high-ranking military official – a deputy battalion commander of the Nanjing Military Region. The deputy commander had earlier arranged for officials at the Jiangxi prison to facilitate the operation.[25]

There is no such thing as 'free and voluntary consent' for organ removal where condemned prisoners are concerned. As soon as suspected capital offenders are caught and charged by the police, they are shackled at the ankles and kept in this condition until the trial. If the prisoner is then sentenced to death, he or she will remain in leg irons, and often also in handcuffs, until the last moments of life. In some prisons they are held in total isolation for months.

'There is a special place inside the jail for holding condemned prisoners – a long chamber comprising several "solitary quarters", one cell for each evil felon,' wrote a retired prison guard who worked in the Tianjin Municipal Jail:

> The door to the chamber is lined with black rubber, very heavy, like an 'entrance to hell' designed by some devil. The corridor is dark and deathly quiet. No sounds at all can be heard apart from the footsteps of guards and the clinking of ankle fetters. Each criminal is kept alone in a tiny, narrow cell. The four walls are lined with thick, springy sheets of leather, and it is as dark as a coffin . . . All of the prisoners are in handcuffs and leg irons, which will not be removed before the time of their execution. In order to eat, drink or go to the toilet, they have to be helped by 'general duties' staff (prisoners serving light sentences).

> Once transferred there, condemned prisoners are denied access to the (communal) latrine and are barred from reading newspapers or listening to

the prison's educational broadcasts. The only recreation left to them is to doze lethargically or just sit there in blank contemplation. In effect, criminals sent to the 'solitary quarters' have lost even their souls, for what awaits them is death.[26]

At around 10 p.m. on the night before execution, a prisoner is placed in an individual interrogation room, still in shackles, and bound tightly to a chair with rope. The judge responsible for announcing the court's final rejection of the prisoner's appeal against execution enters the room, reads the final death warrant aloud to the prisoner and requests that him or her to sign their name to the document. If the prisoner is unwilling, he or she is forced to do so.[27]

Throughout the night, the prisoner is watched over by specially assigned prisoners, who feed him or her the last meal, and perhaps help him or her to smoke a final cigarette. At dawn, the prisoner is untied from the chair, then placed in the back of an open lorry with an armed guard on either side, legs are still in shackles and wrists in handcuffs. During the journey to the execution ground, a thin rope tied around the prisoner's neck is gripped tightly by one of the guards. Before the final bullet in the head, the prisoner is often subjected to the ordeal of a 'mass sentencing rally'.

Mark Baber often witnessed prisoners being taken away for execution from Shanghai Number One municipal prison, when he was a prisoner there from September 1991 to 28 October 1994. Death Row was housed in the building opposite Mark's cell until early 1994, when it was moved into the same building (Building Number Two). 'Prisoners who are to be executed are taken away in the morning in shackles with their heads shaved,' says Mark. 'Around August 1993 I saw thirteen or fourteen prisoners being taken off for execution in one day. I was told that during 1993 a hundred prisoners were taken from Shanghai municipal prison to be executed. In 1994, the number up until October was 120.'

Mark often witnessed prisoners on Death Row being given blood tests by doctors and nurses, and he also saw a separate medical room for the prisoners awaiting execution. 'They are not allowed out of their 1.40 by 2.40 metre cells,' he says. 'They are guarded 24 hours a day by trusty prisoners who keep watch in shifts, with three trusties guarding each prisoner slated for execution. The trusties used for this work are chosen from those serving over fifteen years.' Death Row inmates were not allowed any contact with their families, and it was nearly impossible for them to meet a solicitor.

The constant attention given by medical staff to those awaiting execution is in sharp contrast to the poor treatment given to other prisoners. It is rare for a doctor or nurse to be seen near the ordinary cells, and medical care is often not available, refused or charged for. Mark also recalls that the doctors and nurses are police and sometimes wear police uniforms.

Prisoners at Shanghai Number One generally accepted that Death Row inmates are used as an 'organ bank', with their organs being removed as and when they are ready and a suitable recipient is found. Mark even noticed one day that the diet of Death Row prisoners was superior to the others. While working with other members of his brigade, the 'prison rear supply base', he saw a separate menu called the 'protect health' diet for prisoners on Death Row. Evidently, it is the health of the organs, not the prisoners, with which the authorities are concerned. The human being is merely one link in a grotesque supply chain of the 'organ market with Chinese characteristics'.

Notes

1. Letter to the Editor, *The Guardian* (18 March 1995).

2. Amnesty International, *Torture in China*, (December 1992), ASA 17/55/92.

3. *Ibid.*

4. CICRC, *The White Book on Forced Labour in the People's Republic of China*, vol. 1, The Hearings, p. 175.

5. Tang Boqiao, *Anthems of Defeat: Crackdown in Hunan Province 1989–92*, p. 83.

6. This description is taken from interviews with Chinese dissidents such as Ni Yuxian and appears in Anne Thurston, *A Chinese Odyssey*. Nien Cheng also gives a graphic account of her suffering in handcuffs in *Life and Death in Shanghai*.

7. Amnesty International report, *Torture in China* (December 1992), ASA 17/55/92.

8. Tang Boqiao, *Anthems of Defeat*, p. 99.

9. Amnesty International.

10. Harry Wu, *Laogai*, p. 70.

11. Tang Boqiao, *Anthems of Defeat*, and author interview.

12. Alec Mellors, *La Torture* (Paris, 1949), quoted in Kate Millett, *The Politics of Cruelty*.

13. Liu Qing, *Prison Memoirs*.

14. Amnesty International, *Torture in China*.

15. Such cells are apparently found in Hunan Provincial Number Six prison in Longxi, among others.

16. Liu Qing, *Prison Memoirs*.

17. For further information on Chen see Amnesty International, *Urgent Action Bulletin*, UA 435/94, ASA 17/38/94 (7 December 1994.)

18. Report by Human Rights Watch/Asia and Human Rights in China, quoted in *China Rights Forum* (summer 1994).

19. *Ibid.*

20. Tang Boqiao, *Anthems of Defeat*. Other prisoners took similar drastic measures to commit suicide: they swallowed the handle of their teacups or ate light bulbs (Anne Thurston, *A Chinese Odyssey*). It was a tradition in the Soviet gulag that other prisoners did not interfere when another inmate was carrying out such self-mutilations. In *My Testimony*, Anatoly Marchenko writes that in the prison hospital 'there were plenty of mutilated

prisoners . . . some with ripped open stomachs, some who had sprinkled powdered glass in their eyes and some who had swallowed assorted objects – spoons, toothbrushes, wire. Some people used to grind sugar down to dust and inhale it – until they got an abscess of the lung . . . The surgeon in the prison hospital was a man of rich experience. His most frequent job was opening up stomachs, and if there had been a museum of objects taken out of stomachs, it would surely have been the most astonishing collection in the world' (p. 150).

21. Jia Lusheng and Feng Shou, *The Great Prison of Western China*, pp. 39-41.

22. CICRC, *The White Book on Forced Labour in the People's Republic of China*, vol. 2: The Record, p. 230.

23. Notification on Several Points concerning Implementation of the NPC Standing Committee's 'Decision on the Question of Approval of Death Penalty Cases', Supreme People's Court (11 June 1981), quoted in 'Organ Procurement and Judicial Execution in China', *Human Rights Watch/Asia*, vol. 6, no. 9.

24. Sue Lloyd-Roberts, *The South China Morning Post* (30 October 1994).

25. Hu Ping, *Xue Ji Hong Tudi* [Earth Red with Blood Sacrifice], originally published by the underground press. Quoted in 'Organ Procurement and Judicial Execution in China'.

26. *A Real Life Account of China's Prisons* [Zhongguo Jianyu Jishi] (Tuanjie Press, Beijing), February 1989, p. 334, quoted in Asia Watch report as above.

27. This account is by a former judge familiar with pre-execution procedures in Shenzhen, and quoted in Asia Watch report, details as above.

CHAPTER 5

Loneliness Is the Scalpel
Liu Shanqing

Loneliness is the scalpel used for performing surgery on the soul.

Chinese prison document

Let no one remind us of our mothers, no one tell us a dream of home.

Salvatore Quasimodo (1901–1968)

What happens to the human mind during six and a half years of solitary confinement? At first, Liu Shanqing, who was imprisoned for ten years – six and a half of them in solitary – contemplated suicide. 'Ultimately, I couldn't do it,' he says. 'Shakespeare's words kept turning over in my head: "To be or not to be, that is the question".'

Many prisoners lost their minds[1] in the solitary cells of the prison where counter-revolutionary inmates like Liu were isolated from ordinary criminals.[2] But he maintained his sanity by practising a number of 'survival tactics' he had already contemplated before his arrest, together with a resolute determination in the face of constant psychological pressure.

Liu Shanqing, a bespectacled, young-looking 41-year-old with an informal manner and a broad grin, was imprisoned in Guangdong province for his involvement with the Democracy Wall Movement during the late 1970s and early 1980s.[3] He had been arrested while delivering a jumper for Wang Xizhe, the independent Marxist theorist who was active in the democracy movement.

Because Liu had been born and brought up in Hong Kong, his story became a *cause célèbre* in his home city. His experiences were a bitter reminder of the constant presence of the mainland in Hong Kong affairs, and the human rights implications of the Chinese takeover in 1997. They touched a raw nerve, and so did Liu's fiercely held opinions on Hong Kong's involvement in the Chinese democracy movement: 'With the crackdown [after the democracy demonstrations in 1976 and 1979], Hong Kong people no longer dared to continue to go to the mainland to get involved with the movement. To me, this indicated a serious lapse in moral strength. I was of the opinion that we should struggle and challenge the official bureaucrats to the very end. If we did not persist, the mainland movement activists would say we had no guts.'

Liu Shanqing's courage and obstinacy sustained him throughout his sentence; despite being promised leniency if he confessed and reformed his thought, he refused to give in. He caved in only once, and then retracted his confession soon afterwards. News of his story spread quickly in Hong Kong, and on 27 December 1992 Liu Shanqing was greeted as a hero on his release by a huge crowd at the Canton to Kowloon railway station at Hunghom. For days afterwards, his story dominated the headlines.[4]

Liu, who lives with Christina Tang, the woman who waited for him for ten years, now works in a 'halfway house' home for the mentally handicapped living in the community. In his spare time, he continues his work on behalf of democracy activists still in prison, and for the wider cause of promoting democracy in China. He wants to keep Chinese human rights abuses in the Hong Kong headlines, so the city does not forget. But his political activities are unlikely to be tolerated by China after the takeover. More than ever, as 1997 approaches, Liu Shanqing is aware of the fragile democratic structure of Hong Kong, not to mention his own vulnerability. He talks quickly and breathlessly, as if to make up for lost time; or as if he has a sense of time running out.

Liu grew up in Hong Kong, and feels a particular emotional attachment for his home city. His parents had fled from Canton to escape the Japanese presence on the mainland, and life was not easy during Liu's childhood. There was never very much money for food or other essentials; Liu's father was an uneducated machine – worker who earned very little. But still the family wanted the best for their only son. Liu learnt quickly and was one of the cleverest boys in his class. He passed his exams easily and, after secondary school, gained a place in the University of Hong Kong where he studied physics, maths and engineering.

Liu was studying during the 1970s, when new Leftist ideas were beginning to be disseminated throughout Hong Kong. Many of those whose sympathies lay with the Left, like Liu, began to be critical about the lack of freedom and democracy of the Beijing regime, and also to resent the political power of the old British empire. In Beijing itself, the winds of change were beginning to blow, and in 1976 thousands of people took to the streets in an overt show of homage to the dead leader

Zhou Enlai. The mass gatherings were broken up by the Gang of Four, led by Mao's wife Jiang Qing. The Gang of Four were a political group consisting of Yao Wenyuan, Zhang Chunqiao, Wang Hongwen, and Jiang Qing, Mao's third wife. Jiang was officially blamed for creating and directing the Cultural Revolution, and was the target of a visceral hatred from the people. The four were tried and convicted in 1980, in nationally televised television proceedings. But dissent continued to simmer under the surface of society, and three years later the Democracy Wall Movement was born – the first popular demonstration of its kind since the foundation of the People's Republic in 1949.

These democratic protests were Liu's first awakening into the nature of the bureaucratic system in China. He saw them as the first manifestations of the struggle between the bureaucrats and the people, and, of course, he stood firmly on the side of the people. Liu identified so closely with the people's aims and objectives that he decided to align his fate with the movement activists on the mainland.

He says: 'After I was released from prison and returned to Hong Kong many people asked me, "Liu Shanqing, ten years ago after graduating from university you had such a bright future; why did you get involved in the democracy movement and waste ten years in prison?" Really, if I were an ordinary university student ten years ago, what I did was incomprehensible. The problem is, I was not an ordinary university student. I was a romantic revolutionary.

'In the two years before my arrest, my revolutionary romanticism caused me to venture into China fourteen times to struggle side by side for socialist democracy with the mainland democracy movement activists in south China. Ten years ago, if I had told ordinary people that I was working towards the democratic future of China, surely there would have been hardly a sympathetic ear. But today, after the baptism of the 1989 movement in Tiananmen Square, I believe that many people understand my struggle for China's democratic future. There are always pioneers in history. If it had not been me, it could have been someone else.'

Liu, who had become an underground leader of the Revolutionary Marxist League, became involved with establishing contact with the mainland movement activists, exchanging ideas, and providing material support for the movement. His involvement with the people-run publications on the mainland was particularly sensitive.

Wei Jingsheng, started the magazine *Exploration* and wrote *The Fifth Modernisation* and *Democracy of Dictatorship*, had been arrested in March 1979 and sentenced to fifteen years' imprisonment in October. Wei, a former electrician at Beijing Zoo and veteran democracy campaigner, was unexpectedly released on parole on 14 September 1993 after serving fourteen and a half years of a fifteen-year sentence. He described the conditions of his probation as follows: 'I cannot vote, I have no freedom of expression, I cannot form any kind of organization, even doing business is not allowed' (*New York Times*, 21 September 1993). He confirmed that he had been beaten in prison, had lost all but a dozen or so of his teeth and was suffering from heart and lung problems induced by conditions in prison. According to an Asia Watch source (*Detained in China and Tibet*, p. 509), 'Ordinary police and prison guards had no authority over (Wei) . . . He was watched over by a team of special security officers. No single official was allowed to be alone with him. His condition was reported directly to Deng Xiaoping's office. Deng decided personally on everything related to Wei.' In 1995, Wei was arrested again and has now returned to prison.

Liu Qing, a Nanjing University graduate and former machine-tool operator, was one of the chief editors of *April Fifth Forum*, one of the foremost journals of the 1979–81 democracy movement. He was arrested on 11 November 1979, for producing and distributing transcripts of the secret trial of Wei Jingsheng, and sentenced to a fifteen–year prison term in 1979. In 1980, he was assigned to a labour camp in Shaanxi Province for three years' re-education through labour. Towards the end of this period, Liu smuggled out a long and detailed manuscript, *Prison Notes*, documenting his experiences within the Chinese penal system. He was punished severely by beating and a starvation diet, and was often not allowed to exercise or to talk. Liu Qing was finally released in 1989 and arrived in the USA on 14 July 1992.

Liu Shanqing was instrumental in encouraging mainland activists to continue publishing people-run magazines despite the continual political pressure.

Together with a group of trusted colleagues, Liu risked shipping these magazines out of the mainland so that the Hong Kong and international mass media had access to them. 'Probably most of the magazines that were known to the outside world at the time were smuggled out by us,' he says. 'The more reproductions and analyses of these magazines there were, and the greater the publicity of their cause, the more international support we could generate for the movement.' Just as importantly, Liu also smuggled outside publications into the mainland. 'It was a time when Mao's thought had rapidly collapsed, and the upper levels had not yet come up with a centralized policy while the people were eagerly seeking outside stimulation. When the Democracy Movement began, it was simply natural that in their search for a future for China, the people were receptive to outside knowledge and ideas.'

Liu's other main activity was the building up of a Hong Kong solidarity movement, and discussion with the major mainland activists on the future direction, strategy and organizational matters of the Democracy Movement. 'After returning to Hong Kong, I felt that the support we rendered to the Democracy Movement ten years ago was the precursor of the support the Hong Kong citizens provided for the 1989 movement. The only difference is that the former was on a small scale. It was a kind of rehearsal for a bigger historical event.'

Through his political activities, Liu met his girlfriend, Hong Kong-born Christina, who is two years his senior. They became very close, and shared both political ideals and an intense commitment to the cause. He considered her to be even more extreme in her political opinions than he was.

Usually Christina accompanied Liu on his many trips to the mainland, but when he decided to go to Guangzhou on Christmas Day 1981, she objected for the first time. This time her intuition told her that something was going to happen. She even threatened separation if he insisted on going. Liu recalls: 'My attitude in those days was, to put it bluntly, that of a male chauvinist. She knew there was nothing she could do to stop me.'

The next day at 4 a.m. Liu went to Hunghom railway station by himself. This time, Christina did not go to see him off. Liu knew that her intuition about his trip was well founded. 'By early 1981, the Central Committee thought that to institute the open-door economic policy, it first had to totally suppress the democracy movement. So it thoroughly tackled the movement by its roots, by relentless total suppression,' he says. 'By that time the only form of the movement's activities was publication of unauthorized magazines. Beginning in April 1981, the Beijing authorities launched a nationwide crackdown on the democracy movement activists. As a result, almost all well-known movement activists were jailed and given five to ten years of imprisonment. Inevitably, movement publications disappeared, as did all other forms of related activities.' Liu knew that he was on the authorities' blacklist. 'But I didn't give a damn,' he says now. 'But still, when I reflect upon my actions today, really I committed adventurism.'

Liu first went to visit the wife of He Qui, editor of *The People's Road* (*Renmin Zhi Lu*), to present her with a jumper for her husband, who was being held at Huanghua Detention Centre. He then went to the house of Wang Xizhe, one of China's most famous democrats. Although Liu had been closer to He Qui, after arguing with Wang Xizhe about Marx the first time they met, he still held Wang in high esteem because of his special status in the Democracy Movement.

The moment Liu greeted Wang's wife, he noticed she was behaving differently from He Qui's wife. She seemed upset and disturbed, and at first refused to accept the sweater that he had brought for Wang. After a while she said she had to go out briefly, and told Liu to wait for her return. When she came back, she was crying, and, as Liu left, she urged him time and again to be careful.

He remembers: 'The moment I stepped out of the house, I knew I was being followed. I was frightened. I had been here many times, but never before had anyone followed me so openly. Instead of turning left on to the main road, I turned left towards a vegetable field. I saw some water chives, and said to myself: it could be a long time before I see water chives again.'

Later Liu realized that when Wang Xizhe's wife had left the house for a while, she may have gone to report his visit to the local police station or street committee. At 11 or 12 that night, he was approached by five men. One of them asked: 'Are you Liu Shanqing?' When he replied that he was, Liu was told, 'Then come with us. It is nothing serious.'

'Later I learned that when one is told it is nothing serious, it is more often than not quite serious,' says Liu now. 'So, it had finally happened. I was surprisingly calm. I remember thinking, soon I would be confronting the Communists face to face. So, what was the big deal?'

In the end, it was a big deal. Because Liu refused to confess, he served every day of a ten-year sentence. Enraged by his non-compliant attitude, the prison authorities made him endure six and a half years of his incarceration in solitary confinement. It was in a solitary cell that Liu first descended to 'the bottom layer of hell'.

'In Asia it is said that there are eighteen layers of hell, and the bottom layers are the worst,' says Liu. 'The hierarchies of Chinese prisons are just like layers of hell. People from the Communist Party are on the top level; they can go out of prison occasionally, and some of them can even make love with their wives. Others high up in the hierarchy are so-called active or good prisoners: those the authorities can trust and put into working groups. Sometimes they will build houses for the guards, fix their television sets, or do other responsible jobs. Prisoners like myself – those they wanted to break – were at the bottom of the hierarchy: the lowest levels of hell.'

Liu's isolation began as soon as he arrived at the gate of Meizhou prison after several months in a detention centre waiting for his sentence. 'Director Liu of the prison political bureau, who had been there waiting for me for some time, told me that I was not to talk to the other prisoners, for fear they might bash me up,' he recalls. 'I knew it was because he wanted to isolate me, to keep me apart from the other prisoners. I didn't know until later that Meizhou prison had made special preparations for me. Before I even arrived, the prison staff had commanded the other prisoners to have nothing to do with me.'

Liu Shanqing endured three periods of solitary confinement during his ten-year sentence: the first time was for one and a half years in a detention camp where he seldom spoke to anyone and the guards were warned not to speak to him; the second for about two years in Meizhou prison when he was 'looked after' for 24 hours a day by a fellow prisoner seeking to earn merit points by reporting the slightest of his actions to the authorities. His final three and a half years was spent in Huaiji prison, a solitary confinement 'reform through labour' farm in the Zhaoqing area of north-west Guangdong. He found out that Wang Xizhe and He Qui were also held behind the white walls of isolation cells in the prison, and they were able to communicate with each other through the walls and windows. Liu describes their conversations through the walls in Hong Kong business terms as 'telephoning' and their glimpses of each other through windows 'faxing'. The communication made his last few years bearable.

For his first year in solitary confinement, Liu was imprisoned in a cell only slightly larger than a small toilet with no light except for one small, high window. The wooden floor was partially covered by a threadbare rug, and Liu slept on a wooden 'raft' with one blanket. 'There was a toilet next to the bed instead of a bucket – so you could tell this prison was quite modern,' Liu recalls drily. All of his clothes were taken away and replaced by a thin cotton prison uniform, which was completely inadequate for the Cantonese winter when temperatures often plunged to 2 or 3 degrees Centigrade. In summer, the atmosphere of the cell became stifling, and mosquitoes were a further torment.

Guards who were instructed not to speak to Liu brought him three insubstantial meals a day made up of tiny portions of vegetables, a small bowl of dirty rice and one piece of fat per week. It was only just enough to survive. Every month Liu was given a small bar of soap to wash himself and his clothes. He was not allowed any books or other reading material. 'The worst thing was losing all sense of time,' says Liu. 'After living in Hong Kong I had been used to working to a schedule, attending meetings at certain times and so on. Suddenly everything had been taken away from me. I tried to keep track of the days but I became muddled.

'In solitary confinement we had tactics to survive. You don't think about the past and you don't think about the future – you don't think about anything at all, and you don't make dreams. If you are highly alert you can control yourself in this way. At the detention centre where I was sentenced I had been having nightmares every night. But in solitary I became so successful in controlling my mind that after a while I stopped dreaming at nights.'[5]

Liu tried not to think about Christina; he knew that would create longing, and make his situation worse. But he says he always knew at the back of his mind that they would be together again, and this gave him strength.

He knew in his first few days in prison that, if he wanted to survive, he would have to keep his mind and spirits up. Liu felt he had the strength to resist the psychological pressure political activists are subject to in the labour camps. With his use of the collective pronoun in his description of tactics used to survive, Liu allies himself with the struggle of revolutionaries all over the world. He says: 'The Chinese democracy movement is really a little bit naive, compared to countries like South Africa or Palestine, where the quest for freedom is a great struggle, and activists are prepared to go to jail rather than into exile.'

In the context of warfare, he believes, solitary confinement is a method commonly used by the aggressors to break the spirit of dissidents. Prison documents in China going back to well before the Communist revolution reveal various studies of solitary confinement as a means to encourage reform. In 1934, Zhao Chen wrote:

> *Communication is the inherent essence of the human. But the prisoner is locked into his room and stays alone surrounded by four walls. Thus he will feel incredible suffering. No matter how vicious the criminal, how much they oppose the regulation upon entry, they will all undoubtedly feel regret and fondly remember their past and their family. They will be alone in their room with no one to talk to and herein lies our opportunity to reform them.[6]*

In one Chinese account, it is said, the small punishment cell is 'certainly no guest-house. It is an operating table for felons. Loneliness is the scalpel, used for performing surgery upon the souls of those overly fond of fun and excitement:[7]

> *Day 1: They lock [the prisoner] up in the xiao hao for a period of forced introspection. Day 2: He's still lying on the bed,[8] feeling quite happy . . . Day 3: He feels a little lonely . . . Day 4: He starts to feel rather afraid. The ray of light piercing the little aperture has been mercilessly halved in size by a steel bar. The room is like some dim cave. Day 5: He is plunged into terror. The ghostly shadows of loneliness play over the four walls around, seeming to grin hideously at him. He involuntarily breaks out in a cold shiver. He screams insanely and bangs on the door. He jumps up and down on the bed, and then starts rolling around underneath it. Over the next few days, he begins to repent.*

That's the theory at least. It didn't work with Liu. Although he had no direct experience of imprisonment, Liu drew on the example of other dissidents who had suffered the same fate. 'I think the most important thing is to be optimistic, and you learn to protect yourself mentally. In the situation of solitary confinement, I made a daily schedule. Many prisoners have a large belly because their stomach muscles relax when they are sitting down all the time. So you do not sit down. You have to make a plan to walk every day, perhaps a thousand times around the cell. I counted how many times I walked around, and when I'd finished, I'd walk around again.'

Liu found his inner resources severely tested when he was flung into the 'dark cell' as punishment for refusing to co-operate with the compilation of his year-end summary. At the end of each year, group meetings were called and cadres would put pressure on each prisoner to write a statement recognizing his crime and declaring his submission to the law, his achievement of self-reform through labour, his relationship with the other prisoners and his plans for self-improvement in the coming year. After statements had been written, a small group met to discuss them, and finally they were submitted to the cadres.

Liu was determined to resist the process, despite persuasion and threats from the cadres. Despite being warned that, if he did not make a statement, he would be 'made an example for the masses', Liu stubbornly maintained his stance for a month. 'But the prison authorities would not relent,' he says. 'I had to write a statement or I wouldn't "come through the gate". In a fit of rage I wrote one. The general drift of it was that I was guilty of no crime, that judges, under the pressure of the "Be Strict and Be Fast" campaign, had created crimes out of nothing, had turned small crimes into big ones, and that the judges were the guilty ones.' Prison officials were furious with Liu's statement. 'They referred me to the section head, Liu, to be dealt with,' recalls Liu. 'He swore at me while I read my statement, and I swore back at him.'

Liu was transferred to the 'dark cell' with fetters on his ankles. The cell, which was little more than a cubicle, was black as night and full of mosquitoes and cockroaches. 'The walls were stained with blood, and in some places with defiant slogans,' says Liu. 'To walk into the cell was to sink into total darkness where day and night were the same.'

To be released from the dark cell, a prisoner had to recognize his errors. Liu was told that he would be let out if he wrote a statement admitting his guilt. 'In the beginning of course I held my head high,' says Liu. 'Every day I stuck a grain of rice on the wall to mark the passing of the days. After twenty or more grains of rice, I was weak and dizzy and hardly knew where I was, and couldn't go on counting grains of rice any longer. I had to write a statement. I didn't recognise my crime or declare my submission to the law, merely stating that my attitude had been uncooperative, but they let me out.'

Liu goes on: 'Three types of people suffer the deepest despair in the Chinese prison system: the first two are dissidents who have been labelled as dangerous people to the state, and mentally handicapped people. The Communist Party does not respect human beings, and the Chinese judiciary does not accept that mentally handicapped people exist. They are lumped together with common criminals. And because they do not know how to lie, they cannot confess and show they have "reformed their thoughts". So they receive longer sentences.'

Liu remembers one young man with a mental problem from a poor rural family who was caught stealing a piece of meat from the market. He was so frightened he tried to fight the police who arrested him, and was beaten up badly. He was charged with criminal offences against the police, and sentenced to seven years. One of the other prison inmates used to make a joke and say, 'You're serving seven years for a piece of meat, and now in prison you have a small bowl of meat every week.'

Wang was a mentally handicapped youth who was charged with rape and sentenced to seven years because he was found peering at his sister in the bath. 'Wang's case was more serious because of his poor mental condition,' says Liu. 'In prison, he was so honest he didn't know how to confess his "crime". He couldn't work, and he kept wanting to go home. Sometimes he would just go out towards the prison gates. So because he wouldn't co-operate, guards put him in shackles for a long time. He couldn't have a bath, and because he didn't know how to express himself he was often beaten up. None of the cadres showed any sympathy to him because of their lack of education. In fact, Wang was just the sort of prisoner they didn't want. It was at the time in the 1980s that making money was all-important, and even prisons were expected to increase their productivity. Wang couldn't work, so they just kept him chained up for virtually all his sentence.'

Han was another prisoner who suffered from mental illness. 'He was so mad that he was always yelling, and the guards didn't know what to do with him,' says Liu. They quickly carried out the usual solution by flinging him into a solitary cell. He remained there for eleven years. 'They wanted to let him go, but his family didn't want him back,' recalls Liu. 'He was in such agony that he tried everything to escape from his cell. He even used his hand to break down the door, only to be beaten up and thrown in a more secure cell with his legs shackled. Other prisoners used to hear him screaming and crying all night. He may still be there even now, because if his family do not take care of him, then no one else will.'

The third category of prisoner to suffer the deepest despair in Liu's experience consists of men with small children. 'In Chinese society, it is traditionally the father who has responsibility for the younger generation. Often the children of prisoners would fall behind with their education or fall into bad company, and the father could do nothing. So they would be in great despair.'

Liu's own parents were allowed to visit him every six months during his sentence. Christina was not allowed to visit him even once. Although he had been arrested on 26 December 1981, the authorities had not told his family until his father made inquiries in Guangzhou on 13 March of the next year. Soon afterwards, the Hong Kong government made a statement announcing that Liu was considered a Chinese national and was being detained for engaging in 'unlawful' deeds. The Chinese authorities said that Liu had been convicted at a 'public' trial of collaborating with 'counter-revolutionary elements' to 'attack the socialist system and the people's democratic dictatorship' and of 'violating the laws and regulations of the country'.

Liu's parents were allowed to visit him for the first time two days before his release from the 'dark cell'. Liu didn't know prison cadres had already discussed his case with them. 'When I told them how unhappy I was, my mother nodded her head in sympathy and urged me to do what the cadres wanted, for my own sake,' says Liu. 'I was so angry I felt steam coming from my nose and ears.' Liu understood how it had been possible for his parents to be manipulated by the cadres: 'My mother and father are ordinary people who are not involved in politics. Like most Chinese, they are not so aggressive, not so clear, and they do not defend their civil rights. So it is possible for the Communists to manipulate them. It is also the reason why the Stalinists have been able to control the country for so long.' However Liu admits that he also inherited his strength of mind from his father: 'He is the same sort of character as me, very strong and stubborn, and he understood better than my mother why I had to hold out without confessing for so long.'

Later on in his sentence, his parents – mainly his mother – implored him again and again to confess for his own sake. But the next time they hinted they'd do all they could to get Liu's sentence reduced, and that he could always sort things out after he left prison. At the time, Liu was unaware that a Committee for the Rescue of Liu Shanqing in Hong Kong was campaigning for his release. On one of his parents' visits, Liu managed to slip a copy of the verdict against him into the pocket of his mother's cardigan. His mother took the hint, took off her cardigan, and folded the verdict within it.

'In the end, I convinced my father to publish the verdict,' says Liu.

'When it appeared in the Hong Kong press, I naturally suffered retribution in prison. But this was more than two years later, and I had prepared myself psychologically for it.'

Just as Liu had developed the mental capacity to withstand solitary confinement, prison staff gave him a 'companion', a prisoner called Cai Qian, who was able to gain merit points by monitoring his charge 24 hours a day. For Liu, used to only his own company, it was an abrupt, humiliating change. Cai Quan, a man in his forties from Chaozhou, was fond of 'lighting the ash', reporting other prisoners' misdeeds to the cadres. He was serving more than twenty years for murder, and in prison he had devoted himself to persecuting other inmates. His nickname was Dracula, because he fattened himself by sucking the blood of others.

Liu says: 'He was a difficult man to make friends with, and at first I didn't even try. We were very different: Cai excelled in buttering up the cadres, while I basically took an attitude of resistance. But after a short time I did start to talk to him. I think this was because I'd been isolated for so long, and he was at least human company.'

When Liu began to work in the engineering brigade with the other prisoners at Meizhou, he was treated with immediate respect due to his 'counter-revolutionary' status. They were also impressed to meet a 'Hong Kong fella', a man who had seen a wider world and was still dedicated to the cause of China. 'I was amazed to find that the prison in fact possessed a climate of democracy that far surpassed anything in outside society. The prisoners freely abused the Communist Party and denounced it as useless and soon to fall from power,' says Liu. 'The intensity of their language went well past anything that had been said in my talks with Wang Xizhe. The prisoners not only spoke freely, they acted freely. The prison rules might as well not have existed. It was, to say the least, a state of anarchy.'

Liu understood later that this climate of anarchy originated in the early 1980s, when society outside was also in the throes of change. 'The old ideology had broken up, the first experiments with political openness and economic reform had begun, and, apart from agreeing on the suppression of the democratic movement, many local elites had no unified view on anything. So those below them had no rules to follow. Discipline was abandoned, and embezzling, abuse of office, and all kinds of economic crime suddenly grew rampant. I heard prisoners say that in about one out of every few households in Shantou, someone was in prison for smuggling.'

From 1982 onwards, it had become acceptable in the People's Republic to criticize Mao. For several years, Premier Deng Xiaoping had concentrated his energies on 'opening the door' of China to the outside world. Worship of a former leader had no place in a China obsessed with 'modernization'. As the economic boom began to take off, Deng urged his people to 'keep a clear head, firmly resist corruption by decadent ideas from abroad', and never to permit 'bourgeois ways of life to spread' and 'undermine socialism'. His warnings went unheeded, and the rumours Liu heard in prison were probably true. The new economic incentives, such as the creation of Special Economic Zones, tax exemptions and other benefits to foreign investors, and the upsurge in private businesses, had led to an alarming increase in corruption.

Liu continues: 'While there was no unity among the elite, and the general policy direction was unclear, cadres never know what tomorrow would bring, so the prison cadres had slackened off supervision and control of the prisoners to a degree that was hard to believe.' The result, in prisons across China, was an increase in violence and disorder. As disillusionment set in about Mao and the ideology of Communism, thought reform lost its power to maintain order by controlling the minds of inmates. It was not only Liu, as a 'political', who perceived the regular political study classes as 'bullshitting sessions'. Fights broke out more frequently, not only between prisoners but also between brigades of inmates. Killings were not unheard of.

When Liu arrived at Meizhou prison, this period of anarchy was worrying officials so much that the 'Be Strict and Be Fast' campaign was launched both inside and outside prisons. The campaign was to act as an iron fist to reimpose order: 'to be "strict" meant harsh sentences, and to be "fast" meant the speedy conclusion of cases.' Cadres first set out to make an example of prisoners who had taken part in violence and gang warfare by executing the main offenders. Sentences were also increased, residence rights were cancelled, and others were exiled to labour camps in the north-west.

Guo Yonglong, a high-ranking cell boss who frequently beat up other prisoners at Meizhou, was one of the first targets. Liu says: 'Guo Yonglong and the other prisoners to be dealt with were made to stand, bound hand and foot, in front of us. The cadres then went through a bullshit session about the upper levels' policy. Immediately, Guo and the others were made to kneel and the judgements were read. Guo was sentenced to death. The others either received increased sentences or were transferred to labour camps in the north-west. These sentences had been passed in a court of law, based on material submitted to the court by the prison cadres. The entire process pre-empted any repudiation or defence.

'When the assembly was over, we went back to our cells. From the top floor, we could see Guo Yonglong being led by soldiers to the vegetable plot nearby. They made him kneel, and then fired a shot from behind into his back, thus ending his life. At dinner time, I discovered something amusing. The day someone was executed, the other prisoners were given pork with their evening meal.' At a meeting after the execution, prisoners were expected to voice their support for the punishment. Only Liu stayed silent. The five most insubordinate prisoners were ordered to carry Guo Yonglong's corpse away.

Shen Xueqi was another target of the campaign. Apart from fighting and stirring up trouble, he had managed to avoid working for a year by claiming to have a different medical problem each day. Shen, who was in prison for armed robbery, hated the Communist Party. Once when he heard a cadre talking about him, he was so furious that he grabbed the cadre's genitals and almost did him a serious injury. Liu says: 'One Sunday, Shen and I were playing chess, and someone called Shen out of the cell. When I asked why, he said the boss [i.e. the cadres] wanted him in the factory. But he never showed up again. It turned out that the cadres had gotten together four prisoner bosses – one of them Cai Qian, my master – to put Shen in chains. Shen fought back. The cadres, in fact, had summoned the prisoner bosses to carry out unauthorized private torture on Shen on their behalf. They beat him until his entire body swelled up and he lost consciousness. Then they hung him up and prodded him between the ribs with their fingers. They beat him until he almost stopped breathing, then they took him to the hospital, where his life was saved, with difficulty, by an intracardiac injection.

'Still barely recognizable as a member of the human species, he was sent from the hospital into solitary confinement. All of this happened because the cadre Shen had attacked was seeking revenge.' Later, Shen was executed in the same way as Guo Yong-long. In the 1980s, families of the executed prisoner were no longer sent an invoice for 50 cents to cover the cost of the bullet, as they had been in the early days of the People's Republic.

Another year of Liu's life passed in Meizhou. Although he had 'performed well' in terms of work, his attitude towards reform' was still a big headache for the cadres. He was told that he was the only person who had not confessed to his crime in the history of the prison. Remembering his ordeal in the 'dark cell', this time Liu decided to write a year-end summary. 'This year I had learned my lesson,' he says. 'I put up no resistance and even – to avoid being sent to solitary confinement again – wrote a summary. I talked about hygiene, and about reform through labour, but I said nothing about recognizing my crime and submitting to the law. The cadres knew I would not capitulate and that forcing me would not work. They simply let me "come through the gate".'

The New Year celebrations brought an unaccustomed jollity to

Meizhou. Normally the prisoners would eat dried turnip or salted vegetables for breakfast, and cabbage without a drop of oil for lunch, with two ounces of pork fat added once a week. At New Year, extra food money was distributed to the prison, and there was meat every day. Inmates were allowed to watch films or television, and play cards. A singing and dancing troupe was even hired at 500 yuan for an evening party.

The party spirit did not last long. In 1987, Liu was punished again by solitary confinement for refusing to recognize his crime. This time, he was put in a cell with Chen Shusheng, a former fire brigade bureau chief who had been sentenced for raping a 7-year-old girl. Because he was a cadre, Chen had been given a light sentence of only four years. All other prisoners were forbidden to have anything to do with Liu, and Chen Shusheng supervised him for 24 hours a day. Liu was even watched when he was in the toilet and shower.

Liu was forbidden to work, but was told to study the works of Lenin and Marx. 'This isolation treatment really affected me badly,' says Liu. 'Sometimes the idea of suicide drifted through my mind, but I never seriously considered it. Shakespeare's words kept turning over in my head: "To be or not to be, that is the question." I was in a state of spiritual oppression, alleviated at times by reading; otherwise, nothing much happened to mark off one day from another.'[9]

A month before the Moon Festival, the prison authorities found out that Liu had, via the pocket of his mother's cardigan, smuggled out his verdict, which his father had finally published in Hong Kong. His punishment was an increased spell of solitary confinement.

At first sight, Huaiji prison looked like a hospital morgue. When Liu was brought to Huaiji in 1988, just after the Moon Festival, he could tell that the prison was built specially for the isolation of its inmates. 'There was a single through road with four blocks of isolation cells on either side, whitewashed to a deadly white. It was grimmer still because the prison was located in the middle of a barren wasteland.'

The isolation unit was situated within Huaiji prison, directly under the administrative authority of the Bureau of Reform through Labour. Liu's room had a light well and a small courtyard with a dirt floor; the three meals a day were spartan, sometimes consisting only of a small portion of salted turnip. A long time passed before Liu was allowed books and newspapers. He spent his days walking around the cell, and gazing into the sky outside his window in boredom.

'I started to have nightmares,' says Liu. 'Every night, it would be the same. I would be in a very strange building, a very modern, high and unrealistic-looking building. And every time I would be running, trying to find a way to escape, but I could never find a way out.'

When Liu went to the doctor's clinic one day and caught a glimpse of the list of prisoners at Huaiji, he realized that he was not alone; and that there was a chink of light in the building of his nightmares. He discovered that Wang Xizhe, his old comrade, was in the cell next door. After eight or ten conversations with his former democracy activist colleague, Liu began to make contact with other prisoners, including He Qui and Zheng Qiuwu, who had been involved in the formation of an underground political organization in Hainan.

Liu says: 'Wang Xizhe and I didn't just "telephone" each other by talking through the wall, we also "faxed" each other. Each cell had two windows. The higher one was higher than the wall, and from there you could see the upper window of the next cell. So, if we climbed up the window frames, we could see each other from the opposing windows. This was a great release for us.' Wang Xizhe also discovered a way of communicating in writing: he would insert a strip of paper into a medicine bottle and throw it into the receiver's exercise yard. But this form of dialogue came to an end when a medicine bottle thrown into Wang Xizhe's exercise yard once hit the cadre on duty on the head.

Liu was shocked when he saw Wang Xizhe again for the first time in 7 years. His hair was almost completely white, he was thinner, and he suffered from a heart problem. He had a bad sinus allergy and had lost quite a few teeth. He Qui was also suffering from ill-health. He hadn't put into practice any 'tactics for survival' in solitary, and so, because he had been sitting all day, he developed piles and became weak. Once he had been taken to hospital for emergency treatment, and it had taken 2 doctors working on him to save his life.

Wang's and He's families had suffered too. He Qui's family was in financial difficulties: his wife was looking after their daughter on her own, and her small budget had to provide them both with food, as well as providing He with items not provided in prison such as toothpaste and shaving cream. Wang Xizhe's wife scrimped and saved to feed herself and their son, and gave Wang money each month. The whole family had been persecuted, and Wang's sister was hounded so much by the authorities because of her brother's 'crimes' that she lost her sanity and died. Wang Xizhe echoed the thoughts of China's most famous dissident and fellow democracy activist Wei Jingsheng when he said that what many people in the democracy movement worried about most was that, if they went to prison, their families would suffer. Wei, whose sister and brother had been refused permission to travel abroad, and whose niece had been discriminated against in school, once said: 'Lots of people are ready to sacrifice themselves for democracy. But not to sacrifice their wives, their children.'[10]

The democracy movement in 1989 had a potent effect on life inside prisons throughout China, not only for counter-revolutionary prisoners. Liu, Wang and He kept up with events through day-old copies of the *People's Daily*, the *Southern Daily*, the Shanghai *Wenhui Bao*, the *China Daily*, and other local papers. 'I lived through the movement in the prison, experiencing the same exhilaration, tension, indifference, rage, and grief as everyone outside,' says Liu.[11]

As events unfolded in Tiananmen Square and reverberated through the country, the prisoners took courage from the defiance of the students and began to threaten the authority of the system. Liu recalls: 'When discussing the movement, we didn't whisper stealthily as we used to. We spoke up loud and recklessly, without worrying if the cadres were there listening in or not. At first, the cadres tried to frighten us, telling us to shut up. But we yelled as loudly as we wanted and ignored them; not long after they gave up.'

On the morning of 4 June, a prisoner was cutting Liu's hair when he heard over the prison public address system that the army had put down the students. The broadcast announced that three hundred students and three hundred soldiers had died. 'As soon as I heard that, I shouted, "The Party has committed murder!",' says Liu. "I know, I know," whispered the prisoner who was cutting my hair, thoroughly frightened, "Don't shout so loudly." The cadres nearby heard me, of course, but they didn't do anything. Really, most of the cadres sympathized with the students at the time.' Later, Liu was allowed to see a government videotape of the Tiananmen massacre in one of the cadres' offices. As he watched the footage of burning tanks, people being beaten to death and the resistance of the people, he was filled with rage. 'Stranger still – it didn't matter when I kept on shouting "Great! Great!" or when I yelled, "Down with the Communist Party!" None of the cadres dared say a thing.' Strangely enough, none of the cadres then asked Liu to state his attitude after the film was finished.

Once the movement had died down and was out of the headlines, prison life returned to normal. The prison staff had clearly undergone some 'correction' in their approach; even low-level cadres could be heard claiming that the real villain behind the scenes of Tiananmen was Gorbachev.

The intense emotion – and optimism – experienced during Tiananmen soon faded for Wang, He and Liu, who began to suffer again from the effects of isolation. 'Sometimes, for no reason, Wang Xizhe would let out an enormous yell,' says Liu. 'This really spooked me, and I said to him,

"Don't yell like that, it scares me." We had a bad argument.' Liu's nightmares continued, and, in an attempt to maintain his sanity, he took up the discipline of calligraphy, and practised stretching exercises regularly. 'I realized later that good health strengthened my confidence in myself, and my willpower as well,' he says.

Zheng Qiuwu fared less well. Just after the 4 June massacre, he told Liu and the others that he was ill because his faeces had turned red. He began to beg the cadres to let him see a doctor. Eventually, a prison doctor visited him and gave him some painkillers. But Zheng continued to think he was suffering from a serious illness, and his grasp on reality began to shake. 'He spent the whole day doing nothing, talking to himself, crying out loud that he was sick, that this doctor was excellent but that that one was useless. I was worn down listening to him. Because of Zheng Qiuwu, I could see how easily the isolation cells could reduce a human being into nothing.'

Later He Qui was also affected. He began to spend all day on his bed practising *qi gong* and talking about a civilization founded by space aliens. Liu says: 'When I was in prison I often thought of a famous story of a man punished by heaven for his misdeeds. His punishment was to roll a huge rock up a hill. When it reached the top it would always fall down again, so he had to pick it up and start all over again. In solitary confinement, we were doing the same thing, day after day. We had to push ourselves all the time. And sometimes it was easier to let go.'

The last few months before Liu's release seemed to be the longest. About a month before the due date, Wang, the department head, visited Liu. He had been compiling the paperwork for his release, and said there were still some problems with his 'attitude'. 'He told me that if I didn't confess to my "crimes", they would not let me go,' says Liu. 'I would be free in name but would still be kept in the prison to work. This threat made me think I'd never get out. But then I thought, I've already served ten years; there's no reason to give in when the end is in sight. So I ignored him.'

Several weeks later, threats from a pack of cadres and two deputy prison directors had not persuaded Liu to give in. A few days later, the political officer arrived again and told Liu that he would be entirely responsible for what happened to him. 'I declared that my thoughts were free of crime, that my point of view hadn't changed and that I was not prepared to back down from my principles,' says Liu. 'Hearing this, Wang got emotional, but he realized how stubborn I was, so he backed off. They hadn't said they wouldn't release me, they said, they were merely trying to give me an education. They would act as the law required.'

On 26 December 1991, at 9 in the morning, Liu Shanqing left Huaiji prison.

A strident beep on Liu's pager reminds him of a demonstration outside the Xinhua news agency, the de facto Chinese embassy, in half an hour's time. The Hong Kong Patriotic Alliance for a Democratic China is staging the demonstration in support of fellow activist Chen Ziming, one of the so-called 'black hands' behind the Tiananmen movement. Chen had been rearrested in China, and there were grave fears for his health (Plate 9).

Liu Shanqing has continued to challenge authority ever since he walked out of prison the day after Christmas. He may have been told to leave the country within 24 hours of his release, but he has continued to be a thorn insistently prodding China's flesh. He writes articles critical of Chinese foreign policy and internal structure, and is a member of the committee of Hong Kong's Patriotic Alliance for a Democratic China, one of a network of groups which spans the world. He has also worked in local politics on labour issues. 'I wanted to join the Legislative Council, but the Hong Kong government banned me from joining the elections,' says Liu. 'They told me I had to be a resident of Hong Kong for the past 10 years, and I'd been in jail on the mainland so I didn't count. I was so angry that I took them to court – and won. Now you only have to be a resident for the previous 3 years to qualify.'

He still has vivid memories of the day of his release, and his emotions as the train pulled into Hong Kong station, to be met by throngs of cheering supporters. Christina was in the crowd, but she didn't come forward to meet Liu straight away. 'At that time I just wanted to hold her and kiss her directly, but she did not want to appear when I was surrounded by journalists,' he says. He had not set eyes on her for ten years. 'We met later that day, but she still kept away from the reporters. They surrounded me for 24 hours. In many ways, I didn't mind. I knew that through the media, I could influence people more and gain more support for our cause.'

Liu and Christina finally found time to be alone. 'Some people think it's strange that a love affair could survive those ten years,' says Liu. 'But I never had any doubts about it.' After six months, Liu and Christina married. They had a quiet ceremony, with no guests, out of the glare of publicity. Liu remembers today: 'Christina was very happy to see me when I returned. But she always complained that I left her.' Sometimes Christina still mentions it. But she's just happy to have him back. Liu says with a grin, 'It's not a problem any more.'

Notes

1. Insanity is a technical psychiatric term meaning psychosis, which according to many psychiatrists has a strong biological basis and does not generally occur following acute stress. Hence while the words 'madness' and 'insanity' are frequently used to describe the condition of certain prisoners held, for instance, in solitary for a period, the more accurate description may simply be 'mental illness' or 'mental disorder' (Anne Thurston, *Enemies of the People*).

2. Solzhenitsyn gives many descriptions of the suffering of men in solitary and the descent into madness in the Stalinist gulag. Kosyrev is one of them (*The Gulag Archipelago*, vol. 1, p. 482). For the first five or six days, Kosyrev keeps count of the days. His hearing becomes extremely acute and he begins to hear whispers in the corridor. After the punishment cell, Kosyrev becomes deaf for half a year and began to get abscesses in his throat. His cellmate goes insane from frequent imprisonment in the punishment cell.

3. The Democracy Wall was, literally, a stretch of wall on the edge of the Forbidden City in Beijing, where posters calling for democratic freedom were displayed in 1978–9. The movement for democracy continued underground after the posters were torn down by the authorities.

4. This chapter is based on an interview by the author, and draws heavily on a paper by Liu entitled 'Encounter with Legalized Illegality: Liu Shanqing, the Democracy Movement, and Prison Reforms', *Chinese Sociology and Anthropology*, vol. 26, no. 4 (summer 1994).

5. Anatoly Marchenko, author of an extraordinary testimony about his life in the Soviet gulag, recalls how his cell mates advised him to do the same. 'I'm not looking at any dreams in my new home, so as not to worry afterwards whether the omens are good or bad,' an older inmate told him (*My Testimony*, p. 63). 'As soon as a dream starts to show itself I screw my eyes up nice and tight. . . The old men agreed that none of them thought about the world outside any more, not even in their dreams.'

6. Zhao Chen, *Jianyuxue*, quoted in Michael R. Dutton, *Policing and Punishment in China: From Patriarchy to 'the People'*, p. 162.

7 George Black and Robin Munro, *Black Hands of Beijing*, p. 285.

8. This must have been written about a luxury prison: in most small punishment cells there is no bed, only a concrete floor.

9. Boredom is often one of the worst experiences for prisoners in solitary, when time itself is an enemy. In his memoirs of his 26 months in captivity in Beijing, Reuters correspondent Anthony Grey recalls how he was so desperate for reading material that he saved the reading of an instruction leaflet wrapped round a bottle of TCP liquid antiseptic. 'My first impulse was to sit down and read it immediately,' he said. 'But then I checked myself. I would keep it to read with my supper at six o'clock' (*Hostage in Peking*, p. 211).

10. Interview by Nicholas D. Kristof and Sheryl Wudunn, *China Wakes*, p. 250.

11. Just as prisoners were adept at reading between the lines in Party newspapers in order to discern the true progress of events, so journalists at the time used an oblique style of writing to illustrate own feelings. On 5 June in the *People's Daily* over a story about a handicapped person winning an athletic medal a headline appeared that read: 'The People's Hearts Will Not Be Conquered'. On 7 June, above an old and unnewsworthy story about the poaching of deer in Inner Mongolia, the headline read: 'Guileless Fawns Brutally Slaughtered' (source: Schell, *Mandate of Heaven*, p. 176).

CHAPTER 6

The Wooden Knife
Thought Reform in the *Laogai*

Not to have a correct political point of view is like having no soul.

Mao Zedong[1]

I feel like a cross between Humpty Dumpty and Rip Van Winkle – I have fallen off the wall and suddenly awake I find all the pieces of me, before me.
There are more parts than I began with.
All the King's horses, and all the King's men, cannot put Humpty together again.

Brian Keenan, Dutch Embassy, Damascus, 24 August 1990[2]

There is a moment in the lives of many *laogai* prisoners when their mind splits apart, leading to an irrevocable separation between the inner world and the outer. The Chinese Communists precipitate this split with their perfection of the doctrine of 'thought reform' under the guise of transformation of the self. The potency of thought reform is caused by the penetration by the psychological forces of the environment into the inner emotions of the individual, often involving a life or death struggle of the identity. This aspect of the Chinese *laogai* system has been described as a carefully cultivated 'Auschwitz of the mind'.[3]

When English radio operator Robert Ford was released after a four-year sentence in a Chinese jail following the invasion of Tibet in 1949-50, all everyone wanted to know was whether he had been tortured. 'Of course I had, but I didn't tell them this – because that wasn't the worst punishment. When you're being beaten up, you can turn into yourself and find a corner of your mind in which to fight the pain. But when you're being spiritually tortured by thought reform, there's nowhere you can go. It affects you at the most profound, deepest levels and attacks your very identity.'

The process of interrogation leading to forced 'confessions' can drive people to take actions they would never normally consider. Mark Baber, who was released in 1994 after a sentence of nearly four years in Shanghai jail, became so desperate that he slashed his wrist. 'Teams of interrogators were working on me in shifts after I was arrested,' says Mark. 'After nearly fifty hours without sleep, food, or drink, all I could think of was how I could stop the interrogation. They wanted to know names of Chinese who were anti-government, and said if I didn't make a full confession I'd spend the rest of my life in prison. I wanted to buy some time to think about what to do. So I asked for permission to go to the bathroom, and when I was in there, I broke a glass on the sink and slashed my wrist.'

Mark's captors found him in the bathroom with blood spurting from his wrist and thick clots saturating the carpet. He was rushed to hospital under armed guard. But his attempt to gain a respite did not succeed. His interrogators simply began the process again as soon as Mark was on the operating table, while doctors stitched up the cuts on his wrist. They didn't bother to use an anaesthetic.

This inability to escape participation from the demands of the system, even in a small corner of one's mind, has ground down millions of prisoners since the Communist revolution, and has led to many suicides. It also has far-reaching effects on the individual after his or her release. 'A person caught up in the punitive wheels of a totalitarian system has only two alternatives,' writes Simon Leys:[4]

> *Immediate suicide, or survival. The second option is no less of a commitment than the first, for in this system agreeing to survive means to renounce being oneself. Survival implies adjustment to the milieu . . . [which] requires the adoption of a certain way of acting and thinking.*
>
> *In the initial phase, the prisoner adopts this mode of acting and thinking the way an actor assumes a role; in the second phase, however, the character is gradually substituted for the person, the mask for the face, and the untruth of the jailers for the truth of the prisoner. In other words, to survive you must play the game; by playing the game you are changed by the game. In the final stages of this game, adaptation to the upside-down world can become so complete that if the individual is abruptly reintroduced into an upright world he has an unbearable attack of vertigo, which sometimes defeats his every effort to fit back into a normal environment.*[5]

The concept of 'thought reform' (*si xiang gai zao*) had its origins in the guerrilla warfare of the Communists against Nationalist troops (Guomindang) led by Chiang Kai-shek prior to the 'liberation' in 1949.

Correct thought, pronounced Mao, is the first and essential prerequisite for effective revolutionary action. The *cheng-feng* campaign of 1942-4, which involved the 'rectification' of undesirable ideas and ideologies, was a precursor to the later, more sophisticated techniques.

The emphasis on ideological solidarity was of great strategic and practical importance during a period of guerrilla warfare, where centralized organization is largely absent owing to the nature of the conflict. The creation of unity through common ways of thinking, ideals and ideologies was an essential tool for leaders of often isolated and disparate troops.

Mao's strong nationalistic impulses also led him to believe that a Chinese revolution was synonymous with world revolution. This led to his perception that China's real enemy was foreign imperialism, and that China stood as the only proletarian nation in a hostile capitalist-bourgeois-imperialist world.

Mao was departing in his philosophy from both Lenin and Marx in his belief that the rural peasant masses were the bearers of his internationalist ideals. (For Marx the bearer of socialist consciousness was the urban proletariat, while for Lenin socialist consciousness was to be imposed on the mass proletarian movement by an elite of revolutionary intellectuals.) This faith in the 'peasant masses' opened up an immense pool of potential support for Mao's Communist revolution. The growth of popular support for the Communists leading to their triumphant victory and foundation of the People's Republic further reinforced Mao's faith in 'the people'. The seeds of Mao's hostility to foreign imperialism and urban intellectuals had been sown.

The 'rectification' movements in Yenan in the early 1940s were the beginning of the Communists' 'democratic' method of education and ideological transformation. The principles behind these movements were based on a belief that the individual's thoughts and behaviour are capable of improvement; criminal behaviour has its roots in criminal thought. Throughout the decade, the techniques used were developed and refined as the labour reform system. Mao's words continue to be used as its basis. One quotation of Mao became a key one: 'the objective world which is to be changed [by the proletariat] also includes the opponents of change, who, in order to be changed, must go through a stage of compulsion before they can enter the stage of voluntary, conscious change.'[6]

Chinese Nationalists who were captured by the Communists were some of the first prisoners to experience methods of thought reform, and the 'transformative power' of collective labour. Wang Tsunming, a Nationalist officer who fought the Communists for three years and was captured in 1949, was one of them.[7] Wang and other captured officers became students at the Political Military Academy near Liangshan. From the beginning, Wang and the other soldiers were segregated into a group of about forty people, living with an assigned leader. For the first two weeks, they were seduced into thinking that the Communists would treat them well after all. But then the screws began to tighten.

The main themes of their indoctrination were that the old way was false while the new way brings theory and practice together; and that labour is the foundation of the world. The Nationalist soldiers were also force-fed propaganda on the evil ways of General Chiang Kai-shek. A few weeks later, the airing of grievances and 'self-criticism' began. Participants were made to write up detailed autobiographies and confessions, which were duly stored in their files.

Wang began to realize the price of self-preservation within the Communist system early in the indoctrination process. It was in April 1950, when the Communists were beginning to conduct land reforms in his home town in Shensi province. Four soldiers wrote and told Wang to return home and face land-reform procedures, but Wang wanted to avoid the inevitable purges in the village. He asked the military authorities to allow him to 'learn to be a new man', and stay at the school. They encouraged him to talk to the four soldiers who had written to him and explain his point of view. Wang also wrote a letter for them to take back to the province with them, confessing that he was from the landlord class, that he accepted their practices and that he wished to be a member of the proletarian class. He also wrote a letter to the squad leaders in his old unit, urging these men to accept the Communist programme, so that they might benefit and work for the people.

Wang later concluded that the Communist authorities had set up the entire situation in order to assess which of the soldiers would be more useful to their cause in the villages, or which ones should stay at the military school to set an example of good reform. These techniques, Wang said, were mainly used on those in a position of leadership. In this way the resistance of the commanding officers was broken down, and their willingness to co-operate was used as an example to educate troops both at home and at the military school.

As he told his story, Wang became very emotional. 'They [the Communists] are diabolically clever,' he said. 'They destroy all personal relationships and feelings. I knew that all the men felt guilty in violating the old moral code between officers and men, and I knew that they would not hold me strictly responsible for the letter I had written, because they too had realized that I had been forced to do what I did. Nevertheless, it broke up something between us.'

Wang did not acknowledge at the time that the guilt he was

experiencing about the letter was just the sort of feeling the Communists wanted to foster. It showed that, while he was rejecting the Communists on a conscious level, he had begun to internalize and accept Communist standards of conduct. The splitting of the self between public and private, inner and outer, had begun.

Wang came to the conclusion that the Communists wanted to kill without having the victim's blood on their hands. 'This meant that they wanted physical and mental liquidation of oneself by oneself, so that no one could say that they had done it, but rather the person had brought it upon himself by the nature of his previous actions. I was struck by a great fear.'

Wang had begun to experience the atavistic, overwhelming emotion which is fear of annihilation. This basic fear becomes the final focus for all of the prison pressures; it is fed by every threat and accusation from without, and all the destructive motions experienced within.[8] The creation of this type of fear has been a policy in the Chinese gulag.[9] 'Since the punishment and reform of criminals are compulsory, the best way to maintain strict discipline is to inspire the criminals with revolutionary fear to the highest degree,' admitted a senior official in 1954.[10]

Later on in his indoctrination, Wang witnessed a typical incident aimed at inspiring 'revolutionary fear' in all the prisoners, and setting an example to those who refused to reform. Two of his friends were put on trial as enemies of Communism. After three days of charges, all the men were called upon to vote for their execution. Party members on the platform asked for objections, and they asked all who voted yes to raise their hands. As Party members watched closely, more and more men raised their hands. Everyone knew that they were condemning their friends to death. The two men were shot before their comrades. 'Every Party member and any of the cadre workers there had to walk by and shoot the men too. They mutilated the dead bodies with all of us looking on,' says Wang. 'Later they were buried next to our quarters under only six inches of earth. That night it rained. One of the men tried to clear the water from the grave with a cup. I will never forget this picture.'

Actions like these were a brutal expression of the regime's desire to replace the students' 'old' emotions with 'revolutionary' feelings. 'There is no sentiment between individuals,' says Wang. 'Emotion is only to be built on a revolutionary basis. Revolution purges all decadent thoughts.'[11] Wang notes with some irony that Party members thought nothing of utilizing the concept of 'revolutionary love' as a method of seduction: 'When an old Party member has sought the favour of a young woman of the Party, it is necessary to get her to submit willingly. Other women Party members will persuade her. They will say to her: "We know that this man is ugly and old, but he has contributed greatly to the revolution. You are not going to bed with this man but with what he represents. You will be serving the Party and be duly rewarded for your action. Your refusal will be a refusal of the cause and not the man." Thus you can see that everything between persons – all kinds of sentimental relationships – must always have some kind of revolutionary reason.'[12]

Yue Daiyan, a former Rightist, warned of the consequences of ignoring the existence of non-revolutionary emotions. She tells a story of a male student during the Cultural Revolution who slashed the face of a female student. He had suffered from unrequited love for her, and was determined that no one else should have her if he couldn't. 'It seemed natural to me for the young people to fall in love, and obvious that the official policy of prohibiting romantic emotions had contributed to this tragedy,' said Yue:

> *Clearly, the habituation to violence that was the legacy of the Cultural Revolution, plus utter ignorance and inexperience about how to handle the turbulent emotions of love and jealousy, had precipitated the disappointed suitor's cruelty. The young generation had perpetrated the turmoil, I reflected sadly, but they seemed destined to pay a higher price even than we, the revolution's intended victims.*[13]

The first of the post-revolutionary thought reform campaigns began in 1951, when Mao declared the the 'thought reform of all categories of intellectuals' was essential for 'the thoroughgoing democratic transformation and progressive industrialisation of our country'.[14] As with most of Mao's campaigns throughout the 1950s, it began generally with intellectuals in urban universities and spread to middle and elementary schoolteachers as well as to students and individual writers and artists. Many intellectuals were sent to the countryside for 're-education through labour'. The social and psychological pressures were exacerbated by the external threat posed by the war in Korea, causing an increased concentration on the evils of 'foreign imperialism', and condemnations of 'bourgeois thought'. Mass criticism meetings, 'struggle sessions', public humiliations, self-criticism and confessions were methods of dealing with those showing counter-revolutionary tendencies.

The police technique of the struggle session was later used by the Red Guards to denounce their victims during the Cultural Revolution.[15] In the early years of the Republic, peasants were terrified into submission by the clatter of gongs and tambourines heralding the 'struggle' in their village square. Victims were made to stand in front of a jeering crowd, commonly in the 'aeroplane' position, with arms behind their back and heads bowed. In this humiliating position they had to confess their 'crimes', which often involved exposure of intimate details of their lives, or betrayal by close friends and family. The same accusation meetings were held within prisons, detention centres and labour camps.

A counter-revolutionary prisoner called Lo interviewed by Fox Butterfield recalls taking part in one of these struggle sessions. Their victim was a former Leftist cadre from the Overseas Chinese Affairs Commission who refused to confess. 'We pounded and kicked him so hard he spat blood. A few days later he died,' says Lo. When Lo later refused to write his own confession, the police wrote it for him. His reading of the confession was entirely stage-managed: 'They would tell me, "This sentence you must say very sadly. This paragraph you must say with real emotion." In some places they wrote "pause" for the other prisoners to talk. In other places they wrote "slogans" so people could shout at me.'

When Lo faced the struggle session with his confession, he describes a fear which soon became numbness. 'Eventually I got used to it. When they didn't beat me very hard, it was just like a pig going to market. Since my head was bowed and I couldn't see anybody, all there was was a lot of noise and shouting.'[16]

Jean Pasqualini, a French-Chinese who spent seven years in forced labour camps before being released in 1964,[17] recalls the hatred stirred up during one of these struggle sessions. The victim was a middle-aged prisoner charged with having made a false confession. He sat before Pasqualini and his fellow prisoners on a mat, his head bent low.

'Down with the obstinate prisoner,' they screamed. 'Confess or face the consequences.' In Chinese, Pasqualini points out, these imprecations are terrifyingly real, especially in the context of a prison where a man is friendless and without allies – and when a thousand men are shouting all at once. Every time the man uttered a word, a thousand men would shout further curses at him. 'Is he telling the truth?' howled the cadre. 'No!' shrieked the prisoners.

'The Struggle continued for three more hours like this, and with every minute that passed we grew colder, hungrier and meaner,' writes Pasqualini in his memoirs, *Prisoner of Mao* (p. 83).

'A strange, animal frenzy built within us. I almost think we would have been capable of tearing him to pieces to get what we wanted. Later, when I had the time to reflect, I realised that of course we had been struggling ourselves at the same time, mentally preparing to accept the government's position with passionate assent, whatever the merits of the man we were facing.'

Their victim finally reached a point where he could not bear it any longer, and cried out that he should be punished according to regulations.

The guards came forward with chains, punishment for his stubborn attitude, and hammered home the rivets to his fetters and irons.

The term 'brainwashing' was first used by an American journalist, Edward Hunter, as a translation of the Chinese colloquialism *xi nao* – which means, literally, 'wash brain'.[18] At the height of the Cold War, this was perceived as a sinister, almost magical method for complete control of the human mind. There is no magic involved, of course, but the Chinese concept of thought reform (translated often as 'ideological remoulding') remains one of the most powerful methods of human manipulation ever undertaken and practised in a society.[19]

Ideological remoulding in China extends to all levels of society: from the kindergarten to school, and from the factory floor to the agricultural collective. It emerges in the language of government documents and the stories of children.[20]

In *Thought Reform and the Psychology of Totalism*, the classic text on the subject, Robert Jay Lifton concludes that the unique power of thought reform lies in the 'combination of external force or coercion with an appeal to inner enthusiasm through evangelistic exhortation'. Lifton believes that this gives the process its focused emotional scope:

> *Coercion and breakdown are, of course, more prominent in the prison and military programmes, while exhortation and ethical appeal are especially stressed with the rest of the Chinese population; and it becomes extremely difficult to determine just where exhortation ends and coercion begins.*

Jean Pasqualini gives an example of this subtle manipulation of the psyche in the story of a man who was arrested by mistake. He had the same name as the criminal who committed the offence, but he was innocent. After a few months he had confessed all the crimes of the other man. When the mistake was discovered, the prison authorities found it difficult to persuade him to go home. The man felt far too guilty.[21]

Since the Communist revolution, China has been a Kafkaesque world in which the burden of judge, jury and executioner has been shifted away from the accuser to the accused.[22] Those who had been labelled 'Rightists', 'capitalist roaders' or 'bourgeois individualists' and others who had endured struggle sessions tended to internalize the criticisms. In this way they shouldered the guilt and blamed themselves, rather than the Party – which was after all, infallible.

The Czech writer Milan Kundera illustrates this process by comparing the Communists' totalitarian regime to the looking-glass world of Kafka's novels *The Castle* and *The Trial*. He says:

> *Totalitarian states, as extreme concentrations of these tendencies, have brought out the close relationship between Kafka's novels and real life . . . It is the well-known situation where the offence seeks the punishment. In Kafka the logic is reversed. The punished person does not know the reason for the punishment. The absurdity of the punishment is so unbearable that to find peace the accused needs to find justification for his penalty; the punishment seeks the offence. In this pseudo-theological world, the punished beg for recognition of their guilt.[23]*

Pasqualini claims that over the years Mao's police have perfected their interrogation methods to such a degree that he would defy anyone, Chinese or not, to hold out against them. 'Their aim is not so much to make you invent nonexistent crimes, but to make you accept your ordinary life, as you led it, as rotten and sinful and worthy of punishment, since it did not concord with their own, the police's conception of how a life should be led' (p. 39). When looked at in this way, the prisoner's arrest in the first place is sufficient to prove his guilt.

Wu Ningkun, a political prisoner who served two terms in labour camps, acknowledged this feeling of guilt in his memoirs, *A Single Tear*.

> *Forced labour was only the means [for emancipation], not the end. The avowed end was thought reform of the sinners into new men. A world rid of exploitation of man by man, a brave new world of new men! To be emancipated from myself! What magnificent ideas! What splendid prospects of the future! I was fascinated.*
>
> *Even while tormented on the rack of interrogation and denunciation, I had never felt altogether certain that it was not I who had sinned against the new ultimate truth of Marxism, who had failed the test of an unprecedented revolution. Perhaps it was my mean understanding and vain pride that had blinded me to the incompatible superiority of the socialist system. (p. 95)*

Thought reform consists of two basic elements. Confession is the exposure and renunciation of past and present 'evil', and re-education is the remaking of man in the Communist mould.[24] This can often lead to 'an agonising drama of death and rebirth'.[25] The symbolic death of the old person, and rebirth of the 'new person', has a profound effect on the inner being of the person and his or her sense of identity.

In the early decades of the Communist Revolution, this casting off of the old and acquiring the new was undertaken with an almost religious passion. A French priest, Father Watine, who was imprisoned for three years in China before being released in 1954, recalls slogans on the prison walls about re-education that resembled Christian mysticism in content.

One of them read: 'The luminous way that leads to life, the way of darkness that leads to death, the burden of which one must rid oneself.'[26]

Confession and re-education fall under the labour camp slogan 'Acknowledge your Crimes, Acknowledge your Faults, Submit to Superiors, Submit to the Law [*renzui fufa*]'. Harry Wu quotes an internal Public Security Bureau document as follows:

> *If a criminal does not acknowledge his crimes and submit to the law, then accomplishing thought reform is out of the question . . . Criminals cannot submit to the law until they acknowledge their crimes, and only when they have acknowledged their crimes and submitted to the law can they accept thought reform. Acknowledging one's crime is a prerequisite to submitting to the law, and submitting to the law is the beginning of reform . . . This consciousness must be present throughout the process of reform.*[27]

Before the late 1980s, when socialist modernization changed the structure of life in the *laogai*, prisoners underwent a transition period of group study before beginning physical labour. Public Security cadres selected an older prisoner to manage the group (the administration of Chinese labour camps has always been effective in utilizing prisoners to control other prisoners), and to organize the hearing of confessions and self-criticisms before a Public Security cadre.

The first stage of the process of 'ideological remoulding' is to acknowledge one's crime and one's guilt (*jiaodai zuixing*). In the small study groups each new prisoner is required to relate the story of his crime. Other prisoners are mobilized into applying pressure on the subject. If the subject's story does not agree with the information already given to Public Security, or if he claims to be innocent, he is accused of 'denying guilt and resisting reform'. Usually those who refuse to confess or who deny their guilt altogether are punished by beatings or by being locked into the 'punishment cell' for a spell of solitary confinement. Former prisoners have found that, where the confession is concerned, 'the best course of action is neither to say too much nor too little – to avoid the intimidation, threats, and beatings by telling Public Security only what it already knows'.[28] The policy of 'lenience to those who confess, severity to those who resist' is continuously stressed to prisoners. During interrogation, torture is often used to precipitate suitable confessions.[29]

The second stage of the thought reform process is the recognition and criticism of one's crimes (*pipan reshi*). 'Under no circumstances must the subject make such excuses as "I was momentarily confused", "I was misled by others" . . .,' says Harry Wu. 'One must ruthlessly criticise and attack oneself, while at the same time expressing gratitude for the magnanimity of the Communist Party and the belief that one feels "reformed" and "a new person".'[30]

The third stage is submitting to authority and teachings (*fuguan fujiao*), in which prisoners are forced to study rules and regulations of the system. The one-sided propaganda fed to prisoners within the system was particularly potent during the years immediately after liberation and during the Cultural Revolution. The British Reuters journalist Anthony Grey, who was imprisoned in one room in his Beijing home for 26 months by Red Guards in 1969, recalls the effects of this depiction of 'Triumphant Communism' and 'The Crumbling West' on the mind. He points out that while he was not subject to interrogation or 'brainwashing' as such, the ban on all views except for Beijing's was another form of mental torture. In her letters, Grey's girlfriend Shirley enclosed a copy of the crossword from the *Sunday Observer* to help him while away the hours. 'At the time of the continuing chaos in France when my fears for the fabric of Western society were greatest I turned over the latest crossword and found some adverts in the back,' writes Grey:

> One was advertising for youths to train as showroom salesmen for Ford cars in Piccadilly, London. I was immensely encouraged. Ford's wouldn't be advertising for salesmen in Piccadilly if Europe were plunged into chaos, depression, and revolution, if money was valueless and the masses were marching on Westminster. And in the succeeding weeks whenever I worried about the persistent Chinese reports of deterioration in conditions in Europe and America I remembered that Ford's in Piccadilly still had enough faith in the future to train up young salesmen.[31]

Between 1982 and 1985, political prisoner Liu Shanqing had to attend 'a kind of brain-washing "political education"' for three or four nights a week. Together with a small group meeting of the twelve prisoners in each cell, he also had regularly to attend so-called Livelihood Meetings, led by the cell boss. 'Political study meant agreeing with current policies and campaigns,' says Liu. 'In a small group meeting, the group leader or whoever was leading would first make a speech, then each prisoner had to declare how deeply affected he was by the speech.'[32]

One of the most painful aspects of thought reform is the involvement of the family with the reform process. Liu Shanqing was furious when his own parents were convinced by cadres to tell him to 'reform well'. When Jean Pasqualini was seized by security police from his home, his terrified wife could only cry: 'Go, and learn your lessons well!'[33]

In the late 1980s, however, the effectiveness of thought reform began to wane. New ideas from the West and the power of market forces displaced Maoism as the main ideology. After extensive conversations with Chinese across the country during this period, Harry Wu was one of many commentators to conclude that people were disillusioned with

Communism – even Party chiefs. It no longer held the same sway over the popular imagination. And there appeared to be evidence that as the Chinese faith in the brittle structure of Communism disintegrates, thought reform in Chinese jails is being replaced by increasing levels of physical violence.

The new disillusionment was reflected in the labour camps, where prison authorities were ~~suddenly falling over each other to~~ make money. Liu Shanqing claims that in the *laogai* production brigades became of increasing importance, while the powers of the brigades' political officers declined. The aim of labour became profit, not reform. In Meizhou prison, where Liu was an inmate, prisoners were often expected to work longer hours, and political study classes were dropped or shortened drastically.

Liu Shanqing recalls that, from the mid-1980s onwards, political studies were no longer of any importance to cadres now striving to make profit. With profit in command, nothing else counted. 'The prison had sunk to the condition of one more greedy production unit competing for profits in the impersonal world of the market, looking for ways to extract surplus value from the prisoners' slave labour,' he says.

Other former prisoners report a lessening in the intensity of thought reform with no corresponding decrease in the prison curriculum. In Shanghai jail, Mark Baber recalls that prison officials still supervised ideological remoulding sessions, but were lazy in enforcing any stringent discipline. 'One of the prisoners just used to copy out pages from *People's Daily*, and that was his "reform",' he says. Thought reform is used to make the lives of guards easier, claims Mark. 'The way they use Communist ideology is to justify the guards having an easy a time as possible,' he says. 'Every day there was a political study session, although this was usually just over the intercom into the prison. Usually prisoners had to supervise other prisoners in their reform; the guards were rarely involved.' Every year, a Lei Feng day was held in the prison. Lei Feng, a model soldier who died in 1962 in a car accident, is held up as a model of Communist rectitude: 'In the winter Lei Feng repairs cars regardless of the cold. Lei Feng walks a thousand miles and does 10,000 good things. Working for the Party and the people, his heart is red and never changes.' Prisoners in Shanghai Number One municipal prison were supposed to commemorate Lei Feng day by 'serving the people'. 'In practice this meant that all the prisoners mended things for the guards, such as broken watches,' says Mark. 'The guards took Lei Feng day seriously. But when I told people they were a living Lei Feng, I meant it as an insult.'

Inmates at Shanghai Number One were also meant to say 'have a good reform' rather than hello or goodbye. 'This was even more difficult to take seriously,' says Mark. The prisoners who took all the exhortations to heart, and who made life as easy as possible for the guards, were given reductions in their sentences. The inmate who had the biggest reduction during Mark's imprisonment was the one who created an aquarium in one of the cells. He fitted wall-to-wall tanks and electric fans, so the guards could sit in comfort to gaze lazily at the fish in a cool, relaxing environment. 'The fish were treated better than the prisoners,' says Mark.

If thought reform failed to convince certain inmates who still showed a recalcitrant attitude, guards would use the 'forcing policy'. 'This gave them the licence to use violence, or to imprison someone in the punishment block,' Mark recalls.

This treatment reflects a worrying phenomenon for the Chinese authorities – the increasing problem of resistance to reform. This is linked to a real fear of loss of control in the *laogai*. Resistance to reform lies in the prisoners' refusal to admit their guilt or to accept the justice of the punishment to which they have been sentenced.[34]

Key thinkers in the Party have admitted that juvenile delinquency has become a serious social problem in the course of China's social transformation. They are particularly worried by a trend among young people to replace obedience to the Party by ties of friendship and personal loyalty. Shao Daoshen is a director of the imposing-sounding Criminal Remoulding Psychological Professional Committee of the Chinese Law of Reform Through Labour Society (and author of *The Morbid Psychology of Contemporary Society*). He says anxiously:

> [Young people] are prepared to lay down their lives for their 'friends'. When sentenced to death, a few of them even cry: 'A bullet only makes a hole in me, and I'll become a hero again in another 20 years'. . . As for their outlook on friendship, they devote undue attention to brotherhood, saying . . . 'One should die for one's intimate friends.' In general, they worship the tradition of feudal underworld gangs.[35]

An even more worrying trend for the authorities is the emergence of this sort of brotherly behaviour within prisons and *laogai* camps, not just in the wider society. One prison song reputedly goes:

> As soon as we're liberated and free, we'll become more savage than ever, we'll treat all people on earth without mercy. We'll know better the art of killing, there are tens of thousands of juvenile delinquents in China, I'm only one of their number, so really, I don't feel lonely, just because I have so many prison mates.[36]

A growing subculture within prisons and labour camps is exhibiting behaviour which fits patterns of 'resistance to reform': these include disobeying orders, openly picking quarrels with cadres, copying and circulating pornographic literature and tattooing.

Research carried out in the 1980s and early 1990s indicates that within the labour reform system a substantial proportion of prisoners openly refuse to admit guilt or to accept the justice of their punishment. In the late 1980s, around half the prisoners surveyed by the Ministry of Justice in labour reform units in Guangdong, Jiangsu and Yunnan had openly expressed denial of guilt and/or refusal to accept their sentences.[37]

This increasing resistance to reform is a relatively recent phenomenon in China and is linked to new notions of individual freedom caused by the influx of new ideas, the loosening of central control and the opening up of the economy and culture. However the 1982 description of labour reform camps as 'schools specialising in criminal technique'[38] resonates with Harry Wu's descriptions of camps in the 1950s and 1960s. He says today: 'No hero, like Nelson Mandela, can survive the Chinese camps. I had to become a beast; to learn to cheat, steal, and fight.'

Clearly the shame and self-hatred which can result from these changed perceptions of oneself can be deeply damaging. Just as Jean Pasqualini recognized his capacity to kill during a struggle session, so prisoners have to confront their shadow self in a way many of us manage to avoid in normal life. Released prisoners from the Chinese *laogai* endure brutal- ization on two levels: not only have they experienced violence but they also have to face the dark side of their own nature which renders them capable of violence themselves. Often the sense of loss for their old self, the person they were before imprisonment, is unendurable.

These vivid accounts of spiritual breakdown give an overpowering image of the *laogai* as an 'Auschwitz of the mind', in which the self has to become ashes before change is possible. So, in the words of Brian Keenan, can Humpty Dumpty ever put himself together again? And can imprisonment leave a person with 'more parts' than he or she began with?

Brian Keenan himself, an Irish writer and teacher who was held hostage by fundamentalist Shi'ite militiamen for four and a half years, found that this experience, 'enclosed in a very heightened and very different reality', revealed for him 'so much more of what we are as human beings . . . Such intimate and profound exposure of mind and body was a kind of branding and unholy stigmata, an affirmation of the richness, perhaps even enchantment of humanity.'[39] Keenan also experienced moments of spiritual transcendence in his cell; once when he was confronted by a 'brown button bowl' of fruit left by his captors:

My eyes are almost burned by what I see . . . The fruits, the colours, mesmerise me in a quiet rapture that spins through my head . . . I sit in quiet joy, so complete, beyond the meaning of joy. My soul finds its own completeness in that bowl of colour . . . I am filled by a sense of love . . . For days I sit in a kind of dreamy lethargy, in part contemplation and in part worship. The walls seem to be singing. I focus all of my attention of that bowl of fruit. I cannot hold the ecstasy of the moment and its passionate intensity . . . It seems I can push the walls away from me. I can reach out and touch them from where I sit and yet they are so far from me.[40]

The very absence of such experiences in Chinese accounts of imprisonment testifies to the pervasiveness of thought reform, and its grasp even on the dreaming or unconscious mind. Former prisoners speak of recurring dreams of places they cannot escape from,[41] and fear of giving away 'secrets' in their sleep. (Random accusations of deviations from confessions made in a prisoner's sleep were often held against the subject, and every cell had many ears.)

Lifton's research suggests, however, that prisoners from the Chinese gulag and other subjects of thought reform can make psychological use of their experiences to emerge as a more developed human being, with 'more parts' than they began with. Several of the men Lifton studied, both Chinese and Western, emerged from their ordeal in the *laogai* with a sense of personal renewal. George Chen, for instance, who underwent thought reform at school and university, emerged with a strong sense of identity intact, and a developing creative ability. Father Vechten, a Dutch priest who was imprisoned in China, had developed a general expansion of his emotional horizons, leading to an increased receptivity to his own feelings and those of others.

Mark Baber also felt that his prison sentence in China had broadened his emotional and intellectual experience. 'I found that I had to deal with so many different situations inside prison that I could cope with almost anything outside,' he says. 'But while the ideological reform gave us a particular intellectual dimension, for most of us it was the worst aspect of the prison experience. We would rather have been anywhere – in a war zone, in Sarajevo, suffering in some other jail – any other place where our thoughts could be our own.'

The psychic legacy of thought reform in Chinese society still has to be reckoned with – often in the form of high levels of nervous illness, breakdowns and suicide. An elderly eye specialist at the former Beijing Union Medical College teaching hospital (renamed the Anti-Imperialist Hospital during the Cultural Revolution and now called the Capital Hospital) told one of his patients that Chinese mental hospitals are packed with victims of the Cultural Revolution and other campaigns. 'What do you expect?' he said to Li Yikai, whose husband Wu Ningkun was imprisoned during the Cultural Revolution. 'All the stresses of the years would take their toll on your system one way or another.'[42]

When the mental pressure was lifted after Mao died and the Gang of Four was deposed, the psychological cracks and tears repressed over the years began to show. It was said that some people expressed their relief by drinking so much alcohol that they suffered brain haemorrhages. Fox Butterfield reports the case of one man who laughed so hard he became hysterical and couldn't stop laughing for weeks.[43]

Martha Avery, who translates the novels of Zhang Xianliang, refers to a term in Chinese which means 'to be made to accompany to the execution ground'. This refers to a person who is taken to the execution ground, believing he is going to be killed. Instead, people around him are shot, while he is left alive. Zhang writes: 'Although the gun may never have been fired, the bullet of fear and repression has lodged inside the brain. Every intellectual in China lives with this kind of bullet in his brain.' Zhang's novel *Getting Used to Dying* is narrated by two voices of the same person, and according to Avery is hence a portrait of what would be a psychosis in Western eyes, created by the bullet of fear and repression.

During thought reform campaigns in the community, mental health problems and psychoses were often evident even without physical abuse or imprisonment. Hu Weihan, a native of Hubei province in central China and a graduate of North China University just outside Beijing in the 1950s, told the psychologist Robert Jay Lifton that at least two students had to be sent to mental hospitals, having apparently become psychotic during the intensive ideological remoulding campaign.[44] Hu estimated that about a third of the student body were suffering fatigue, insomnia, loss of appetite, vague aches and pains and upper respiratory or gastrointestinal symptoms. Hu himself suffered from fatigue and general malaise: when he visited the school doctor, he was given a (psychologically sophisticated) diagnosis: 'There's nothing wrong with your body. It must be your thoughts that are sick. You will feel better when you have solved your problems and completed your reform.'

Other common symptoms of stress resulting from psychological pressure include neurasthenia, or weakness of the nerves, which Western psychologists identify as nervous tension, depression and anxiety. And just as terrifying dreams and insomnia are common among prisoners in the *laogai*, so these same disturbances of sleep persist among released prisoners as they attempt to reconcile the outside world with the disturbing emotions released within.

Author Zhang Xianliang had to endure an intensive process of thought reform before understanding what the 'renegade Zhu Zhenbang' meant when he talked about using a wooden knife to kill a man. 'Such a knife was aimed not at a man's throat, chest or stomach,' he wrote in his autobiographical novel *Grass Soup*. 'Instead it attacked the invisible feelings that tied him to the world around him. A wooden knife could not enter a man's flesh, but it was plenty sharp enough to cut immaterial things.'

Notes

1. 'On the Correct Handling of Contradictions among the People', 1957.

2. Brian Keenan, *An Evil Cradling*, p. xi.

3. Harry Wu.

4. Simon Leys, *Broken Images*, p. 146.

5. While Leys points out that this idea originated more than two thousand years ago in Ssu-ma Ch'ien's famous 'Reply to Jen An', the statement still rings true today as a depiction of those who have survived the system.

6. Mao Zedong, 'On Practice' from *Selected Readings of Mao Tse-Tung*, p. 81.

7. His testimony, 'Wang Tsun-Ming, Anti-Communist: an Autobiographical Account of Chinese Communist Thought Reform, is in Samuel M. Meyers and Albert D. Biderman (eds), *Mass Behaviour in Battle and Captivity*, p. 121.

8. R. J. Lifton, *Thought Reform and the Psychology of Totalism*, p. 70.

9. The writer Zhang Xianliang was referring to his background in labour camps during the Cultural Revolution when the narrator of his novel *Getting Used to Dying* refers to 'the constant terror that lives inside all Chinese'.

10. The official was Lo Juiching, Vice-Chairman of the Political and Legal Affairs Committee of the Government Administrative Council, in a report read before the 22nd Session of the Government Administrative Council on 26 August 1954, included in CICRC, *White Book on Forced Labour in the People's Republic of China*, vol. 1, p. 289.

11. Meyers and Biderman, *Mass Behaviour in Battle and Captivity*, p. 132.

12. Other sources emphasize the importance of exploiting the prisoner's emotions for the good of the proletarian cause. In his recent textbook *Labour Reform Law* [Laodong gaizao faxue], Yang Diansheng writes that part of the responsibility of the labour reform cadre is to 'make a good combination of education appealing to the reason [*lixing jiaoyu*] with that appealing to the emotions [*ganxing jiaoyu*], using concrete facts to educate prisoners. For instance, organize the prisoners to tour factories and villages, so that they may see with their own eyes the great accomplishments of Socialist construction and the huge changes taking place in the motherland . . . Do a good job of running the prisoners' cafeteria . . . and so on' (p. 192), quoted in Harold Tanner, 'The Theoretical Bases of Labour Reform', *China Information*, vol. 9, nos 2/3 (winter 1994/5).

13. Yue Daiyan with Carolyn Wakeman, *To the Storm*.

14. *People's Daily* (24 October 1951).

15. The Red Guards were groups of school and college students with a strong allegiance to Mao who banded together and were active agents in the destruction of homes, families and individuals during the Cultural Revolution. Their aims were to attack 'feudal' and 'reactionary' elements of society. In the late 1960s, the Red

Guards turned in on themselves and engaged in conflict between their different factions and also against the People's Liberation Army.

16. Fox Butterfield, *Alive in the Bitter Sea*, p. 468.

17. Pasqualini is now a Director of Harry Wu's Laogai Research Foundation. He lives in Paris.

18. Lifton, *Thought Reform and the Psychology of Totalism*, p. 3.

19. *Ibid.*, p. 4.

20. A book recently published by New World Press, Beijing, entitled *Mummy, Daddy, and Me: Chinese Children Talk about Their Parents*, contains various whimsical essays which 'open a window into the innermost recesses of the Chinese family life'. An editor's note solemnly exhorts parents to compare themselves with the parents in the book and learn what their own youngsters might expect of them. A story by a grade six student, 'Don't Rest on Your College Degree', chides a mother for laziness: 'In the evenings, sister and I do our homework under the lamp. Dad reads a book attentively. Everyone studies except you, the college graduate. You never study. Instead you see movies, watch TV and go to bed early every night . . . You yourself don't set a good example for us.' This essay is signed by Chen Xin, 'your daughter who wishes heartily that you could overcome your shortcomings'. In another essay, a child pleads for her imprisoned father to 'get rid of all your defects and become a good person'. Other stories preach about the evils of materialism, the 'Communist style of being selfless in the public interest', and the value of honest toil on the land through various nauseating exchanges between seemingly perfect 'little emperors' and their parents.

21. Pasqualini, *Prisoner of Mao*, p. 40.

22. Orville Schell, 'The Reemergence of the Realm of the Private in China', in *The Broken Mirror*.

23. Milan Kundera, *The Art of the Novel* p. 90.

24. Lifton, *Thought Reform and the Psychology of Totalism*, p. 5.

25. *Ibid.*, p. 66.

26. CIRC, *White Book on Forced Labour in the People's Republic of China*, vol. 2: The Hearings.

27. Labour Reform Work, CCP Internal document, Beijing, 1985; quoted in Harry Wu, *Laogai: The Chinese Gulag*, p. 28.

28. Wu, *Laogai*, p. 29.

29. This was even admitted in an edition of *People's Police* [Renmin Gongan], 2 August 1991, p. 3. Liu Siqi, 'Causes for the Persistence of Forcing Confessions under Torture in spite of Repeated Bans', quoted in Tanner, 'The Theoretical Bases of Labour Reform'.

30. Wu, *Laogai*, p. 30.

31. Anthony Grey, *Hostage in Peking*.

32. 'Encounter with Legalised Illegality: Liu Shanqing, the Democracy Movement, and Prison Reforms', *Chinese Sociology and Anthropology*, vol. 26, no. 4 (summer 1994), p. 48.

33. What a contrast to the departure of Irina Ratushinskaya, the Russian poet, for a seven-year sentence in the Soviet gulag. Her husband Igor's glance before she was taken away sustained her emotionally and mentally during her imprisonment: 'Just before they managed to hustle him out [of the courtroom], one last look at me. Tell me, dear comrade-judges, has anyone ever looked at you like that? . . . Or at you, Prison Governor Petrunya? No, of course they haven't. And that is why you cannot understand how I can face the journey to the camp with a smile.' Chinese prisoners arrested during purges and counter-revolutionary campaigns would rarely have such sustenance. *Grey Is the Colour of Hope*, p. 20.

34. In 'The Theoretical Bases of Labour Reform', Harold Tanner points out that it may be a simplification to speak of resistance to reform, because what appears to be on one level to be resistance may on a deeper psychological level be linked to a self-hatred based on acceptance of the state's condemnation of the offender. This particularly applies to actions such as self-injury (p. 50, note 27).

35. Shao Daosheng, *Preliminary Study of China's Juvenile Delinquency*, p. 31.

36. Ding Haihai, 'Reflections inside by an Especially Serious Prison Bombing Case', quoted in Tanner, 'The Theoretical Bases of Labour Reform'.

37. 'The New Situation and Characteristics of Criminals in Custody in the New History Era', *Fanzui yu gaizao yanjiu* (1990), no. 4 (internal), p. 4, quoted in Tanner, 'The Theoretical Bases of Labour Reform'.

38. Fang Bo, 'On the Factors in the Shaping of Criminal Psychology', quoted in Tanner, 'The Theoretical Bases of Labour Reform', p. 52.

39. Keenan, *An Evil Cradling*, p. xiii.

40. *Ibid.*, p. 69.

41. See Chapter 5 on Liu Shanqing; and Lifton, *Thought Reform and the Psychology of Totalism*, p. 187.

42. Wu Ning-kun, *A Single Tear*, p. 365.

43. Butterfield, *Alive in the Bitter Sea*, p. 511.

44. Lifton, *Thought Reform and the Psychology of Totalism*.

CHAPTER 7

Return from Hell
Harry Wu

Dwell on the past and you'll lose an eye. Forget the past and you'll lose both eyes.

Russian proverb

Harry Wu was on an ox cart leaving the graveyards beyond Qinghe farm when he made the promise to himself. He was returning to 585 barracks after burying his friend, Chen Ming, a mild-mannered, reserved man who had been arrested as a 'thought reactionary'. Two nights before, Chen Ming had been unusually talkative. He had told Harry about his past: how he had left his village to become a geography teacher in Beijing, and about his sadness when his girlfriend left him to marry someone else. And then about his arrest in Tiananmen Square and his imprisonment as a 'reactionary' for having spoken favourably about Taiwan to his pupils at school.

Chen Ming had drifted off to sleep. That morning he didn't move, and he didn't sit up for the 4 o'clock meal. His cellmates assumed he was dead, like so many others in the prison camp – which housed inmates in an advanced state of starvation, kept apart from the healthier prisoners. An hour later, the duty prisoners arrived to take away Chen Ming's body. At midnight, he came back. Harry was told that a duty prisoner in the storage room had seen a hand reach up and shake the door. It was one of the seven bodies piled up before being taken by ox cart to the mass graves. Everyone thought it was a ghost – but it was Chen Ming. He was not quite dead.

Harry persuaded the guards to feed his friend. 'He is not an ordinary prisoner – he has come back from hell,' he told them. Chen Ming was given two corn *wotou*: he grabbed them from the plate and stuffed them both into his mouth at once. Fragments of corn clung to his lips and his hands were sticky with moisture from the steaming buns. A few seconds later, he clutched his stomach in pain and dropped to the floor. He was dead. His stomach, weakened from months of starvation, could not digest so much rich corn so quickly.

All night, Harry watched over Chen Ming's body. In death, his face had taken on a rosy, ruddy hue, looking healthier than he had done in life. Prisoners recognized the condition as typical of the last stage of oedema; it was called the 'last redness of the setting sun'.

As he sat beside his friend's corpse, the other prisoners sleeping soundly in the dormitory next to him, Harry began to think. Usually he would save his energy by making his mind a blank. Tonight he began to wonder what his own life was worth – what his friend's life had been worth. 'If I die tomorrow like Chen Ming, I thought, my life will have been worth nothing,' says Harry. 'But somehow I didn't want to give up, I didn't want to surrender. Something inside me cried out, where is my God, my Father? Help me. Guide me. Bless me. Then my mind emptied. The rest of that night I slept peacefully.'[1]

The next morning, when the duty prisoners came to take Chen Ming's body to the ox cart, Harry refused to let go of his friend. The surprise of the security captain on duty at Harry's emotions – an unusual occurrence in a prison camp where the living and the dead were often indistinguishable – outweighed his anger. 'No one can respond to so much dying,' says Harry.

He climbed into the ox cart and sat next to Chen Ming's body, wrapped in a quilt and lying between six other corpses. The cart rolled into a section of the camp known as 586, dotted with small pieces of wood marking the graves with names written in black ink. Some of the holes had been dug up, perhaps by wild dogs, and Harry could see scattered scraps of clothing or belongings. When they had finished burying Chen Ming, pieces of the quilt stuck out from the earth. Harry recalls: 'That last glance at 586 seared itself into my memory. Suddenly my mind became animated, and I had what seemed almost a revelation. Human life has no value here, I thought bitterly. It has no more importance than a cigarette ash flicked in the wind. But if a person's life has no value, then the society that shapes that life has no value either. If the people mean no more than dust, then the society is worthless and does not deserve to continue. If the society should not continue, then I should oppose it.'

Harry made a promise to himself that he could not 'slide into nothingness'. 'One day we are all going to be a handful of dust. So we mustn't waste our life.' He had to reclaim some value from the fear and death that defined his life in the *laogai*. He decided to do this by remembering everything he could about the camps, and by publicizing the truth about them when he was finally free. Harry began to exercise his mind by practising elephant chess in his head, and retelling the plots of his favourite novels – *Les Misérables* by Victor Hugo and Dickens's *Tale of Two Cities* were two. He used the 'prisoners' telegraph system: attentiveness, memory, chance meetings'.[2] Whenever he was beaten during struggle sessions in the Cultural Revolution, he would shield his head from the blows. And when he was pulled from a coal mine after an accident, his first anxiety was that it might have affected his brain, and therefore his memory.

Harry's promise was formed in his childhood, by the father he loved and respected, and who blamed himself for the family's suffering. It did not waver despite the disillusionment he suffered through rejection and broken relationships. And it was this promise that finally caused Harry to disappear again in China after a decade of freedom in exile.

The water in Harry Wu's swimming pool is pale blue, reflecting the clear Californian sky above. Beyond the neat filing cabinets and bookshelves in his study in this peaceful part of Silicon Valley, just forty minutes' drive from San Francisco, stretch the San José hills, and then the desert where it is 'hotter than hell'. Harry dreams of isolating himself in the desert in a small caravan, alone, writing a book. But it never happens. Fifty-nine-year-old Harry, who spent nineteen years in the Chinese *laogai*, is driven by a desire not to waste time. He can never have those nineteen years back. So he is determined to make the most of the life he has left, before he becomes a handful of dust.

Harry doesn't relax by his pool; he wakes up early and has a brisk twenty-minute swim to keep his body in condition. His gruelling work schedule is a testimony of his mental and physical stamina. He is awake for most of the night as sleep brings nightmares, and he travels tirelessly. He becomes edgy if he is away from a phone and a fax for more than three days (Plate 10).

Harry's self-declared mission – fulfilling the promise he made in the ox cart after leaving the mass graveyards at Qinghe – is to reveal to the world the true nature of the Chinese *laogai* system in the hope that one day it will take its place in history beside Treblinka and Dachau. He wants the word *laogai* to enter the English dictionary, just as the acronym *gulag* has come to signify the Stalinist labour camps.[3] In an attempt to achieve this Harry has had to 'cross the line between life and death' once again.

More than four years after his release from camps, Harry arrived in San Francisco with $40 in his pocket. His sister had arranged for him to be a visiting scholar at Berkeley, California, but she couldn't support him financially. 'I worked in a doughnut shop to make money,' he says. 'If I made enough doughnuts I had enough money for lunch, then I made some more doughnuts and I could afford dinner. Today, I never eat doughnuts.'

When Harry first came to America, he wanted to forget the promise he made at Qinghe and to start life afresh. He says: 'I am a very normal person, and just like anyone else. When I first came to America, I just wanted to turn the page over and forget the past. I wanted to enjoy life. I wanted to work, to have a nice house and car, to have a family. I thought, 'I'm free – I can do what I want.' But the wounds in my heart wouldn't heal. Still I had nightmares at night, and I couldn't forget the people I'd left behind, or the prisoners who had died. I want to be free of these nightmares but the problem is the nightmares will never get rid of me. So I began to think, if I don't go back, who will?'

Harry was awarded a research scholarship at the Hoover Institute at Stanford University, and he began the work he had prepared for during his imprisonment. He travelled the length and breadth of the USA to compile the first database of its kind of the experiences of *laogai* prisoners. With endless patience, Harry listened to former prisoners, often reliving his own experiences of suffering in the camps, or reminiscing about friends and family. Some *laogai* survivors entrust him with precious manuscripts: diaries detailing thirty years of imprisonment and other precious records of their experiences.

Harry lobbied the US Congress and British Parliamentarians about the *laogai* camps and their exports to the West; he ploughed through Chinese internal documents for hours to find the smallest details or the most shocking truths. And he found time to visit Auschwitz and Dachau.

The depth of anger against the Chinese authorities Harry still felt, however, and the guilt about those he had left behind, drove him on. Lobbying and fact-finding in libraries were not enough for him. He decided he had to go back to China, risking his life, freedom and happiness to revisit the labour camps and gather evidence which would prove to the wider world that they exist. He found a willing and devoted ally in a woman called Ching-lee, a gently spoken, strong-minded Taiwanese secretary for the Minister of Economic Affairs in Taipei. Although Ching-lee had never heard of the *laogai* until she met Harry in a coffee bar in Taipei, she soon became as passionately committed to his cause as he was. In 1991, they spent their honeymoon filming labour camps undercover in China.

Before they left, Ching-lee and Harry practised videoing each other walking on the beach on a windswept day. This practice would give them the necessary ease and familiarity to attain the footage they needed in China. Days before they left on their 'honeymoon', Harry made a will. He knew what the consequences of his capture would be.

Harry made five perilous journeys into China on his own and with Ching-lee. In making these journeys, he has done more than any other Chinese to expose human rights abuses in the Chinese *laogai*. For parts of the trip, he was accompanied by journalists from the American CBS network and Yorkshire Television, and Sue Lloyd-Roberts of the BBC. Each visit produced extraordinary footage of the *laogai*, and gave the West its first glimpse inside the Chinese gulag. For the BBC news broadcasts, Harry spent six weeks travelling from the far west to the far east of China, as well as the deserts of the north-east. He visited at least 27 forced labour camps.

Harry says: 'After the CBS TV programme *Sixty Minutes* was aired, I was put on a blacklist within China. Most of the other dissidents on the blacklist had been involved in the 1989 democracy demonstrations at Tiananmen Square. But going back to China once was not enough to collect the information I needed to expose the *laogai* system – the core of human rights abuse in China today. So in 1992 and '93 I returned, with other TV journalists. I wanted to use TV as a tool to expose the ugly truth of the Chinese Communists. And I wanted to go and see everything with my own eyes.'

Harry Wu's work forced the US and European governments to take human rights abuses in China seriously. It also affected trade between China and the West. It is illegal in Britain and the USA to import prison labour. US Customs, under pressure from Congress, began to make seizure orders on suspicious goods coming in from China. Companies were prosecuted and fined tens of thousands of dollars for importing goods from factories Harry Wu had proved to be *laogai*. Ignorance was no longer an excuse.[4] Harry incurred even greater wrath from the Chinese when he provided conclusive evidence of organs being transplanted from executed prisoners into the bodies of wealthy Chinese expatriates from Hong Kong who travel to China for transplant operations. His research was corroborated by Human Rights Watch and Amnesty International.

Despite being known as China's most-wanted man, Harry claims: 'When I am in the country, I am just a little fish in a big sea. They can't find me.' He developed a complex system of evading detection. For the first trips, he travelled into China with fake travel documents. Once he disguised himself as a Chinese public security officer to enter a camp; at other times he posed as a US businessman and a tourist.

On his most recent trip, Harry had the protection of his US citizenship, registered under his legal name of Peter H. Wu. He applied for a Chinese entry visa, which was granted on 11 March 1995. However, this time, Harry knew that he was one of 49 dissidents who had been named on a secret government blacklist in May 1994. On this list, issued by the Ministry of Public Security, Harry is labelled a 'category 3' person. 'If subject attempts to enter China, [he is to] be dealt with according to the circumstances of the situation,' states the document. This means in effect that border authorities are to seek immediate instruction from higher authorities on how to handle the case, while their charges are kept either in isolation or under close surveillance.[5]

BBC reporter Sue Lloyd-Roberts says: 'Harry was always nervous crossing the border into China. When we crossed from Kazakhstan together last year [1994], he asked me to stand at least ten places behind him so that I could act as a witness if he was arrested and alert the necessary contacts. He was fully aware that he is probably China's most wanted man, and would rely on immigration inefficiencies to get across the frontier.'

On 19 June 1995, just after 11 in the morning, Harry's luck ran out. He was detained at the Chinese border post of Horgas when he tried to enter from the former Soviet republic of Kazakhstan, together with a companion, North Carolina law student Sue Howell. Howell had been accompanying Harry as a witness, in case he was arrested, imprisoned or worse. Harry comments wryly that he was arrested by 'a computer, not a person'. His documents and visa had been logged into the new system by border officials, and a warning immediately flashed on to their screens. They became aware that they might have netted a big fish. 'I knew it had been a big risk, going into China again with a legal visa,' Harry says. 'Maybe it was a trap. Economic development has helped the Chinese public security system to modernize and to use improved technology. So it now uses computer screening on border checkpoints.' The police who arrested Harry all had Motorola cell phones – another sign of increasing affluence.

On 23 June, Ching-lee woke up at 5.30 in the morning, unable to sleep. She had endured five restless nights without hearing from her husband, and usually he would phone every day. Several hours later, the news came through from the US State Department that Harry was being held by the Chinese.

After his arrest on the 19th, Harry and his companion had been escorted beyond the customs point and into Xinjiang by five members of the border police. They were locked into a guesthouse nearby, under constant guard. They were not allowed to communicate with the US Embassy or anyone else. Before dawn on Friday, 23 June, officials of more senior rank arrived at the guesthouse. Soon afterwards, Sue Howell was expelled.

After she left, Harry asked one of the guards what would happen to him: he made a gesture of a throat being slit. 'We just want to get rid of you,' he was told. Sue Howell took back a message for Ching-lee from her husband: he told her that she should remember China was his home. His parents and his brother had died there under the Communist regime, and they were buried there. That was his place, and if he died there, that was OK, he had said.

Ching-lee was determined that this should not be his last word. Within days of his arrest, an international campaign in the USA and Europe was gearing up to free him, with Ching-lee as its public face. Supporters organized press conferences, lobbied Congressmen and arranged demonstrations. In answer to its daily queries, the State Department was told first that the validity of Harry's travel documents was being investigated, and then that officials were looking into 'possible criminal offences' supposedly committed on previous trips to China.

Harry, too, put pressure on the security officials guarding him. 'Every day I told them, I need to see someone from the US Embassy,' he says. 'A representative should have been allowed to see me after 48 hours. The police told me they had forgotten to arrange it. "You're a very special case," they said.'

There was more than an element of the surreal about the whole experience. 'For the first part of my detention, I was driven around China with a number of security officials in an Audi car,' he says. 'It was a very nice car. Sometimes I travelled by train. They took me to restaurants when I wanted to eat, and they took care of me. No one knew who I was or recognized me.'

One of the police chiefs in Xinjiang, where Harry had been attempting to enter when he was arrested, admitted that Harry had just been in the wrong place at the wrong time. 'He told me he was just following orders from Beijing, and that he just had to take me somewhere,' says Harry. Finally he was taken to a lakeside villa in Wuhan, a major industrial city on the Yangtze River in Hubei province. Wuhan is the last place in China where Wu worked before leaving for the United States. In China, those accused of national crimes are often taken back to their work unit locale for trial. The news that he had been taken back to his former residence was greeted with unease by his friends and family in the USA. They knew that this might mean he was being treated as a Chinese, not an American, citizen, and they feared the consequences.

'In Wuhan, about sixty policemen were looking after me,' says Harry. 'There were about thirty guarding the outside of the guesthouse with machine-guns and dogs. I was the only guest.' Three young lieutenants stayed with Harry in his room 3 by 4 metres square, dogging his every move – even when he went to the toilet. 'They stood by me when I was in the toilet, and at first it was hard for me to relieve myself,' says Harry.

'I asked them, "Don't you care about the smell?" After a few days I complained to the supervisor, who said, "OK, we'll do something about it." So the next time the lieutenant stood outside the toilet door when I went in.'

Every day Harry was interrogated. Security officials told Harry that they wanted him to solve his 'problem'. 'We'll just pick a few crimes from your activities,' they told him. 'You can help us with this.' 'There were two major charges against me,' says Harry. 'One was stealing state secrets and passing them on to television companies or foreign institutions such as the US Congress and the European Parliament. They also wanted to charge me as a spy, but they dropped this because they realized the BBC and CBS are not intelligence services!' Officials also charged Harry with posing as a policeman, sneaking into a camp and filming. Harry admits to breaking the law where this was concerned, believing the ends justify the means: 'The law is made by Communists, so I'm very honoured to break the law,' he says. 'I did this to expose the truth.'

By the time Harry's interrogation began at Wuhan, his case had become an international *cause célèbre*. The media coverage exceeded the expectations of campaigners. 'Expect no favours from China's rising Stalinists,' thundered headlines. 'Why China Won't Crush Harry Wu!' He even became immortalized by cartoonists: in the *International Herald Tribune* he was depicted in convict outfit entering a room in a Chinese prison full of convicts busily sewing 'Free Harry Wu' T-shirts. 'Prisoner Wu! You'll be assigned to Machine 309 on aisle 9! . . . And step on it – a big rush order just came in' read the caption.

Among the high-level US supporters for Harry were Newt Gingrich, House Speaker, and Senator Jesse Helms, Chairman of the powerful Senate Foreign Relations Committee, who – in the words of one of his aides – 'just loves Harry'. In the UK, Margaret Thatcher showed a personal interest in his case and Ching-lee met officials from the Foreign Office. On Harry's eventual return to the USA, he was told that he was the one man who had been able to unite the Republicans and the Democrats in a common cause. 'We wanted to make Harry a bit more valuable,' says Jeff Fieldler, a director of the *Laogai* Research Foundation. 'And this is what we achieved.' The stakes had effectively been raised.

Harry's case exacerbated an already strained relationship between China and the USA. One man locked away in a lakeside villa guarded by men with machine-guns had become the focus of a storm which some said could result in a new Cold War. In July, former Foreign Minister Henry Kissinger warned that relations between Washington and Beijng were 'in free fall'. The mutual savaging between countries had really begun with the visit of Taiwan's President Lee Tenghui to Cornell

University only weeks before. Beijing was furious with the Americans for allowing such a visit to take place. China's visceral animosity towards Taiwan dates back to the defeat of Chiang Kai-shek and the Nationalists by the Communists. When the Taiwanese talk political independence from the Republic of China today, this rubs salt into an old wound and led to China firing 'test missiles' at the island in 1995 and also in 1996, in a dubious attempt to dissuade voters from electing Lee Teng-hui in the country's first democratic elections.

In the midst of the storm, Hong Kong officials co-operated with US business leaders in Washington to put pressure on US Congressmen not to impose sanctions on Beijing. In Beijing itself, it was reported that executives from Boeing had been warned that US aircraft manufacturers could miss out on $100 billion worth of future Chinese orders because of the bad bilateral relationship. In the USA, there was evidence that at least one business deal involving a US company might have fallen victim to the downtown in Sino-US relations.

In mid-July, there was further public outrage when Beijing released a video of Harry making a 'confession' to camera. He looked haggard and lean, as if he had lost a great deal of weight and was under severe pressure. On the video, he admitted to 'falsifying facts' in the BBC news broadcasts about the *laogai*. By discussing details of the BBC footage, Harry's covert message was that the substance of the broadcasts was correct. 'I hoped that the omissions in the "confession video" – such as their failure to interview many key witnesses – would tell the world that the video itself was a fabrication,' says Harry. 'For example, they omitted to mention the patient in Wuhan who said his doctor told him that his kidney was from an executed prisoner, or the Chinese government document detailing the procedure to extract organs from executed prisoners.'

Harry had not been tortured in order to extract the confession. However, he had been under severe pressure and he knew that, the more convincing his confession, the more leniency he was likely to receive. The official statement on his case released by Xinhua[6] acknowledged that 'Wu Hongda's attitude towards admitting his crimes was quite good and he showed signs of repentance and that he was also made use of by other people in committing his crimes'. In his confession statement, Harry admitted that his actions 'have done harm to the Chinese government and people and have violated China's laws'. He said that 'in the face of facts', he felt remorse for the consequences of what he had done. 'I even told them I would withdraw from and disband the *laogai* research I have been doing,' he says. Those who know Harry also know that he has no intention of doing so. 'I had to play the game,' he explains.

When Harry was arrested in 1957, he didn't have the benefit of a trial.

In 1995, the situation had improved. 'This time I had a four-hour trial and a lawyer, even though I only saw the lawyer two or three times,' he says. 'The first time was just to ask him to fax my Embassy – to ask them for 6,000 yuan to pay him.' At the trial on 24 August, Harry reports, the police were 'very kind', and treated him with respect. During the proceedings he was taken into a waiting room. 'After twenty minutes a judge came in with three others,' Harry adds: 'One of them was a woman, and she wasn't bad looking. They asked me about my health, and told me that Chinese judicial procedures gave me the right to appeal against his sentence in ten days, with a second trial. I told them that of course I wanted a second trial. I was told maybe I didn't need a second trial, maybe I would be given an additional sentence which I could take first.'

When Harry told them that he was still entitled to his rights for a second trial, he was accused of being very stubborn. 'We're concerned about your health, and about your family waiting for you,' they told him. Finally they just handed him his sentence: fifteen years in jail for 'having committed the crimes of stealing and spying out state secrets and illegally supplying them to overseas institutes, organizations and figures, and of passing himself off as a government worker for deceptive purposes'. The second clause of the sentence was expulsion from China. Harry didn't know whether this would mean he served ten, twenty or fewer years before expulsion. He was genuinely astonished when they told him the expulsion took place immediately. 'I had no choice,' Harry says with a straight face. 'So I went back to the USA.'

He was put on the next flight to San Francisco, and, within hours, the world's media featured his release as their leading story. On the plane, Harry was working out how to get home. He decided he'd call Ching-lee from the airport, and then hire a car to drive home. He was shocked and moved when he was greeted by hundreds of supporters wearing yellow ribbons and waving 'welcome home' banners. He disembarked from the plane wearing jeans and a baseball cap, and quoting Hemingway. 'If I wasn't American, I wouldn't be free now,' he told everyone.

Harry's recent arrest and imprisonment is a story about international politics, and a strained relationship between the world's biggest superpower and a country which wants to be the world's biggest superpower. It shows how the fate of one individual can illuminate the divisions or desired unities between leaders responsible for more than a billion people, and it is also a story of the relationship between the media and politics. The BBC had already attracted the ire of China by its controversial documentary on the sex life of Mao. Diplomatic relations with Britain suffered after this broadcast because the Chinese hierarchy was unable to understand the notion of an independent broadcasting company operating separately from the government. The Chinese assumed it was a deliberate, government-sponsored attempt to make the Chinese 'lose face'. Their fury increased with the release of Sue Lloyd-Roberts's broadcasts.[7]

But most of all, Harry's experience is a story of a man's quest to expiate his guilt and to find meaning in a pain which is still raw more than fifteen years later. Harry has been described by some as 'admirably crazy',[8] and by others in even less flattering terms. Others see him as a determined saboteur of USA-China relations, or as a spy for the CIA. He is often isolated even within the Chinese exile community, sometimes because of his forthright criticism of dissidents' concern only for political prisoners, to the exclusion of ordinary prisoners, in the Chinese *laogai*. 'In China in the 1980s, all the time my father had gone, I never shed a tear. But when I began to write, and retrieved all these details, and realized that all these people were missing, I felt very sad. And after that, I felt guilty. These people were honest and straight, and they were destroyed. But when we were actually sharing the situation, I had not really liked them. So I felt very sorry and guilty, and decided that the world had to know about it. These people were very ordinary human beings like you and me. Like Bigmouth Xing . . . he was a peasant, he was a criminal, but he was a good guy. That is why it is so amazing that these "dissidents" say to me, "We are only concerned about political prisoners".'

To return to China, not once but several times, might appear to some to be an act of unbelievable idiocy. When asked why he goes back to relive the hell of his past, Harry's answer is: 'guilt that I survived'. Another answer could simply be "because I had to'. His way of coming to terms with his trauma is to go through it again and again. Freud described a similar phenomenon as the 'repetition compulsion'. He was referring to the psychological need to re-enact, symbolically or otherwise, a highly disturbing experience. Erikson explains: 'The individual unconsciously arranges for variations of an original theme which he has not learned either to overcome or to live with', and deals with the stressful situation by 'meeting it repeatedly and of his own accord'.[9]

In Harry's case, it is not so simple. Trauma, guilt, shame and compassion all lie behind his actions. He is a man who experienced a loss at an early age with the death of his mother (Harry was only 5), and who now witnesses similar loss in the broken lives of *laogai* survivors. After experiencing abandonment by members of his family, Harry now witnesses that betrayal in a regime.

In his autobiography, he describes how, after seventeen years away from home in the labour camps, he arrived in Shanghai to see his family. The first reaction of his 'number four' sister was to ask why he came back, and whether there was any problem. 'Did you get permission to leave? Show me your travel certificate,' she demanded. Harry's youngest sister came to the door, grabbed his papers, and immediately ran off to report to the police station. After seventeen years without seeing his family, Harry had expected a very different welcome.

Harry is an emotional man who speaks with passionate eloquence, and his feelings frequently spill over into tears when he is interviewing *laogai* survivors for his research. Sue Lloyd-Roberts remembers that, during their undercover trip to China in 1994, Harry met a 29-year-old prisoner who had been sentenced to nineteen years in a labour camp for taking part in a street brawl. He was 23 when he was arrested, the same age as Wu when he was first detained in the late 1950s. 'Harry emptied our Jeep of food and gave it to the young man, who lived in a tiny shack guarding the piles of cotton picked by the prisoners,' says Lloyd-Roberts. 'He sat with the prisoner, tears running down his cheeks, reliving and sharing the desolation and hopelessness that had overwhelmed him when, still in his twenties, he saw no future outside China's prison camps. Our driver and I had to force him back into the Jeep before the guards returned and arrested us.'

Harry's own self-image lies somewhere in the divide between the degradation of his life in the camps and the fame he has enjoyed since his release. 'A hero couldn't survive the labour camps,' he often says. 'You have to become like a beast to survive. I learnt to be like an animal – to fight, to steal food, to survive.' Since his return to America in August, Harry has been a feted guest on chat shows, including *Larry King Live*, and a popular figure on the human rights cocktail party circuit. The contrast between the two lives could scarcely be more profound, and it often gives Harry a feeling of isolation and detachment.

The writer Victor Frankl, who was imprisoned in Nazi concentration camps from 1943 to 1945, wrote that, in his experience, the inmates who managed to survive such horrors were those who could attribute meaning or purpose to what they had to endure. 'Meaning makes a great deal of things bearable – perhaps everything,' he said.[10] And he quotes Nietzsche: 'He who has a why to live can bear with almost any how.'

Harry is focused on his own 'why', his own purpose, but other longings and desires intrude upon his life too. As a child, his spiritual awareness was kindled by the kindness and teachings of the Jesuit priests at his school in Shanghai (one of them gave him his English name, Harry). Later, in the camps, he clung to his love of literature and the imagination by maintaining possession of his small collection of books, despite the danger if they were discovered. Today, he loves art; particularly Rembrandt's treatment of light and the limpid colours of Monet. 'If my life had been different, I would have liked to be a painter,' he says. But the ugliness of what he has witnessed still lives in him. When that last glance at the graveyard numbered 586 seared itself into Harry's memory, he was giving his experience of suffering a meaning. His life is still focused on this purpose today, and for him, it is a mission of life and death. There is no time for art galleries, or for going on retreat in Wyoming.

On some days, the memory of his father is fresh in his mind. Harry has not forgotten his stern questions after two older boys picked a fight with him in the schoolyard one day all those years ago in Shanghai. 'Did you give in? Did you stand up again?' Since then, Harry has heard the same voice inside him: 'Someone has to stand up.' If his father was alive today, he would be proud of his son.[11]

Notes

1. Harry Wu, *Bitter Winds*, pp. 124–9.

2. Alexander Solzhenitsyn, *The Gulag Archipelago*, vol. 1.

3. The word *gulag* originates from the Russian acronym for Chief Administration of Corrective Labour Camps.

4. In May 1993, the Commissioner of US Customs told Congress that Customs investigators interviewed Harry Wu on the publication of his report *Cruel Money*. 'As a result of this interview, and a careful analysis of the report itself, by early September Customs issued detention orders for chain hoists from two locations, surgical gloves, condoms, raincoats, rubber boots and shoes, and rubber vulcanisation accelerators.'

5. Human Rights Watch/Asia and Human Rights in China report: *China: Enforced Exile of Dissidents – Government 'Re-Entry' Blacklist Revealed*, vol. 7, no. 1 (January 1995).

6. SWB FE/2392 G/1, 26 August 1995.

7. Statement from the *Laogai* Research Foundation, 'Response to Chinese Accusations Regarding BBC Video'.

8. Richard Cohen, 'An Admirably Crazy Fight Against China's Gulag', *International Herald Tribune* (12 July 1995).

9. Erik Erikson, *Childhood and Society*.

10. Victor Frankl, *Man's Search for Meaning*.

11. The full story of Harry Wu's return to China and recent imprisonment will be told in his autobiography, to be published in autumn 1996.

CHAPTER 8

The Most Dangerous Counter-revolutionary

Religion in China and the Story of David Chou

I can see that in the midst of death, life persists.
In the midst of untruth, truth persists.
In the midst of darkness, light persists.

Mohandas Karamchand Gandhi

In the light of recent religious purges carried out by the Communists, it is sobering to contemplate that, historically, the Chinese state has been tolerant of religion. Major religious institutions in China have been separate from the control of the state, unlike in the West, and until the twentieth century a wide variety of religious beliefs flourished.

However, Mao saw religion as a cancer in the body politic: a poisonous threat to the state and the supremacy of Party ideology. Influenced by Stalin, Mao instituted a series of terrifying purges virtually as soon as he came to power in 1949. In the *laogai* camps, Catholics and other Christians often endured worse torture than murderers, thieves or political Rightists.[1] Their faith is still being severely tested today, despite the current revival of religion which has resulted from the loosening up of controls accompanying Deng Xiaoping's 'socialist modernization'.

For most of Chinese history, Buddhism was the main religion of China in both rural villages and urban areas. Chinese Buddhism has a distinct spiritual philosophy which can be distinguished from its Indian and Tibetan counterparts. In Tibet, the spiritual and the secular were fused in the government of the country. But in China, although they played a major role in education, monks and nuns had no real political power. Tens of thousands of monasteries and nunneries were content to run schools and act as community centres and even banks.[2] Although the Communists tried their utmost to destroy the roots of this ancient belief system, many of the religious sects enjoying increasing popularity in 1990s China are quasi-Buddhist in nature.

Daoism is similar to Buddhism in its basic tenets, and today its believers tend to follow split-off sects which utilize ancient Daoists texts and liturgy. These sects include the Bai Yang Jiao (White Sun Sect), the Da Dao Hui (Big Sword Society), the Hua Zhai Dao (Way of Flowers and Vegetarianism) and the Chang Sheng Dao (Way of Eternal Life).[3] Most of these peasant-based religious sects bear no relation to religious 'cults' as we know them in the West, such as the Moonies or the Scientologists. They represent one of the most ancient cultural traditions in China. Although these sects were virtually wiped out during the 1950s and 1960s, the loosening up of control – particularly in rural areas – following Deng Xiaoping's economic reforms in the 1980s led to an upsurge in traditional and neo-traditional groups.

However, human rights groups internationally sounded the alarm when a September 1983 amendment to the Criminal Law made the 'crime' of 'organizing and using a reactionary sect or secret society [*fandong hui-daomen*] for counter-revolutionary purposes' punishable by death. According to Asia Watch, the typical sentencing range for traditional sect leaders in China lies somewhere between ten years and life imprisonment. Others are executed.[4]

Buddhists in Tibet have been persecuted by the Chinese ever since the invasion of the People's Liberation Army under Mao in 1949-50. This persecution is not only religious; it is a result of the entanglement of politics with religion in this formerly independent country. Monasteries or nunneries are traditionally centres of education in Tibet, and for many Tibetans are also the places where they become politically aware through learning about their heritage. A recent speech by the Chinese Communist Party Secretary for Tibet made it clear that it is a political requirement for Party members to have no religious beliefs whatsoever.[5]

The role of the Catholic Church in the recent political change in Poland was also noted by the Chinese Communist Party. One Chinese official said: 'The church played an important part in the change [in Eastern Europe]. If China does not want such a scene to be repeated in its land, it must strangle the baby while it is still in the manger.'[6]

Islam is another religion in China closely associated to political activities, particularly concerning independence from China. Islam is primarily found among the non-Chinese-speaking people in the vast desert to the west of China's heartland, known as 'China's Siberia' owing to its concentration of labour camps. This immense and bleak area forms Qinghai, Xinjiang, Gansu and Ningxia provinces, and is home to many national minorities.

Christianity was first brought into China in AD 635 by Nestorian missionaries, but it initially failed to capture Chinese hearts and minds.

The Pope attempted to spread the Christian net wider by sending a group of Franciscan friars to China in 1294. However, the Church was more successful in gaining followers among foreigners living in China than it was among the Chinese themselves. The Italian literary scholar and gentleman Matteo Ricci was the most famous of the Jesuits to establish himself in the court of the Qing emperors in Beijing in 1601.[7] Ricci succeeded in winning several high officials to Christianity, and even members of the imperial family. Many churches were set up in different parts of China.

The modern missionary movement began in 1842, when the Opium War opened China to foreign trade and then Protestant and Catholic influences. Mission schools, hospitals, universities and clinics were established. Many Chinese established links with churches overseas: families with these foreign connections were often the first to suffer under Mao.

The purges began virtually as soon as the People's Republic declared its existence in 1949. In his autobiography, *Bitter Winds*, Harry Wu recalls two new courses appearing in the school curriculum in 1950, one about Darwin's theory of evolution, and another teaching the Marxist theory of social development. Gradually the foreign Jesuit priests who taught at his school, St Francis's in Shanghai, were sent home by the government. Wu remembers his horror in 1952 at seeing an elaborate exhibition of photographs and documents revealing the 'crimes of the foreign imperialists who use religion against the Chinese people'. Wu says:

> One laid out an assortment of weapons – knives, pistols, even a grenade – supposedly discovered in the city's Christian churches, which allegedly proved the foreign missionaries were really imperialist agents and spies. Another was a collection of photographs of suffering Chinese children at missionary orphanages. I remember one picture of an American nun sitting down to eat a big meal of bread and milk while several starving Chinese children stood by looking on. Another picture showed the graveyard for Chinese children attached to a missionary orphanage. I didn't know then that the children had been deposited at the orphanages in advanced stages of illness and starvation and that the nuns had been unable to save them *(Bitter Winds, p. 8)*.

Wu, who had admired and respected his Jesuit teachers, was also shocked by the Party's allegations of illicit sexual relations between foreign priests and Chinese women.

Throughout China, priests, missionaries and ordinary religious believers became the focus of hatred, whipped up by a government which called them 'wolves in religious clothing', as if they were about to devour the souls of the innocent. To keep the wolves at bay, millions were sent to labour camps or to do labour with peasants in the villages. Some of them are still there today.

Liu Bainian, lay member of the Standing Committee of the Catholic Patriotic Association, claims that no one has been detained in China for religious reasons since the Cultural Revolution. Testimonies collected by Amnesty International and Human Rights Watch from bishops, priests and members of Buddhist, Daoist and other sects who have suffered for their beliefs expose the hollowness of this claim.

Bishop Fan Xueyan became well known as the most influential of China's underground Catholic bishops. For the greater part of his adult life, since his ordination by Pope Pius XII, Bishop Fan had been held in labour camps and detention centres. He died in police custody in April 1992, the day before his ten-year sentence would have expired. His body was reportedly delivered to his family by Public Security officers who did not give any explanation as to the cause of death.[8] His corpse was wrapped in a plastic bag and the legs so tightly wrapped with a white cloth that it was difficult to unwrap them.

Bishop Fan, who was born on 11 February 1907 in a village in Hubei, studied for the priesthood in Beijing and Rome. After being ordained as a priest in 1934, he went to serve in Wanxian diocese in Sichuan province. During the war against Japan, he contributed medical and material services to the Eighth Route Army (the name given to the Red Army when it was placed under nominal Guomindang command during the second Communist-Guomindang united front against Japan in 1937–45).

In 1958, seven years after being ordained by the Pope, Bishop Fan was sentenced to fifteen years' hard labour for his opposition to the Chinese Church's 'imperialist, self-governing policy' and for 'stubbornly refusing to accept' the official Catholic Patriotic Association. He served his sentence in labour camps in Laishui, Huanghua and Anxin counties, and in 1969 was released to live in his home village – albeit under supervision. He was arrested again in April 1978 and detained without charge in a county jail in January 1980. On his release from his second imprisonment, Bishop Fan secretly ordained three bishops and several priests, and secretly continued other underground church activities.

On 13 April 1982, he was arrested again, and charged with 'colluding with foreign forces to jeopardize the sovereignty and security of the motherland'. This time he was sentenced to ten years, and jailed in Hebei Number Two prison in Shijiazhuang, the capital of the province. Following an intervention by Cardinal Jaime Sin of Manila, Bishop Fan was finally released on parole in November 1987, but forced to remain under house arrest. On 3 November 1990, the bishop was 'disappeared'. For a year and and half until his death at the age of 85, he was moved from place to place by the Chinese authorities. Although relatives were allowed to visit him at the beginning of his detention, in 1991 a government statement said Bishop Fan would henceforth 'be staying at a pleasant location' where he apparently did not wish to be disturbed.

His corpse was released to his family in April 1992. Colour photographs of the body taken after death show that he was very emaciated, which could perhaps be attributed to age; they also reveal large pinkish-purple marks on his forehead and on one cheek. Both legs appeared to be dislocated below the knee. The marks were consistent with violence inflicted shortly before death.

The body of Bishop Liu Difen, a Catholic bishop from Anguo diocese, Hebei province, was given back to his family bearing similar marks of violence. Bishop Liu Difen had disappeared in December 1990, at the age of 78. On 15 November 1992, his corpse was handed over to his family, who were told that he had died from high blood pressure and a brain embolism.

Asia Watch has noted the existence of extrajudicial detention for bishops like Fan and Liu Difen, known euphemistically as 'old-age homes'. These appear to be run by the Religious Affairs Bureau in conjunction with the official Catholic Patriotic Association. Elderly clergy are often forcibly removed to these homes, where medical care, if received, is basic. Clergymen and women confined to these grim establishments, in secret locations throughout China, are clearly open to all forms of physical and mental abuse.

Relatives examining Bishop Liu's corpse found two unhealed wounds in the middle of his back, scars on his left shoulder and two holes under his left armpit. It was not difficult to conclude that his death had been due to severe maltreatment.

During the Cultural Revolution, Catholics – who were associated with imperialism where the Party was concerned – endured severe harassment, and thousands were sent to carry out hard labour in the countryside. George Mo, whose story is told in Chapter 2, has compiled a file with evidence of abuses against both the clergy and believers. 'They not only arrested, tortured and killed those clergy who resisted their "reform" but also defamed them by every means,' he says. 'Priests and nuns with firm faith were questioned for days and nights without rest. After the worn-out priests and nuns fell asleep, the Communists carried them into the same bed and took pictures'.[9]

George also reports the death of Liu Deming, a monk of Beijing's Notre Dame, who was beaten to death when he refused to deny his Christian faith. Father Ma of Holy Mother Cathedral at Zou Sa, 30 miles south of Shanghai, also suffered a horrifying fate. His hands were bound behind him and he was then pushed head first into a well, just wide enough to accommodate his body (Plate 11). He drowned within seconds.

Although Communist propaganda claims that prisoners in labour reform camps have freedom of worship, in reality freedom of religion is non-existent in the *laogai*, because it is opposed to the four cardinal principles (a belief in Maoism, a belief in socialism, faith in the Communist Party and the democratic dictatorship of the people) and labour reform regulations. Harry Wu points out that while, for instance, Muslims in *laogai* camps are provided with separate food prepared without pork fat and are given days off in accordance with Muslim holidays, this is an example more of traditional customs and practices than of religious freedom.[10] In the labour camps, 'studying the Bible, worshipping, or spreading of religion are prohibited'.[11]

During the Cultural Revolution particularly, those with religious beliefs suffered severe persecution. Christians who dared to pray were forced to endure struggle sessions and were punished by torture, beatings or solitary confinement. Often their faith was an inspiration to other prisoners, despite the authorities' attempts to the contrary.

Yih Leefah, a Chinese-born American citizen who was imprisoned at White Grass Mountain, a camp in southern Anhui, remembers how a Shanghai bishop saved him from suicide.[12] Yih, an intellectual, was forced to work tending the pigs by shovelling out excrement and scooping up the resulting fertilizer into piles. He became so miserable and desperate that he was tempted to commit suicide. But Monsignor Kong Pingmai, the Roman Catholic Bishop of Shanghai – who was also a prisoner in the camps – dissuaded him. Bishop Kong retained his faith even when he was informed upon for praying and forced to undergo struggle sessions. While he was standing, head down, before the mob of prisoners, Yih said to him, 'You old fool, why should you pray, if there is a god in heaven you would not be here.' 'Then he looked at me with very disappointed but loving eyes, like Jesus must have looked at Peter when Peter denied him three times after he had been arrested. I felt terrible.' Later on the Bishop told Yih that he forgave him, and encouraged him again not to give up on life.

In his memoirs, *Prisoner of Mao*, Jean Pasqualini recalls a moving Christmas service in the camps by Father Hsia.

As I looked down the embankment I saw that he was just finishing up the mass, in front of a mound of frozen earth which he had chosen as an altar. He was making the traditional gestures of priests all over the world. But his vestments here were ragged work clothes; the chalice, a chipped enamel mug; the wine, some improvised grape juice; and the host, a bit of wo'tou he had saved from breakfast. I watched him for a moment and knew quite well it was the truest mass I would ever see.[13]

Zhou Dawei prefers to be known by his Christian name, David Chou. It is the name he was christened with following his birth in 1934 in Hubei province, and he is proud of it because it is symbolic of his deep religious beliefs. 'I have been a Christian since I was born,' says David, a burly, bespectacled 62-year-old whose conversation is peppered with gruff, gravelly laughs. 'The name David is from the Bible. Have you heard of the London Mission? My grandfather used to worship there. He was an ordinary Chinese farmer, but then the church gave him enough financial support to train as a doctor. He was 50 years old at the time!'

David works as the night manager for a drug rehabilitation unit in Los Angeles. The job is tough and dangerous. 'But it's OK,' he says with a grin. David is used to dealing with the seamier, shadow side of life after serving over a decade in the *laogai* for his beliefs and family background. It is his third extended sojourn in America, and David hopes that this time he'll be able to stay. His first visit was in 1984, when he came to visit his uncle. In 1988, he came back again at the invitation of the Philadelphia Chinese Cultural and Community Centre, where he worked as their manager for nearly a year. But he was back at home in Beijing early enough to participate in the 1989 democracy movement. 'I marched with the students for several days to show my solidarity with the democracy movement,' he says. 'I was the only one over 50 years old!'

Like everyone else, he was devastated at the outcome in June 1989. But at his core, he was not surprised. He knew what the Communists were capable of. 'People think that the economic reforms mean there is a new society. But with the old men in charge, there can be no freedom or democracy. The current dictator is no better than the last. If these old men do not die, China will remain a feudal society, as it has been for eight hundred years.'

Before the Communist takeover in 1949, David was studying in Hong Kong, and staying in the house of 'a rich, famous gentleman called Sir Y. K. Gan, much decorated by the British'. His father was working as a manager in the British-supervised Maritime Customs Office in Wuhan city, Hubei province, and his brother was in the Nationalist air force. At the age of 15, he returned home to be with his family. During 1955 to 1956, David's father was detained during the counter-revolutionary campaign under suspicion of being an imperialist spy. However, no evidence was found against him, and he was sent to work in the countryside. After the family protested, he was 'retired' instead at home.

In the same year, David graduated from the Beijing Institute for Foreign Languages, after studying Russian. He utilized his language skills by working as a translator and editor for a Chinese construction publication, and he continued his study of Russian. Russian advisers had been appointed across the country and were involved in many different industries, and also with implementing Stalinist security and legislative policies.

This was all to change with the Hundred Flowers Movement in 1957. Mao urged the people to 'let a hundred flowers bloom and a hundred schools of thought contend'. The overt agenda was for the people to offer constructive criticisms of the government. The government boasted that they wanted to work with the people to the best of their ability, and in the spirit of mutual progress. Students and workers alike were encouraged to criticize the Party's work boldly in order to help it to correct mistakes and eliminate any previous 'erroneous tendencies'.

The reassuring language of the campaign was aimed at quelling the anxieties of those who were unused to speaking out. Mao said it would be:

> a movement of ideological education carried out seriously, yet as gently as a breeze or a mild rain. It should be a campaign of criticism and self-criticism carried to the proper extent. Meetings should be limited to small-sized discussion meetings or group meetings. Comradely heart-to-heart talks in the form of conversations, namely exchange of views between individuals, should be used more and large meetings of criticism or 'struggle' should not be held.[14]

Those who had suffered in the severe Elimination of Counter-revolutionaries campaign in 1955 and in other campaigns were suspicious of the government's promises of 'heart-to-heart talks' and warm exchanges of viewpoints. But young people, including David, found themselves inspired by new feelings of their own empowerment. Excited by the opportunity for debate, they didn't pay attention to the possibility of becoming 'snakes' to be flushed out of the long grass – in other words, dissidents and opponents to the Party line.[15]

If people didn't make any suggestions because of their fear of the consequences, they were 'persuaded' to do so by Party bosses, teachers or the heads of their work unit. David remembers feeling an initial wariness about participating in the criticisms, but ultimately he did so. He knew that he was in a vulnerable position: as a Christian, he had not been allowed to join the Youth League or the Party, even though he had wanted to do so. 'I was very young and wanted to join the League,' he says. 'I was thinking about my future.' To him, it was not incompatible with the religion his family had adopted. In the 1950s, before the

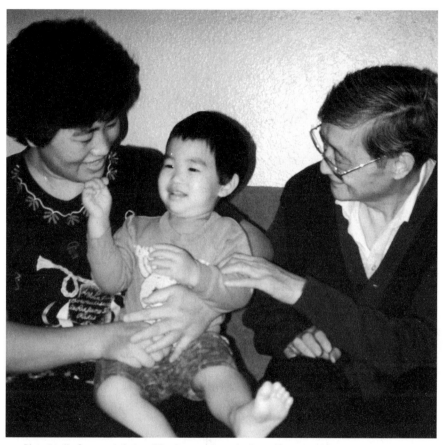

Plate 1 Jie Quansue's father did not return from the *laogai* for more than twenty years. Now he lives with her family in Los Angeles (*photo:* author).

(a)

(b)

Plate 2 Prisons and labour farms are found throughout China: generally they have both a factory and a prison name. Some are surrounded with barbed wire and have obvious watchtowers with an armed sentry (a), and others, like Quincheng prison (b), look like ordinary factories (*photo:* Robin Munro).

(a)

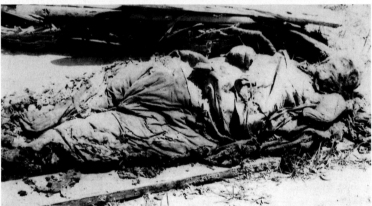

(b)

Plate 3 *(above)* (a) George Mo with his family in 1945. Top row: his father Paul Louis Mo, grandmother and mother Cao Dezhen. Front row: his second sister, brother, older sister and George *(photo: George Mo's personal collection)*.

(b) The body of George Mo's father, Paul Louis Mo, taken from the Tsao-Tsun graves for the prisoners of Da-Tsen-Yao coal mine in Wan-Tsun, Daton, Shanxi. George's father died on 4 April 1969 *(photo: George Mo's personal collection)*.

Plate 4 *(left)* Today George Mo works as a security guard in a motel in Los Angeles *(photo: author)*.

Plate 5 *(above)* John working in the camps (*photo:* John's personal collection).

Plate 6 *(left)* John (Liu Xinfu) (*photo:* author).

Plate 7 *(opposite top)* Former Tibetan prisoner Palden Gyatso demonstrating a variation of the 'Su Qin carries a sword on his back' position used for torture in the *laogai* (*photo:* John Hooper).

Plate 8 *(opposite below)* Torture weapons used in Chinese prisons. From the catalogue of a Chinese security company (*photo:* Yorkshire Television, courtesy Roger Finnegan and Tim Tate).

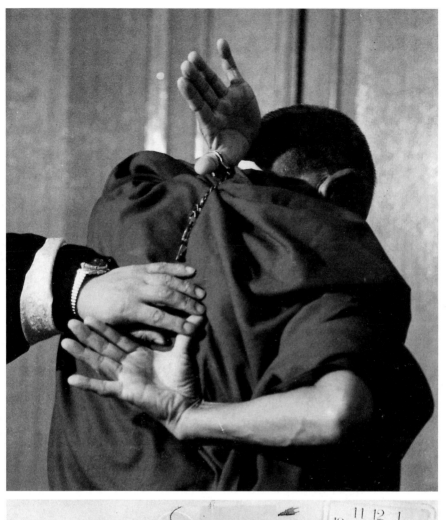

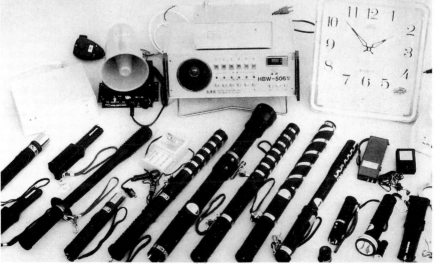

Plate 9 *(above)* Liu Shanqing (second from right) and colleagues in the Hong Kong Patriotic Alliance for a Democratic China stage a demonstration in support of political prisoner Chen Ximing in summer 1995 (*photo:* author).

Plate 10 *(left)* Harry Wu at the Hong Kong/Chinese border (*photo:* Yorkshire Television, courtesy Roger Finnegan and Tim Tate).

Plate 11 *(opposite)* A well in the grounds of the Church of the Holy Mother, Zou Sa, thirty miles south of Shanghai. During the crack-down on 'imperialist running dog' priests, Father Ma's hands were tied behind his back and he was pushed head-first into the well, where he drowned (*photo:* George Mo's private collection).

Plate 12 *(above)* Zhu Xiaodan, the young democracy activist, is now living in Los Angeles and hopes to be granted political asylum (*photo:* author).

Plate 13 *(above)* Palden Gyatso during his visit to London *(photo:* John Hooper).

Plate 14 *(left)* Han Dongfang in Hong Kong *(photo:* Annie Knibbs).

Cultural Revolution, they were allowed to attend church, even though it was strictly controlled by the Communists. But by the time of the Hundred Flowers Movement, they were allowed no contact with the London Mission. Foreign connections were deeply suspect.

When David was encouraged by his teachers to open up with his deep feelings about the Party, he finally told them that he thought the Party should not be so suspicious of overseas links. 'Because I had studied in Hong Kong, I suggested that we expand our foreign connections for the good of the country,' he says.

Several weeks later, the crackdown on 'snakes in the grass' began in earnest. David and his classmates, even the keen Party members, became aware of the real nature of the Hundred Flowers Movement. 'We had been so idealistic, so full of hope about the Communist government,' he says. 'Gradually we realized how oppressive the regime was, and we became disillusioned. Nobody dared to say anything again. Even family members suspected each other.'

David was in a particularly sensitive position. It was a period of ambiguous Sino–Soviet relations, and he could be targeted at any point according to whichever position the Party was taking on Russia. The relationship between the two countries had always been complex and difficult, mingled with layers of distrust. It had survived Mao's disagreement with Stalin in the 1920s on the need for a mass-based rural revolution. As Mao built up his People's Republic, he had become dependent on Soviet technical assistance in creating a communications infrastructure, power supply and industry. The heavy losses suffered by China in the Korean War (1950-3), and the accompanying mistrust about the threat from the capitalist and imperialist West, only increased China's reliance on Soviet involvement in building up a new army and navy. In 1957 and 1958, however, resentment had begun to build about the price China was paying the Soviet Union for aid in industrial development. China needed a large agricultural surplus to meet the terms for repayment of Soviet loans.[16] Cracks in the Sino–Soviet relationship became more evident. And those in labour camps who had suffered for their views against Russia in the 1950s were often left to rot there, despite being vindicated.

David was forced to undergo a struggle session over two days in which he was verbally harangued, and declared to be the 'biggest Rightist' in the local area. 'On the first day I argued with the people I was struggling against, but by the end of the day I just saw that these were people who were controlled by the Party. On the next day I didn't attend because I was ill, and I was criticized in my absence.' His new status as a 'counter-revolutionary Rightist' blackened his name and his future. He was fired from his job.

David's greatest crime was regarded as being a petition he had organized in his Russian class. During the Hundred Flowers Movement, he had made a speech at his school saying that the government were training Russian-speaking personnel but that there was no work for them. The speech resulted in more than a hundred students organizing a rally, demanding to meet Premier Zhou. The students had also refused to continue studying Russian. David's crime was 'to agitate the students to demonstrate'. 'I didn't think that what I'd spoken about was wrong,' says David. 'I spoke from my conscience.'

Even so, David was frightened. For six months he stayed in his dormitory in Beijing, waiting for the inevitable. His arrest finally came on 13 March 1958. For one and a half months he was held in a detention centre in Beijing. Conditions were so bad that he longed, finally, to be sent for labour reform in the countryside. Twenty people were packed into a cell with a 60-centimetre-wide strip each. The daily diet consisted of a meagre two meals: two small corn buns plus a watery porridge. 'The worst thing was the hunger,' he says. 'The amount of food we were given was one-third of our daily needs, so everybody was starving. We had to do constant self-criticism; the brainwashing began as soon as we entered the detention centre. Even the families and friends of prisoners who visited the detention centre were encouraging us to reform and to repent. There was a lot of pressure from all sides.'

David still believed he had done nothing wrong; and his faith in a higher (and divine) authority sustained him. But he knew he wouldn't survive the system for very long if he didn't make a full confession and acknowledge his guilt.

Six weeks after his arrest he was taken by truck with a group of other prisoners to the mountains north of Beijing, beyond the Great Wall. The group of prisoners were guarded by armed security personnel at each corner of the truck. David and his fellow inmates were relieved to be leaving the detention centre; they had high hopes of better food, improved conditions and fresh air at their destination, Quinjung farm, Hubei province.

Their expectations were not fulfilled. During David's initial sentence at Quinjung, from 1958 to 1965, he endured virtual starvation, beatings and solitary confinement. Because he refused to reform at the beginning of his sentence, David was handcuffed to a bed in a small single room for several days.

'When I arrived at Quinjung we were given small portions of salt, vegetables, rice and buns,' he says. 'After a few months the diet decreased even more. Instead of vegetables, we would have weeds from the fields. We also ate leaves from trees in the camp. I had weighed about 160 pounds before my sentence there began. After two years I was down to 96 to 98 pounds. Now I weigh about two hundred pounds. We were like bones, dragging ourselves around. I was so weak sometimes that just walking to the door only feet away took an hour. I couldn't even sit down because there was no flesh on my backside. In those days, personal morality didn't exist in the camps. We were just concerned with self-preservation.'

Out of a group of about two hundred in David's labour troop, only thirty were capable of going out to work during the famine. And David believes that from the two thousand prisoners held at the camp during that time, seven or eight hundred people died during those three years. David believes he survived because he was younger and stronger than the others, and because of his belief in God.

Once David's uncle in Hong Kong mailed him a food parcel. He may have mailed more, but they were possibly intercepted and eaten. This one reached David. 'I tore it open, and it smelt so good,' he says. 'Even now, I can still smell that food. But I didn't waste time smelling it. I just devoured the entire contents of the package in one sitting. It took half an hour. I didn't know what I'd eaten; I had no sense of taste. I just needed food. Later on my uncle wrote to me asking me if I'd received the kilo of lard he had sent me.'

After being held at Quinjung for four years, David became very depressed. He had survived the famine, which he now feels is 'a miracle', but he had lost all hope for his future. Because his sentence was extrajudicial, no limit had been imposed, and he feared he might be in prison for the rest of his life. He spent most of his days quietly longing for Mao to die.

In 1965, he was released from the camp and allowed to go home. Life had not been easy for his family during his imprisonment. Like millions of ordinary families in China, they had suffered severely during the famine. David's younger brother didn't even want to know him because of the political pressure the whole family had endured. Economically, life was easier. David was able to buy food and plant seeds for the coming year in a small plot of land. 'Things were changing slowly,' he said. 'There was food in the shops again. The only other things in the shops were bicycles and beer!'

David was still under heavy surveillance owing to his counter-revolutionary status. Perhaps the authorities were looking for an excuse to pounce on him again. David doesn't know this for sure. He admits that he played the game and didn't look for trouble. He prayed silently and worshipped on his own, rather than making a public display of his faith. When two elderly American friends came to visit him, David wasn't at first aware of the danger.

'I had known the ladies as a child, when one of them worked at my middle school,' says David. 'My father knew them too.' They took advantage of the more open political climate in China to visit the Chou family in 1973 (a year after President Richard Nixon travelled to China and met with Mao).[17] Days after their visit, on 3 August, David was arrested and sentenced to labour reform for counter-revolutionary crimes. The sentence was intended to 'teach him a lesson' and warn him against further contacts with foreigners. It was an indication of the atmosphere in a country ruled by the 'Gang of Four'.

For the first seventy days of his sentence, they kept him in solitary confinement at Hanzhou prison. This form of isolation at the beginning of a prisoner's sentence is often used as a psychological technique.[18] The idea is that before even beginning his or her 'reform', the prisoner suffers extreme loneliness, uncertainty and abandonment. Interrogation and self-criticism become their only form of direct communication with others. It is therefore both a punishment for those whose crimes are deemed particularly serious and a means of encouraging prisoners to confess.

'They suspected I was one of the biggest counter-revolutionaries of the Cultural Revolution,' says David. 'But they investigated nothing, and there was no evidence. After a few months, I was summoned before a woman – who I suppose was a judge – in a small house near the labour camp. It was very strange. There was no one else in the room. She pronounced sentence on me on behalf of the court, telling me I was anti-Communist, anti-Cultural-Revolution, and anti-Proletarian-Dictatorship. I was terrified. For any one of these offences I could have been shot. They were very serious charges. But to my amazement she sentenced me to only one year for each one, which made three altogether.'

After pronouncing judgement, the woman asked David if he agreed with the sentence. He had little choice but to agree. He was escorted back to the prison farm under armed guard. 'I was 40 years old, and I was not frightened of hard labour,' he says. 'What I was frightened about was starvation. I knew that I could not endure another prolonged period of hunger.'

This time David did not have to endure the same conditions of virtual starvation. Although the diet was poor, it was just sufficient to give prisoners energy to labour. His life in the camps for the second time around revolved around work. 'We did ten hours of labour and then two hours or so of study sessions before sleeping,' he says. 'The Party controlled people, and so we all had to criticize each other. They didn't want us to become united as a group or to form friendly relationships with each other so they tried to separate individuals from the group. The whole process of self-criticism is like a game you have to play. You're not telling the truth, you're just playing the game.'

Even in his blackest moments, David did not consider suicide. 'There was an electrified wire fence around the camp. I saw some prisoners, particularly during the famine, throw themselves on to it. They were immediately electrocuted. That happened. But I never thought about it for myself.' David's Christian faith did not waver throughout his two sentences. 'I hoped – believed – that God would help me through my ordeal. My faith gave me a reason to live.'

On 9 September 1976, at ten minutes after midnight, the Great Helmsman finally 'went to meet Marx'. Mao's death came a month after the massive earthquake at Tangshan. Superstition had not been wiped out with the Cultural Revolution. Many people, including David, linked the natural disaster to the end of an era. He points out that the earthquake happened in a leap month according to the lunar calendar, which is also unlucky, and that Mao, Zhou Enlai and Zhu De, General of the People's Liberation Army, died at this time. The Tangshan earthquake killed even more – claiming four hundred thousand lives.

Hundreds of thousands of people filed past the lifeless body of Chairman Mao on display in the Great Hall of the People during a week-long mourning period. Although public grief was expressed, there was no outpouring of emotion as there had been after the death of the widely loved Zhou Enlai, who was thought to have been a moderating influence during the excesses of the Cultural Revolution.[19] This time, people felt confused and uncertain about the future. Prisoners in labour camps for ideological crimes hoped for freedom. Others feared for theirs under the continuing reign of the Gang of Four, who had terrorized the country during the Cultural Revolution (see page 55). Some of the uncertainty was brought to an abrupt end on 6 October, barely a month after Mao's death, when Party Chairman Hua Guofeng ordered the arrest of Mao's third wife, Jiang Qing, and her cohorts.[20]

The year 1976 was also the one in which David's sentence was completed. His joy at the fall of the Gang of Four was short-lived; he was assigned to labour in the countryside for another one and a half years. When he was finally released, he was allowed to go back home to Beijing. 'It was only after the death of Mao that we spoke out freely about the labour camps, and about our experiences,' he says. 'Before then, we were too frightened.'

Three years later, a series of political rehabilitations cleared the names of many thousands who had suffered in labour camps or re-education units during the upheaval of the previous decade. David's name was also cleared, and he was allowed to return to his old job as an editor and translator. At the end of 1980, at the age of 46, David married a woman called Xing Yingzhang.

'After 1980, when it began to be safe to meet up and talk about these experiences, we held a reunion in Beijing,' he says. 'We brought together old friends who had also served long sentences in the labour camps, professors and intellectuals, and we had some drink and some food. That first time we met, we just comforted each other. Every month after that I would meet one of those men, an old friend from the labour camp, a man who is 75 years old. We used to have a drink together, and talk all afternoon or all evening. Those are my real friends, friends in suffering.'

Notes

1. Harry Wu witnessed this during his imprisonment. Catholics and members of other faiths often receive longer sentences than the non-religious.

2. Susan Whitfield (ed.), *Religious Persecution in the People's Republic of China*, joint report by the Jubilee Campaign and June 4th China Support, October 1994.

3. Asia Watch Report, *Detained in China and Tibet*, 1994, p. 269.

4. *Ibid.*, p. 255.

5. Speech given on 8 September 1994 by Chen Kuiyuan to the 6th Enlarged Plenary Meeting of the 4th Tibet Autonomous Region CCP Committee and broadcast on Tibet TV on the same day. Translated and reproduced in summary of *World Broadcasts, the Far East* (23 September 1994), quoted in *Religious Persecution in the People's Republic of China*, p. 5.

6. Puebla Institute, Washington DC, 'China: Religious Freedom Denied' (June 1994), p. 13, quoted in *Religious Persecution in the People's Republic of China*, p. 4, note 8.

7. In the sixteenth century, a Spanish missionary who had repeatedly failed in his attempts to reach China declared that it was as difficult as trying to trying to reach the moon. In *The Burning Forest*, Simon Leys concludes: 'In fact, reaching the moon proved to be a much easier task – and also a far less interesting one. Whereas the exploration of our dead satellite is a mere technological venture that can only yield scientific data, a true spiritual encounter between the West and China not only would provide mankind with a deeper understanding and knowledge of itself, it might even ensure that our planet enjoys a civilised future' (p. 42). Matteo Ricci was one of those who attempted to make a fruitful encounter with this separate culture.

8. Details of Bishop Fan's life are obtained from Asia Watch, *Detained in China and Tibet*, and Amnesty International, *Torture in China* (ASA 17/55/92).

9. Perhaps this sort of manoeuvre was behind the pictures shown to Harry Wu alleging sexual misconduct among the clergy.

10. Harry Wu, *Laogai: The Chinese Gulag*, p. 33.

11. *Ibid.*, p. 52 note 45, from *Laodong gaizao gongzuo* [Labour Reform Work], Beijing, CCP internal document, 1985.

12. Fox Butterfield, *Alive in the Bitter Sea*, pp. 497-8.

13. Jean Pasqualini, *Prisoner of Mao*, pp. 261-2.

14. *The Secret Speeches of Chairman Mao from The Hundred Flowers to The Great Leap Forward* (Cambridge, MA: Harvard University Press, 1969), pp. 181-2.

15. This idea of weeding out traitors appears to be the subtext of Mao's words

when taken in context. However, in his book *The Search for Modern China*, Jonathan Spence argues that the Hundred Flowers was, rather, a 'muddled and inconclusive movement that grew out of conflicting attitudes within the CCP leadership. At its centre was an argument about the pace and type of development that was best for China, a debate about the nature of the First Five-Year Plan and the promise for further growth. From that debate and the political tensions that accompanied it sprang the Great Leap Forward' (p. 574).

16. *Ibid.*, p. 575.

17. For a useful account of Nixon's visit to China and behind-the-scenes US–China relations, see Jonathan Spence's *The Search for Modern China*.

18. R. J. Lifton, *Thought Reform and the Psychology of Totalism*, p. 486.

19. For an enlightening commentary on Zhou's supposed benevolence, see Simon Leys's book *The Burning Forest*.

20. Jiang Qing, a former film actress, was a major political figure in the Cultural Revolution of the late 1960s. Also known as 'Madame Mao', she became leader of the 'Gang of Four' and was arrested in 1976 after Mao's death. Her death sentence was commuted to lifetime house arrest.

CHAPTER 9

A Dream of Democracy
Zhu Xiaodan

You can surmise how those of us who have spent our best years in prison regard our lives these days. There are no words to describe to innocents the mysterious density of terror.

Unnamed democracy activist describing the crackdown after
Tiananmen.[1]

Zhu Xiaodan still bears the psychic and physical scars of torture in a Shenzhen detention centre. Just below the knee of each leg, the skin is pockmarked with small dark patches where he was burned with cigarettes. A sewn-up gash the shape of an open mouth is all that remains on his arm after his flesh was slashed with a knife by police during the Tiananmen Square demonstrations. On the back of his head are three and a half deep cuts and a small bald patch on his skull. When Zhu takes out his set of false teeth, gaping holes show where four of his front teeth were knocked out.

Zhu Xiaodan looks younger than his 33 years. He is tall, skinny and full of energy; when he talks, he leans forward in his chair with glittering eyes. Zhu has lived in the USA since 21 September 1992. He knows the exact number of days he has spent in the States; his precision indicates both his insecurity about staying in America and his desire to do so, as well as his fear of returning to China.

After studying at Utah State University for a Ph.D. in economics when he first arrived in the States, Zhu is now living in Los Angeles. Although he misses his girlfriend and family, and his long-term situation is uncertain, Zhu is happier to live in a country he considers to be free. It is the natural wish of someone who dedicated most of his student years to the cause of democracy – and had the courage to stand before thousands of students and argue openly with the man who is now China's premier.

In 1986, Sichuan-born Zhu was studying for an MBA at the Management School of Shanghai Jiao Tong University. Together with some classmates, he organized a general demonstration which was supported by thousands of ordinary citizens as well as students. Their actions reflected a restlessness and dissatisfaction with the system shared at that time by students across the country. 'I had a deep feeling for freedom,' says Zhu. 'I wanted a better life, and a better future. I felt democracy was the only way to achieve these things.'

In 1979, the electoral laws had been modified from the 1953 original structure. The laws established a four-tier system of government: at the base were congresses in each of the communes (or administrative townships) elected every two years. Then came the congresses in China's 29 provinces, autonomous regions, and Shanghai, Beijing and Tianjin. Above these were county congresses, elected every three years. At the top of the tier system was the National People's Congress, which described the system as 'democracy under leadership centralism'.[1] All congressional candidates, of course, had to follow the Party line. Some students who fought for seats in congressional elections in order to assess the democratic process were prevented from taking their seats. Despite the presence in Congress of some reform-minded officials – notably Hu Yaobang – no reform of the system appeared to be taking place.

When election time came around in 1986, a spate of student protests blew up across the country. In Hefei, students wrote wall posters with slogans like: 'No democratization, no modernization'; 'Almost every day the newspapers talk about democracy. But where can we actually find any?'

In Shanghai, thousands of citizens and students took to the streets. The situation in the city became so severe that the Mayor of Shanghai, Jiang Zemin himself (he is now the president of China) came to Zhu's campus to persuade the students to call off their protest. About five thousand students from all the universities and colleges in Shanghai turned up to hear Jiang Zemin speak to the student leaders. Zhu was so passionate about the aims of the movement that he didn't stop to think of the consequences of his actions. For more than an hour, Zhu and other students stood onstage and argued with Jiang. 'We listed the reasons why the protests were taking place,' says Zhu. 'We wanted to show the people that we didn't want to keep silent.'

Several days later, many students fled. Zhu, and about thirty other students who were perceived as ring-leaders of the protest, were made to undergo a period of 're-education'. They were kept in special dormitories, away from other students and university staff. 'In the morning we had to study special Communist Party materials, and in the afternoon we had to do labour such as cleaning the toilets and classrooms,' says Zhu. 'I wasn't beaten – I just had to do self-criticisms.' He was finally released in 1987 and allowed to go back to normal student activities. He knew he had been lucky. 'I heard that the General Secretary had told local authorities not to arrest me, but to keep me in the neighbourhood so I could be supervised. In the past, my crime would have landed me in jail for ten years. However, the Party was aware of the sensitivity of the situation.'

Zhu was allowed to go to Guangdong province, where he found work as an English translator. But his political ideals had not faded. He found a focus for them in 1989, when the whole country erupted with democratic fervour – beginning in Beijing. 'I organized three protests in Shenzhen, Guangdong province, and raised funds for the students at Tiananmen,' says Zhu. 'At the end of May, I travelled to Beijing to deliver the money, and to show solidarity with the demonstrators.'

When Zhu arrived in the capital, the situation was tense. Government troops were massing on the outskirts of the Square,[2] and students were blocking their way. 'The crackdown began on 4 June, at about midnight,' remembers Zhu. 'The day before there had been gunshot, but it was only a "phut-phut-phut", half-hearted sound. On 4 June it began in earnest. I had been asleep in a street adjoining the Square because I was so tired from the events of the day before. I woke up to see troops coming straight for us. They were pouring through the barricades. Before, the soldiers had been sitting down, several metres away, waiting for us to disperse. Now they were really coming. This time it was real.

'Somehow I still believed they were not going to kill us. I just didn't think it was possible. I kept saying to myself, don't panic, nothing will happen; they're just coming to make us leave. Then it happened. Before I could think about running, seven or ten soldiers were around me, beginning to kill me.'

Zhu's memory of the exact details is hazy. His mind went blank with fear, and, after a few seconds of being bayoneted with the rifles of the soldiers, he lost consciousness. In those few seconds before he blacked out, he was cut by a bayonet on his arm, four of his front teeth were broken, and his head was cut badly in three places.

Finally the soldiers moved on and Zhu was taken to hospital – he still doesn't know who took him there, although he believes either students or local people helped him. He was unconscious for several days. When he woke, he was in terrible pain and was scarcely coherent. Zhu says: 'Several soldiers surrounded my bed and kept asking me who I was, where I was from, and whether I was an American spy. They told me that, if I gave them the details, they would let me walk out of hospital without any repercussions. All I told them was that I was one of the common people, and that I wasn't a spy.'

When the Public Security Bureau found Zhu's identification papers from Shenzhen, and as soon as he could get up from his hospital bed, they sent him to a detention centre in the city. He was escorted back to the centre from Beijing by armed guards. He was to spend the next eight months imprisoned there.

'As soon as I arrived, still weak from hospital, they began to interrogate me again,' says Zhu. 'Every day I would wake up, and at a set time would be taken to the interrogation room. They would just repeat over and over again "confess, confess". They beat me as well. Sometimes other people came into the room; they would tie me to the bed and beat me with sticks.'

Zhu was told that, if he confessed everything about his involvement with the democracy movement, he wouldn't be tortured. It is uncertain whether this was true or not. In any case, Zhu did not tell them everything they wanted to hear. And so his torture continued.

'In the south of China there are many mosquitoes. However only a few prisoners who were "well-behaved" could sleep under mosquito nets,' says Zhu. 'I didn't have one as a punishment. Sometimes they would bend me forwards, and tie my arms to my feet, which were attached to the chair. They kept me like that for a whole day, without any food or drink, or going to the toilet. All the time I was being bitten by mosquitoes. I couldn't stand it. In that period, my mind almost broke, exploded.' Zhu's legs and arms became completely insensitive for days afterwards, and were weakened so much that he could scarcely walk.

On other occasions, Zhu's legs were bound to a chair and burning cigarettes were pressed into his skin. He was imprisoned for sometimes an entire week in the "dark cell": a tiny room with no light and black walls. 'There was no sound except for a rushing in my ears,' says Zhu. 'I felt like I was going crazy.'

At around this time, Zhu's interrogators told him that they knew he had organized student protests and that they already had video footage of him. But they wanted him to admit he was a US spy. 'I still insisted that I wasn't,' says Zhu. 'And I told them I didn't want to bring down the government; I had organized only peaceful protests. But they still persisted in believing that I wanted to destroy the Communist Party, and that I was a spy. I was scared that, if I told them what they wanted to believe, they would execute me – I knew there was a death sentence for spying.'

Occasionally Zhu told them he wanted to do hard labour in the prison, thinking that might end the torture. But they told him that he couldn't do this until they sentenced him. And they couldn't sentence him until he confessed. And when he did confess, he would probably be sentenced to death.

Zhu was finally released after eight months. He believes this was due to international pressure over his release, and concern from the authorities that they didn't have enough evidence to convict him. Although he wasn't allowed to be employed in a state-owned company, he found work in a company owned by a foreign firm. His ordeal wasn't over; every two weeks he was required to report to the Public Security Bureau, and his family and friends were put under pressure not to associate with him.

'My girlfriend still loved me, and of course I still loved her,' says Zhu. 'But she couldn't withstand the pressure. After I was released all of my friends kept away from me. Including my girlfriend. They were too scared to even say hello to me in the street – they were so anxious about being seen associating with me. I felt very depressed and very frustrated.'

Like so many other young democracy activists, Zhu felt that he had no future in China. He decided to escape from China, and in 1992 left for the USA, where he is now applying for political asylum. He still suffers from sleepless nights when memories of his imprisonment loom large in his mind. And his new friends in the USA cannot make up for the absence of the girlfriend he left behind. 'I miss her a lot,' he says. However, he is strengthened by the knowledge that those who knew him in China respect what he was trying to achieve with his fellow students. 'One day, when I go back to China, people will welcome me as a hero,' he says. He may have to wait for some time.

Notes

1. See Jonathan Spence, *The Search for Modern China*, p. 723.

2. Robin Munro and George Black, *Black Hands of Beijing*, give a detailed analysis into the events at Tiananmen in 1989.

CHAPTER 10

Sentence First, Verdict Afterwards

The Legal System in China

For want of something to do, a prisoner gleaned from the sweeping of the shop floor tiny bits of glittering wire, which he deposited in a bottle. Years passed. On the day he was freed, there was nothing to take with him to mark the passage of those years except the bottle, and so he carried it away.

Back home, he rose and he ate and he slept at the exact hours the warden had decreed. Too old to work anymore, he spent his days pacing, the exact space of his long confinement — four paces forward, four paces back, four paces forward, four paces back.

For want of something to do, one day he smashed the bottle to count how many tiny bits of glittering wire he had collected. He wept. At his feet lay broken glass, and a clump of wires rusted solid in the shape of a bottle.

Story of a Chinese dissident now held in prison[1]

Looming above the doorway of a typical Qing dynasty prison was an immense, scowling creature resembling a stripy cat with tusks. This so-called *bi'an*, carved into stone above the entrance, is a legendary animal which was one of the nine offspring of the dragon, a traditional metaphor for China. Each of these offspring had tasks to perform on earth. The *bi'an*, which was the fourth child, came to be associated with social control owing to its ferocious nature and the terror it instilled in those who saw it.

Once the criminal had walked into the doorway underneath the offspring of the dragon, life would never be the same again. The *bi'an*, which represented the surveillance of the state, signified that a prisoner's fate was sealed.[2]

In revolutionary China, the *bi'an* had no place above the doorway of prisons. The agenda behind the system had become reform: an individual's destiny was no longer set in stone. The Communist Party had decreed that redemption was possible for even the most hardened criminals.

China's penal system may have developed and changed over the centuries. But the symbolic, glowering *bi'an* still casts a shadow on today's prisoners. Whether the inmate of a forced labour camp today chooses to commit suicide or survive, his or her life will be altered irrevocably. There is no going back. Even after their release or 'reform', a former prisoner's sense of freedom is often severely compromised by the experiences which live within him or her.

Throughout Chinese history, punishments by the state have ranged from physical mutilation to fines, executions and penal exile, depending on the perceived severity of the crime. Between 936 and 942, prisoners who had been reprieved from death sentences were sent to border regions as corvée labour or conscripts.[3] In the mid-Ming period, criminals were forced to join the military in border areas in a new form of military exile.[4] If lifelong exile was enforced, the criminal and their family were made to remain in exile until the criminal died. When eternal exile was the penalty, the exiled criminal's sons and grandparents were also forced to remain. This form of banishment foreshadows the exile of prisoners today, often to Qinghai, otherwise known as China's Siberia. Here, millions of prisoners are forced to labour until the end of their lives, even after their sentences have expired. One recent government document boasted about a resolution which decreed that groups of criminals should be deported to outlying regions and that their city-based registration should be cancelled. 'These elements endanger social order and are difficult to reform,' a statement read. 'They will therefore be sent under escort to outlying regions to carry out reform through labour. This is an important measure in the educational transformation of the criminal.'[5]

The *Wu-Xing* (Five Punishments) devised by the Miao tribes dates back to earliest times, and included the cutting off of a foot or nose, castration, branding of the face, bastinado (or flogging to death) and exposure in public places. Victims of these punishments included traitors, thieves, bandits, raiders of villages, robbers and forgers. Between 770 and 476 BC, a sentence of death involved horrific mutilation: *peng* entailed boiling the victim alive in a huge pot of boiling water, while *huan* involved five horses being used to rip the victim limb from limb. *Xiaoshou* entailed the decapitation of the body and public display of the head, and *hai* was the mashing up of the body until it resembled mincemeat.

Clan punishment (*zuxing*) involved the whole family in the crime of one individual. *Zuxing* was an ancient sanction for treason, recorded in the time of the first emperor in the second century BC and retained by following dynasties. Zhang Jinjian writes:

> Clans were to have responsibilities for the crimes committed by clan members . . . If a person commits a serious crime . . . then three categories of clan member (sanzu) that is the parents, brothers and wife of the criminal would be held responsible and executed. If it was an extremely serious crime all his clan, as well as relatives who held the same name, would be executed. This family or clan death sentence, was one of the cruelest punishments devised.[6]

Similarly, if an individual enjoyed good fortune, this would reflect on the entire family as the following old Chinese proverb shows: 'When a man becomes an official, his wife, children, dogs, cats and even chickens fly up to heaven.' The proverb adds: 'When he falls, they fall with him.'

Often the chief perpetrator of an act of treason was first mutilated and tortured, then his head was cut off and exposed in a public place. His parents and children were strangled. Under the Ming dynasty, hundreds of members of a single clan were reported to have been executed. The punishment was designed to prevent revolt and, in cases of treason, to preclude revenge by the family clan. Zuxing was also an expression of a deeply held belief in China that family training was responsible for the behaviour of the individual in later life.

In his Notes and Commentaries on Chinese Law, Ernest Alabaster writes:

> The most ignominious of all penalties is slicing to pieces (lingchi) and extinction of the family (zuxing). Here the offender is tied to a cross, and, by a series of painful but not in themselves mortal cuts, his body is sliced beyond recognition. The head of the offender is subsequently exposed in a cage for a period.

> This punishment, known to foreigners as 'lingering death', is not inflicted so much as a torture, but to destroy the future as well as the present life of the offender — he is unworthy to exist longer either as a man or a recognisable spirit, and, as spirits to appear must assume their present corporeal forms, he can only appear as a collection of little bits. It is not a lingering death, for it is all over in a few seconds, and the coup de grâce is generally given with the third cut; but it is very horrid, and the belief that the spirit will be in need of sewing up in a land where needles are not, must make the unfortunate victim's last moments most unhappy. In short, though the punishment is severe and revolting, it is not so painful as the half-hanging, disembowelling, and finally quartering, practised in England not so very long ago.[7]

This concern with family lineage and the afterlife was evident in many of these early punishments. Castration (*gong*), for instance, is a literal example of a family line being brutally drawn to a close. The various types of execution which involved slicing and mashing the body to pieces would be a sign in the spirit world of the individual's crime. The *bi'an's* eyes were upon the criminal, sealing his or her fate. Eternal redemption was as impossible as redemption on earth.

Forced labour and banishment have been used as punishments for criminals in China since AD 936, and possibly even earlier. Mao's policies of sending prisoners into distant provinces to labour was undoubtedly influenced not only by tradition, however, but by the Soviet Union. Soviet law stipulated that 'as a rule' prisoners should serve their sentences in the republic where they were convicted. However persons convicted of 'especially dangerous crimes against the state' might be sent to distant camps.[8] The *laogai* system is now accepted as a part of Chinese society, and has become an important bulwark of China's economy.

Although the Chinese wrote the Soviet influence on their penal system out of the history books following the Sino–Soviet split, it was undoubtedly important in the early development of the *laogai*. After 1949, Soviet advisers were key figures in the administrative organizations of policing and justice. Soviet advisers carried out training of police, based on Soviet models. Thus similar techniques of interrogation and detention would be promulgated by the Soviets.[9]

The 1954 regulations on the labour reform system – which remain essentially unchanged today – drew heavily on the 1933 Soviet corrective labour legislation.[10]

These regulations are as follows. First, Labour Reform Policies, approved by the People's Republic of China State Council on 26 August 1954, and promulgated on 7 September of the same year. Second, Temporary Disciplinary Methods for the Release of Criminals Completing Their Terms and for the Implementation of Forced Job Placement, approved by the twenty-second plenary session of the Government Administration Council on 29 August 1954, and promulgated on 7 September of the same year. Third, Re-education through Labour Policies, approved at the seventy-eighth plenary session of the National People's Congress (NPC) and promulgated by the State Council on 3 August 1957. These were amended on 29 November 1979 by the issuing of Supplementary Re-education Through Labour Regulations.[11]

While the legislation is similar, and despite the former involvement of Soviet advisers in training security personnel, the *laogai* developed very distinct characteristics, notably in thought reform. Re-education through labour was developed exclusively by the Chinese. While the horrors of the Soviet gulag were profound, inmates at least did not suffer this particular form of mental torture. In *The Gulag Archipelago*, Solzhenitsyn writes:

> It is a good thing to think in prison, but it is not bad in camp either. Because, and this is the main thing, there are no meetings. For ten years you are free from all kinds of meetings! Is that not mountain air? While they openly claim your labour and your body, to the point of exhaustion and even death, the camp keepers do not encroach at all on your thoughts. They do not try to screw down your brains and to fasten them in place. And this results in a sensation of freedom of much greater magnitude than the freedom of one's feet to run along on the level . . . A free head – now is that not an advantage of life in the Archipelago?[12]

The Criminal Law of 1979, the Party's attempt to restore order in the aftermath of the lawlessness of the Cultural Revolution, was also influenced by Moscow policies. It bears some resemblance to the 1960 Russian Soviet Federated Socialist Republic (RSFSR) Criminal Code, although much of it is distinctly Chinese.

Leng Shaochuan and Chiu Hungdah[13] point to the Chinese Criminal Law's emphasis on punishment of wrongdoers rather than wrongful acts and its use of highly moralistic words such as 'heinous' and 'monstrous' to describe some offences. Another difference from the Soviet code lies in its inclusion of many types of crimes closely related to specifically Chinese circumstances, such as the reselling of ration coupons and the 'brutalization' of family members.

The 1979 Criminal Law at least provides detailed procedures for dealing with 'criminal' behaviour which forces institutions formerly involved in the brutalization of human beings to deal with a legal language. However, much of the Law violates international standards of fair judicial process. It does not, for instance, meet international standards for preliminary detention. The International Covenant on Civil and Political Rights requires that in criminal cases any person arrested or detained has to be brought 'promptly' before a judge or other judicial power. Since Tiananmen, the Chinese authorities have, if anything, flouted the theory behind this Covenant even more outrageously.

Sixty-year-old Bao Tong, a leading political reformer and former adviser to dismissed Chinese Communist Party Secretary-General Zhao Ziyang, was detained for two and a half years before being notified of his formal arrest. He was held incommunicado for much of the time and without charge. He was not tried until July 1992, more than three years after his detention. His trial, which Human Rights Watch described as the most important political proceedings in China for twelve years, reportedly took only hours to complete. Although a report from Xinhua, China's official news agency, implied that Bao's wife, daughter, brother and sister had attended the trial along with some 230 others, his family were in fact allowed in the courtroom only to hear the ten-minute verdict.[14]

The labour leader Han Dongfang, head of the Beijing Workers Autonomous Federation, was detained in June 1989 and held for 22 months without trial. He was released only on 28 April 1991 with advanced tuberculosis contracted in prison (see Chapter 17). He believes that only international pressure secured his freedom: the Chinese authorities did not want a dead prisoner of conscience on their hands.

With these cases and thousands of others, the Chinese are violating their own laws. Instead of seeking formal arrest they are applying a parallel system of administrative detention which was widely used against counter-revolutionaries after Tiananmen and in times of political insecurity so as to maintain order. The system of 'shelter and investig-ation' (*shourong shencha*) is a form of 'preventive' administrative detention to detain dissidents and suspected opponents arbitrarily without charge. 'Re-education through labour' is another form of arbitrary detention, imposed as a punishment by local government committees without any judicial process. The accused are not charged under the Criminal Law, do not appear before a court of law and have no access to a lawyer.

Over the last few years, human rights and political activists, members of unapproved religious groups, and others classified as 'hooligans', 'sexual hooligans' or 'trouble-makers' have been sentenced without trial to several years of 're-education through labour'. Many of them literally 'disappear': their families may not be told of the trial, and they may not know until it is a foregone conclusion where their spouse, sibling or child is being held.

Zhou Guoqing was a bespectacled, slim poet and lawyer living in Beijing. He was sponsor of the League for the Protection of the Rights of the Working People (LPRWP), an independent labour rights group which applied unsuccessfully for legal registration in March 1994. After the rights group had been discovered by the authorities, Zhou was taken into police custody on 3 March together with his wife Wang Hu, who was released after a week.

In September 1994 Zhou was sentenced without trial or charge to three years of 're-education through labour'. Wang learnt of her husband's sentence only in December 1994, when he wrote to her from the labour camp in Heilongjiang province, hundreds of miles north of Beijing, where he had been sent to serve his sentence. At the time of writing, Zhou is still being held in the camp.[15]

Chinese with religious beliefs have suffered imprisonment and persecution ever since the Communists founded the People's Republic, and this continues today. Amnesty International reported on a recent story of arbitrary detentions and torture of Catholics in two mountain villages in northern China.[16] In an appeal addressed to Amnesty, Catholics in the village claimed that the villagers had been subjected to arbitrary detention, torture and heavy fines by local officials for breaches of the birth control policy. Many Catholics in the villages of Fengjiazhuang and Lontiangou in Lingshou county, Hebei province, reject abortion and sterilization because of their religious beliefs, and had been fined in the past for having more children than permitted. However, a new family planning programme had been initiated by local officials in spring 1994. Targeted individuals from the villages were taken away to county government offices, where they were detained and tortured, the appeal to Amnesty claimed. If individuals who had been targeted could not be found, their relatives were detained instead as hostages and similarly tortured or ill-treated.

Liu Qing, a democracy activist, was detained under 'shelter and investigation' for about 180 days, the first five months in solitary confinement in Beijing's Banbuqiao detention centre. Liu witnessed officials from the Public Security Bureau taking the law into their own hands when one of the policeman read out his 'detention order'. '[The order] was [written on] newsprint-quality paper, and the text on it was mimeographed in black . . . Later I talked to people with more experience in these matters, and what they told me proved beyond doubt that the piece of paper the PSB had shown me was not a real detention-order at all. Formal detention-orders have to be properly printed on bond paper . . . The "order" on cheap paper was apparently a sort of internal document used by the PSB. It had no external validity whatsoever' (from his prison memoirs and an interview).

Liu, who later served three years in a re-education through labour camp without trial, adds: 'The reasons given for my detention ranged from the absurd to the shameless. The regulations and punishments for the maintenance of "social order" have become the most efficient possible blunderbuss for the PSB . . . I tried to find out from my interrogators, their minions and the guards, which rules I had actually violated. They were either embarrassed, and tried to change the subject, or were plainly startled and rendered speechless by my questions.'

The *Alice in Wonderland* world of 'sentence first, verdict after'[17]is reflected in the People's Republic's position of 'no presumptions' of guilt or innocence. In theory, the law is applied to the facts to reach a correct result, using the maxim 'Taking facts as the basis and the law as the criterion'. Despite this philosophy of non-presumption, a student of legal jargon in the People's Republic can observe a different language in the courts. A Public Security Bureau arrest notification in a 1989 case, for example, stated that the suspect, 'having *committed the crime* of counter-revolutionary propaganda and incitement was arrested by this office according to law'.[18] In reality, China operates a 'presumed guilty and found guilty' system of legislation.[19] Court authorities reject the internationally accepted legal principle of 'presumption of innocence' because they say that if this was enforced Chinese policemen would never arrest anyone.

The International Committee of Lawyers for Human Rights has noted that pleading a defendant's innocence is an audacious action for a lawyer in China to take. In the post-Tiananmen period, local justice bureaux have required official approval before allowing a defence of innocence. It has been suggested by the People's Republic's legal press that in some areas lawyers are even required to obtain the approval of the bureau party committee before presenting a defence of innocence. Pressure from government officials reportedly caused lawyers defending Peng Rong, a Beijing University student charged with 'counter-revolutionary propaganda and incitement' and 'colluding with hostile forces' to withdraw a plea of 'not guilty'.[20]

In a circular to the All-China Lawyers Association, members were informed that 'experience has proved that the lawyers to be selected [for political cases] must possess high political consciousness [among other characteristics]. Only in this way are lawyers capable of maintaining unity with the party central leadership in politics'.[21] In the aftermath of Tiananmen, both the Shanghai and Beijing lawyers' associations indicate that lawyers were often unwilling to take on cases of students or workers involved in the demonstrations. The Beijing Municipal Lawyers Association Research Department admitted frankly that some lawyers, 'still haunted by terrible memories, feared that if they did not do the job well, they could commit political mistakes'.

The fears of lawyers were well-founded. Often those who had the courage to put up spirited defences of political prisoners were subject to harassment and temporary loss of their licence to practise. This happened to the lawyers of Chen Ziming, one of the so-called 'black hands' of Tiananmen. Ziming was thought to have been one of the principal instigators of the 'turmoil' at Tiananmen Square in 1989.[22] His lawyers, Ji Suwan and Gao Xiaofeng, were prevented from practising law after Justice Ministry officials refused to renew their licences.

The satirical writer Hah Gong has suggested that the only way of protecting the law in China is for all lawyers, 'and indeed anyone possessed of a basic understanding of bourgeois law, to be executed forthwith'. Hah Gong's acerbic pen was inspired by a recent case in which a lawyer in China was expelled from the courtroom for 'aiding and abetting the accused's attempts to avoid incrimination'. 'Who needs lawyers anyway?' he wrote scornfully in the Hong Kong publication *Ming Pao*.[23]

> *Lawyers are mere lackeys working to protect the interests of the ruling class. We don't even need law. Our exalted Motherland has thrived for five thousand years without a single lawyer ever setting foot in a courtroom. Take for example the story 'Judge Bao Cuts Chen Shimei in Two at the Waist'. Did Chen Shimei hire a lawyer to defend him in court? All Judge Bao had to do was to bring down the gavel, take out his tiger-head scimitar, and Chen Shmei's head rolled off to a new address.*

> *Naturally our influential/bourgeois/reactionary lawyers will claim that the good Judge Bao didn't understand the real principles of jurisprudence, and that this is merely a moral tale and not a legal precedent. They will ask what right Judge Bao had to chop Chen Shimei in half so arbitrarily? Do you see how wonderfully subtle our traditional system of law is? Even 'illicit sexual relations' can get you thrown in the clink for fifteen years . . . In the future all a judge need do is tap his gavel once and say, 'Bring in the accused and give him sixty strokes of the bamboo rod.' Beat the shit out of them, and they'll deliver their confessions on a golden platter. Other possible methods that can be used to induce confessions are the chaining of the accused to a pole or the application of heated steel rods . . . With time-honoured methods like these, who needs lawyers?*

The reality illuminated by Hah Gong's satire is that the law in China is still an instrument of state repression.

The widespread economic reforms of the 1980s in China have not been matched by increasing opportunities for political participation – despite the initial promise of law reforms which resulted from the opening up of the market. Laws were called for in previously unheard-of areas such as stock market legislation, privatization, foreign joint ventures and commercial contracts. Legal reformists seized the opportunity to address other issues, too.

In 1986, for instance, in response to the concerns of legislators, Chinese citizens were for the first time given the right to challenge in court a decision by public security to detain or otherwise penalize persons for a misdemeanour offence.[24] In 1988, the notorious and all-pervasive sections of the Criminal Law on state secrets were addressed by reformist lawyers. The 1951 Provisional Act on Guarding State Secrets enabled such arcane information as 'meteorological forecasts' to be classed as a state secret. Two all-embracing categories of the Act included: 'all state affairs which have not yet been decided upon or which have been decided upon but have not been made public' and 'all other state affairs which should be kept secret'.

This of course could mean almost anything not publicly released. In 1982, a Chinese editor was sentenced to five years' imprisonment for leaking details of the agenda of a Communist Party meeting to a Japanese reporter. As we have seen, the state secrets clause of the Act was invoked after Harry Wu, the Chinese-American human rights campaigner, was arrested on the Chinese border in June 1995.

Drafters of a new law on the protection of state secrets sought to eliminate the extremely vague definitions of the existing law by imposing relatively objective standards on the concept of a state secret, and establishing a way of disseminating information on the types of material that could be revealed. However, the changes were not substantial, and the charge of stealing or leaking state secrets can still be imposed arbitrarily by the state and used to justify long-term imprisonment and often execution.

Also in 1988, the legal community began a discussion on the sacred cow of Chinese law: the ambiguous crime of 'counter-revolution'. They wanted to replace it with more legally definable concepts such as 'harm to national security'. Article 90 of China's Criminal Law defines counter-revolutionary crime as 'acts done for the purpose of overthrowing the political power of the dictatorship of the proletariat and the socialist system and endangering the People's Republic of China'. Among the multitude of sins covered by the Act are conspiring with a foreign state to jeopardize the sovereignty and security of China, plotting to overthrow the government or split the country, instigating an armed rebellion, committing espionage or supporting the enemy and carrying out sabotage with a counter-revolutionary motive. Using 'counter-revolutionary slogans, leaflets or other means to spread propaganda inciting the overthrow of the regime of the dictatorship of the proletariat and the socialist system' are also counter-revolutionary offences. In practice, the definition of counter-revolution is still widely used in China to justify arrest and imprisonment of those the state wants to silence. They can even be imprisoned for a counter-revolutionary 'attitude'.

Legal reformers in China may have their work cut out for many years to come. However, at least the number of them is on the increase. Growing numbers of dissidents and legal reformers are speaking out in China itself, and attempting to reform the system from the inside. Although the number of lawyers in China is still outrageously small – just over seventy thousand for a population of 1.2 billion – this figure is still a great leap forward from the state of affairs during the years of 1959 to 1966.[25] At this period the number of lawyers in the entire country shrank from four to none because of the Anti-Rightist campaign. Judges and lawyers alike were sent to the countryside, executed, struggled against or given lifetime sentences of hard labour in the far north. Many of them, as 'historic counter-revolutionaries', are still there.

By mid-1983, however, 2,350 legal advisers' offices and more than twelve thousand professional and part-time lawyers were reportedly operating throughout the country.[26] Leng Shaochuan and Chiu Hungdah point out the opening headline 'Welcome the New Year of Rule of the Country by Law' in *China's Legal System Paper*, a publication of China's Justice Ministry in December 1982. It's quite a contrast to the headline in the *People's Daily*, only sixteen years before, which proudly declared itself: 'In Praise of Lawlessness'!

For the first time in the history of the People's Republic of China, the Criminal Law and the ongoing attempts at reform offer hope for the future legal system. The mere existence of criminal laws is an improvement on the chaos and lawlessness of the Mao years. However we need to look no further than the cases of legal reformists being harassed by the state for their genuine attempts at peaceful change to understand the power of entrenched Party ideals fed by a paranoia and fear at losing control.

Wang Jiaqi, a tall, forceful and idealistic young lawyer, is one of those reformists. Now living in New York, Wang studied Criminal Procedure Law at Beijing Univeristy. While still a student, he started to handle cases in which individuals had suffered harm as a result of official abuses. By 1994, Wang was helping to draft the documents for the establishment of the League for the Protection of the Rights of Working People for the People's Republic of China. He believes in reform of the existing Chinese system:

> The construction of the Chinese legal system is far from complete. But many of the laws are relatively progressive and the constitution contains guarantees for human rights. So it is not so much that there are defects in the laws themselves; the problems emerge from the system as a whole, since law has not been given a very authoritative position from which to regulate government organs and society. So I think that the people who despair of Chinese law are wrong.[27]

Wang believes that one of the problems is that China is still essentially feudal with its reliance on rule by man. 'Deng Xiaoping gives power to [former CCP General Secretary] Zhao Ziyang, then takes it away, and gives it to [current General Secretary] Jiang Zemin.' As a popular saying in China has it: 'policy is better than law, and leadership is better than policy'.[28]

Before the League even had a chance to submit its application for registration to the Ministry of Civil Affairs – as all groups wishing to function in China are required to do – Wang and several other founding members were secretly arrested. Wang gave his interrogators such a hard time on the first night, telling them about the string of procedural errors that they were making, that they abandoned questioning him. After six days, he was taken to Tangshan steel works, and then moved to a People's Armed Police barracks in the city. On 27 March 1994, Wang was joking with three guards about what they would do if he escaped. They took it in good humour, with one of them even saying that he wouldn't bother chasing him. Wang decided to make a run for it on a trip to the communal toilet. Because the building was a barracks, the guards were looking out rather than in, and so Wang was able to jump on to the back of a passing truck and escape. He lay low for several days, and arrived in Hong Kong nearly three weeks later.

The crackdown at Tiananmen shattered the hopes of many for a true reform of the legal system. In March 1992, the People's Supreme Court President Ren Jianxin told the National People's Congress that 'The people's courts are an important tool of the people's democratic dictatorship . . . We must strengthen our usefulness against enemies of the dictatorship.'[29]

After Tiananmen, even the promise of China's economic *glasnost* has not extended into the political sphere – and some critics fear it may even have made the system even more corruptible. The monitoring group Human Rights in China claims that in areas such as Shanghai, Guangdong and Fujian where reform has been proceeding at rapid rates there has been no decrease in abuses or any loosening of political control. In some cases, they report, the decentralization of power has actually led to more abuses, since officials do not fear central intervention.[30]

Clearly the rule of law in China is still a goal rather than a reality. One of Mark Baber's experiences after his arrest in Shanghai in 1991 indicates just how rotten is the state of law in contemporary China. Several months after his arrest, Mark had finally been granted access to a lawyer. He had an agenda of complaints. The official in charge of Mark's investigation had denied him medical treatment, beaten him up, framed him, threatened to arrest his mother, refused to pass on all the statements on his case and stolen all his money. The man is totally corrupt, Mark explained, eager for some professional legal support. But his lawyer merely replied, 'What's corrupt about that?'

Notes

1. Quoted in Bette Bao Lord, *Legacies*, p. 1.

2. A picture of the *bi'an* is included on p. 103 of Michael Dutton's *Policing and Punishment in China*.

3. *Ibid.*, p. 130.

4. *Ibid.*, p. 140.

5. *Ibid.*, p. 253.

6. *Zhongguo lidai xingming kao in Guoli zhengfa daxue xuebao* (17 May 1968), p. 52, quoted in *ibid.*, p. 109, note 24.

7. *Ibid.*

8. Amnesty International, *Prisoners of Conscience in the USSR: Their Treatment and Conditions* (London, 1975), p. 48.

9. Lawrence Hinkle and Harold Wolff, 'Communist Interrogation and the Indoctrination of "Enemies of the State"', *AMA Archives of Neurology and Psychology*, vol. 76 (6 December 1956), p. 151.

10. Luo Ruiqing, the Minister of Public Security at the time, acknowledged that the work of preparing these laws was carried out in collaboration with Soviet legal experts, and contained many of the same principles as the Soviet legislation (Lo Jui-ching, 'Explanations concerning Reform through Labour in the People's Republic of China', 26 August 1954, in CIRC, *The White Book on Forced Labour and Concentration Camps in the People's Republic of China*, vol. 2, pp. 289–93).

11. These policies are included in *Gongan fagui huiban 1950-1979* [Collection of the Public Security Regulations of the People's Republic of China, 1950–1979] (Beijing: Legal Press, 1980), pp. 195–206.

12. Alexander Solzhenitsyn, *The Gulag Archipelago*, vol. 2, p. 589.

13. Leng Shochuan and Chiu Hungdah, *Criminal Justice in Post-Mao China*.

14. Amnesty International, *China: Appeal on Behalf of Bao Tong*, ASA 17/45/92, August 1992, and Asia Watch, *Detained in China and Tibet, a Directory of Political and Religious Prisoners*. Bao Tong was finally convicted of 'leaking state secrets' and 'counter-revolutionary propaganda and incitement' and sentenced to seven years' imprisonment.

15. Amnesty International report, *China – Six Years after Tiananmen: Increased Political Repression and Human Rights Violations* (June 1995), ASA 17/28/95.

16. Amnesty International Urgent Action bulletin UA 62/95, ASA 17/15/95 (14 March 1995).

17. When the Red Queen says: 'Now, are you ready for your sentence?' Alice replies: 'Sentence? But there must be a verdict first.' The Red Queen merely announces: 'Sentence first, verdict afterwards' (Lewis Carroll, *Alice in Wonderland*).

18. *Criminal Justice with Chinese Characteristics*, note 43.

19. As described by Fox Butterfield, *Alive in the Bitter Sea*.

20. *Criminal Justice with Chinese Characteristics*, chapter on Criminal Procedure.

21. *Ibid.*

22. For Chen Ziming's full story, see Munro and Black, *Black Hands of Beijing*.

23. Quoted in Geremie Barmié and John Minford, *Seeds of Fire*, p. 182.

24. *Criminal Justice with Chinese Characteristics*, p. 2.

25. In its report *China Human Rights Practices, 1994* (issued February 1995), the US State Department claims that China plans to increase the number of lawyers to 150,000 by the year 2000. As of July 1994, there were 70,515 lawyers working in 5,885 law firms. In many cities, private law firms are being organized outside the framework of established government legal offices. These firms are self-regulating and do not have their personnel or budgets determined by the state. At the end of 1993, there were 502 such firms. However, claims the report, many defence lawyers – like other Chinese – still depend on an official work unit for employment, housing and other benefits, hence are often reluctant to be viewed as over-zealous in defending individuals accused of political offences.

26. *Zhongguo Fazhi Bao* (27 August 1982), quoted in *Criminal Justice with Chinese Characteristics*, p. 75.

27. Interview in *China Rights Forum* (fall 1994).

28. Quoted in Harry Wu, *Laogai*, p. xiii.

29. 'Beijing Clamp on Crime', *South China Morning Post* (29 March 1992).

30. *China Rights Forum* (Spring 1994).

CHAPTER 11

In Defence of the Fifth Modernization

Tang Boqiao

You were the sons and daughters of loving parents, you were the students of proud teachers. You were brothers, sisters, friends, sometimes even enemies. But how many dreams you still had to dream! You would have been fathers and mothers, you who still had so many new roads to travel down.

Oration delivered by Tang Boqiao at the 8 June mass mourning meeting at Changsha for the democracy movement at Tiananmen.[1]

Tang Boqiao will never forget the peasant who helped him to escape while he was on the run from the security police in summer 1989. After organizing democracy demonstrations in his home city in support of the Tiananmen movement, Tang was the most wanted man in Hunan province. Posters bearing his name and face were plastered all over the area. The crackdown had begun in earnest, and security police were combing the country for him.

For thirty days, Tang was on the run, staying at different places in Guangdong province every few days and then moving on, dependent on the protection of a network of supporters. On the night of 4 July, he was staying with a peasant family who were relatives of a friend. At about 11 p.m. that night, just as Tang was going upstairs to sleep, he suddenly heard knocks on the door. A middle-aged man came in and talked quietly and urgently to his host. Tang recalls: 'Running up the stairs, my host told me in poor Mandarin: "Pack your stuff and leave here with me now. The village cadre just told me that the public security men are here to get you." My heart missed a beat and I had a premonition that I would not be able to get away this time. I hardly remember anything of our departure from the village apart from the ghostly howls and barking of

139

dogs. That night, the peasant, whom I will never forget for the rest of my life, and I trudged along in the wilds, breathless with anxiety, for nearly 60 kilometres.'

Tang's premonition proved to be right. That day they took refuge in Jiangmen city; Tang was so exhausted that he immediately fell asleep in the sitting room. At two in the morning, there was a hammering on the door. 'Before I had time to react, a swarm of heavily armed public security personnel and officers of the People's Armed Police swarmed into the room like a pack of mad dogs. "This is Tang Boqiao," snapped one of them. I made a futile attempt to defend myself, asking, "Why are you arresting me?" but the next thing I felt was a series of hard objects clamping down on my throat, and my whole body, upside down, being hoisted into the air. Fists and cudgels (probably electric batons) rained down on me, and I felt as if I was dying.'

Tang was pushed out of the house. Following him were the husband and wife he had been staying with, who had also been arrested. 'As I looked around me, I felt a sense of deep and tragic solemnity welling up within me. There before me stood a vast array of over a hundred military police, all armed to the teeth, and a row of police cars glowing with a steely, cold light. The police were all scurrying around as if in some rapid-deployment military exercise against an enemy army – and at that moment, I realized with great clarity my own value and the strength of democracy. We had made the butchers of the people frightened!'

The province of Hunan – which has a population of more than 55 million – has a history of violent and tragic political upheavals led by famous Hunan figures like Tan Sitong. An intellectual who helped lead the '100 Days Reform' movement in 1898 against the Manchus, Tan was later executed after he refused to flee from the ensuing repression. Tan's words, 'If I don't shed my blood, then who will?' still have the power to inspire a younger generation of Chinese patriots. (At Tiananmen Square, a constant refrain from the students was, 'If we don't speak out, who will?' And student leader Chai Ling's words to the masses were awash with the language of bloodletting and sacrifice.) Tang, who was born in Lengshuitan, points out that Hunan has bred many tyrants, too – from Zeng Guofen, the 'Butcher of Hunan', to Mao Zedong himself, born in 1893 to a farming family in Shaoshan, and a former pupil of the First Normal School in Changsha.

Ever since the foundation of the People's Republic, the people of Hunan have played an active role in political movements both for and against the government. The 1980s, when Tang was growing up, were no exception. Tang was 13 when Deng Xiaoping made his historic visit to the USA in January 1979: a symbolic beginning to the institution-alization of his 'reform and open door' policy. (Some members of Deng's entourage made an unforgettable, if surreal, impression by being photographed dancing with Minnie Mouse at Disneyland.) Tang's formative years were spent in a climate of new economic fervour and Western cultural influences, from the Pet Shop Boys and Proust to milk shakes and McDonald's. Philosophy, literature and political ideas from Europe were being enthusiastically translated into Chinese. (The 85-year-old translator of James Joyce's *Ulysses*, Xiao Qian, who once denounced the book as 'a self-indulgent novel that served none of the purposes of China's Communists', now claims that he resisted translating it today not for political reasons but because 'on every page there was something not found in the dictionary.'[2]) The opening up of the economy and exposure to new ideals led to a deeper hunger for other freedoms. Television sets and washing machines were not enough for Tang's generation, who were not prepared to accept the same set of rules as their elders. They were not willing to 'bend with the wind' and suppress their own individuality in order to conform to the state.

During the decade, a series of student protests spread in Changsha, demanding political reform to be stepped up to keep pace with economic reform, and seeking to promote democracy. In Tang's account of the movement for *Asia Watch*[3] he describes the first as a campaign in the summer of 1980 to elect student representatives freely to the local People's Congress. The protest involved mainly students from Tang's own school, Hunan Teacher Training College (now Hunan Normal University), and it was led by Tao Sen, a student, and Liang Heng.

All the campaigns of the 1980s were part of the nationwide pro-reform drive partly inspired by the opening of China to the West. They were strongly influenced by the messages of freedom which appeared on a slightly crumbling, yellowing strip of blank wall in Beijing known as the 'Democracy Wall' in 1978. The messages, written on sheets of paper and pasted on the wall (which lay just west of the former Forbidden City) ranged from simple couplets to sophisticated epics penned by intellectuals and poets such as Bei Dao. At the beginning of the movement, a huge 94-page wall poster entitled 'God of Fire Symphonic Poems' was pasted up on a high fence along one side of Tiananmen Square. The sequence of poems, which was written by Huang Xiang, a worker in a knitting mill in the city of Guiyang, described the China of the Gang of Four:

The war goes on in everyone's facial expression.
The war is waged by numerous high-pitched loudspeakers.
The war is waged in every pair of fearful, shifting eyes.[4]

But the writing on the wall with the most impact had been scrawled on to posters by a young electrician called Wei Jingsheng. It was Wei who first coined the phrase 'the Fifth Modernization', meaning democracy itself. It was a direct challenge to the Chinese Communist Party leadership and to Deng himself, who had declared that the Four Modernizations – in agriculture, industry, national defence, and science and technology – were sufficient to transform the country. Wei believed that, until China embraced the 'Fifth Modernization', the other four would be merely 'another promise'. 'What is true democracy?' asked Wei in his famous poster of 5 December 1978. 'It means the right of the people to choose their own representatives [who will] work according to their will and in their interests.' Wei, one of China's most famous dissidents, even went to the length of lambasting Deng as a 'new dictator'. This criticism was too much for the authorities. He was arrested and sentenced to fifteen years in prison, on charges of 'counter-revolution' and, according to the *People's Daily*, 'ultra-democratization'.

Wei Jingsheng's brave challenge to the regime inspired democracy activists and ordinary citizens throughout China. As the 1980s progressed, each movement was larger and more influential than the last, infused with the courage of so many Wei Jingshengs.

In 1989, students in Hunan – including Tang – felt the beginnings of a new restlessness and discontent radiating from Beijing, the centre of political activity. Orville Schell, an American writer and veteran China-watcher, arrived in the city that February:

> By the time the Chinese New Year ushered in the Year of the Snake in February 1989, the city of Beijing was seething with a discontent so poisonous that many people began to whisper that the government's heavenly mandate to rule was running out. The optimism that had been generated in 1978 when Deng Xiaoping formally proclaimed his ambitious programme of pragmatic reform and 'opening up' to the outside world had been all but dissipated by deepening economic problems and a growing disillusionment with the slowness of political change.[5]

In the eyes of the world, China had become an economic power to be reckoned with – statistics showed that it was the world's third fastest-growing economy of the decade. To its own people, the country was riddled with corruption, and the fluctuating, unstable economy was creating new evils of unemployment and inflation. Students and intellectuals found it particularly difficult to eke out a living, and were resentful about the privileges of party members. Anti-establishment verses were common.

One read:

A Japanese limo that costs big bucks,
From the blood and sweat of the people is sucked,
And inside a fat son-of-a-bitch is tucked.[6]

Others looked back with a strange nostalgia to the tormented times under Mao:

Mao Zedong was so bad, so bad,
But if you had a dollar you knew what you had.
Deng Xiaoping is fine, so fine,
But a dollar's only worth a lousy dime.

In addition to the economic frustration, students, intellectuals and workers were impatient about the sluggish pace of political reform. Their hopes had been raised by 'socialist modernization', and the revival of codes and courts – then dashed. The system was still the same, with the judicial process still under the control of the Party. The Party could still arrest and imprison anyone it wanted, and there was still no real freedom of speech, assembly or worship.

The death of former Party Chairman Hu Yaobang on 15 April became the focus of the students' grief and the complex emotions that surrounded their philosophies of political reform.

Tang Boqiao was a reluctant leader of the student democracy movement in his home province of Hunan. When students began to mass in Tiananmen Square in May 1989, the 23-year-old student of political science was already a veteran of smaller, local protests at his college, Hunan Normal University. And this time, he didn't want to get involved.

'As chairman of the Hunan Students Autonomous Federation, I'd already been an activist in the 1987 and 1988 political movements at college,' says Tang, a tall, slim graduate who now deals in stocks and shares in New York. 'Many students had been expelled for their activities over those two years. I had many reservations about the developing movement at Tiananmen. I was worried that the students were moving too fast – I preferred a gradual step by step process. Unlike the others, I was not so excited about the prospects of becoming involved with this movement.'

Although Tang didn't want to represent the students at his college, he was persuaded to do so. 'Finally I came forward after the urging of students and friends,' he said. He was soon in the thick of the action. On 15 May, he arrived in Beijing to distribute funds for the movement, and to meet fellow student activists.

When he arrived, hunger strikes had begun and the crowd in the square was approaching a million people. Citizens of Beijing and workers had joined in the protest. Doctors and nurses flocked from nearby provinces to care for the hunger strikers, and peasants brought buns and cakes for the students. Orville Schell watched a father bathing his fasting daughter's face with a cloth, all the while begging her to return home:

She steadfastly refused to go. And eventually her father departed in tears. He was so overcome with emotion that as he walked away, he dropped his thermos bottle. Helping him pick it up, I tried to console him, only to find that he was weeping not because he had failed to convince his daughter to abandon her fast, but because he felt so proud of her determination to risk her life for the sake of her country. 'My generation never dared to speak out, much less to act out what we really believed,' he told me, half-sobbing, half-laughing. 'Now my daughter is doing it for me. How can I not thank her?'[7]

Tang quickly sensed the potential of the gathering at Tiananmen, and realized that the students were making the most of a great opportunity for political change. But still he had reservations. 'I felt there was no one leader who embodied the spirit of the movement; who fused the students together, and who could help them carry out their aspirations,' he says. Tang still feels the same today, looking back. 'Despite all their emotions, their hopes and fears, the students did not succeed in articulating what they really wanted,' he says. 'At college, we learnt that political movements can either lead a nation forward very quickly, or result in disaster. I very much hoped the Tiananmen demonstrations could help facilitate the economic development China so badly needed, but I had my doubts.'

Tang's doubts were not strong enough to overwhelm his own desire to participate in the deepening democratic movement. On the train back to Hunan on 20 May, he was sufficiently encouraged to work out a strategy of local support for the Beijing movement. 'I left because I sensed the tension between the students, the public and the government, and I didn't want to increase that tension,' he says. 'Also I wanted to save my own energy to organize a solidarity network at home.' The reluctant leader was back in the political fray.

He returned to Hunan with the students' slogans of freedom and patriotism – from the lofty 'democracy or death' to the more mundane exhortations to Deng, 'Step down and go play bridge!' – echoing in his ears. When he arrived at Changsha, he immersed himself in the local movement. The organized countrywide protests against the regime spread across China, involving both workers and peasants as well as students. They were the worst nightmare for a ruling party which feared *luan*, or chaos and disharmony, above all else.

'During the 1989 Democracy Movement, Hunan province experienced the largest and best organized student and worker-led campaign for democracy of any part of China outside Beijing,' says Tang. 'The demonstrations and solidarity groups in virtually every city and district in Hunan attracted tens of thousands of people.' The demonstrations were held mainly in support of the Beijing movement. But there were other items on the Changsha agenda. 'We wanted the government to recognize the legitimacy of certain student groups,' says Tang. 'There was also the issue of salaries for intellectuals at universities: we supported an increase in the wages of professors.'

In May, the students founded the Hunan Students' Autonomous Federation: Tang Boqiao and fellow student Fan Zhong were elected joint leaders.[8] 'The students chose us as their leaders after a formal democratic process,' says Tang. 'First we reformed and restructured the student governing bodies of all the participating colleges, then we had each college reselect their delegates to the SAF, and formed a standing committee from among those delegates. By then, the SAF had effectively established itself as the unified voice of the province-wide student movement. Students came to Changsha from many other colleges to join us. And we sent "democracy propaganda teams" to all areas of Hunan.'

While students in Beijing had often been directly hostile to the workers' attempts to participate at Tiananmen, the Students' Autonomous Federation realized the power of solidarity with the workers early on. On 24 May, it joined together with the Changsha Workers' Autonomous Federation to organize a massive city-wide demonstration. Drivers from Changsha's private taxi companies were among the participants, with more than forty taxis altogether taking part in the demonstration column.

When four leaders of the Changsha Workers' Autonomous Federation were arrested after participating with the students in a peaceful sitdown protest, the SAF leadership organized a student march to the Hunan government offices. They succeeded in attaining the release of two workers, Li Jian and Zhou Yong (who were both re-arrested after 4 June). The other two were not freed, and one of them, Zhang Jingsheng, received a thirteen-year sentence.

On the evening of 3 June, the news that troops had opened fire in Beijing was broadcast into the SAF headquarters via the Voice of America. 'The sound of gunfire on Tiananmen Square shattered the nation's illusions,' says Tang. 'A third of the people in Hunan came out on to the streets in a spontaneous outpouring of grief and anger.' Road traffic in all major cities in the province was brought to a standstill. For almost a week after 4 June, Changsha was in chaos.

Tang and his colleagues held an emergency meeting, and decided that they would hold a public memorial meeting at Changsha railway station to mourn the dead of Tiananmen Square. All the students knew they were in grave danger: government news bulletins had announced the launch of a nationwide search and arrest operation against leaders of the pro-democracy movement. 'We decided the mass meeting should also serve as an oath-taking ceremony at which SAF members would pledge their loyalty to the pro-democracy cause and bid a temporary farewell to the people of Changsha,' says Tang.

On 8 June, Tang and Zhang Lixin (representing the Beijing SAF) presided over the meeting at Changsha railway station. They stood on a stage piled high with floral wreaths and thin white banners inscribed with funeral couplets before an audience of 140,000 people. When the main memorial oration was read out, the sound of weeping and wailing from the crowd filled the air.

'Was it the indignant, still-beckoning spirit of Qu Yuan from more than two thousand years ago that took you away? Was it the heroic spirits of seventy years ago that called you?' Tang read amidst the outpouring of grief. 'Was it the loving heart of your numberless predecessors before the Monument to the People's Heroes that moved you so? You have suddenly gone, suddenly gone. You have left behind only a river of fresh blood, you have left behind only a deep love, and a deep hate. You have gone. Spirits of Beijing, where do you rest? Oh where do you rest? The mountains and rivers weep, the sad wind whirls. Before the evil gun muzzles, before the ugly face of fascism, before my people in suffering, and before the calm, smiling face on your death mask, I can do no more than make this offering to your spirits with vibrant, leonine nerve.'

As leader of the SAF, Tang also assured the masses that the students would never waver in their struggle for democracy. They vowed they would not be beaten by the 'thugs in thick glasses . . . the gun-wielders' in government who 'outnumber the pen-pushers'.

The next day, all the students remaining on the campus went to ground. On 14 June, Tang escaped to Guangdong province with two other students, and went into hiding in Guangzhou, Xinhui, Foshan and Jiangmen. But Tang had mixed emotions about his escape. On the one hand, he wanted to save himself by escaping abroad, and, on the other, he felt duty-bound to stay in China and continue his work. On 4 July, he decided to 'enter the jaws of the tiger' and go back to Hunan to distribute among other pro-democracy fugitives some of the donations that he had received from people overseas to help him escape. He boarded a train to Hunan, and during the journey he was horrified to see a police officer on the train, inspecting people's travel documents. The danger was averted when a friend he had met on the train nonchalently started chatting with one of the police officers, whom he knew as a friend. He told the police that he was with Tang, and that they were selling cigarettes. The police officer glanced at Tang. 'I'm not sure if he recognized me or not,' he says now. If the policeman did, he kept it quiet.

When Tang arrived near his destination, he realized that it was just too dangerous to disembark from the train. An arrest warrant for him had been posted up on the entrances and exits of the railway stations in Hunan province, and all passengers getting on and off the trains had to go through security checks. He returned to Guangzhou, and the home of the peasant family. The next day Tang was arrested, and taken to Jiangmen City Number One jail in Guangdong province. The stress of the past thirty days and the difficult physical conditions he had endured on the run combined to make him fall immediately ill, with a high fever of 39.6 degrees Centigrade. Cadres informed him that he was not entitled to medical expenses, and so no treatment could be given. Tang just had to clench his teeth and survive as best he could; he is still not fully recovered from the illness today.

In the next few days, Tang was transferred from another jail in Guangdong, the Guangdong Provincial Number One jail in Guangzhou city, back to Changsha – where he was held at the Changsha City Number One jail. On arrival at Changsha, a Toyota Corolla Super Saloon raced up to the platform to meet Tang and his jailers. He was bundled into the car and driven out of the station through an underground passageway direct to the jail.[9] The use of such heavy security for Tang's journey emphasized his importance in the eyes of local and national officials. It also indicated a fear of public unrest: security officials had already lost control in Hunan, and did not want the arrest of prominent student activists to create more security problems. Tang had not expected the level of anxiety that existed about 'turmoil elements'.

Interrogation began virtually as soon as Tang arrived at Changsha. It lasted for several months, and each session lasted about ten hours – sometimes twenty. Three cadres of section-chief level from the pre-trial investigation division of the Changsha city Public Security Bureau carried out the interrogation, and the aim was to break down Tang's resistance until he would answer any question they asked.

Because they were Party officials who had survived the Cultural Revolution, they were able to bring extra tricks and devices to their grim work. One of these was to interrogate in shifts, so that Tang was constantly exhausted. This lasted for four months. 'At one stage they tried to make me admit that I had contacted Wang Dan, the Beijing student leader, by cipher telegram. The charge was based on two things: that I had been in Beijing during the mass hunger strike there; and someone had informed against me. The interrogators grilled me on this matter for over ten hours a day for more than twenty days, but got nothing from me,' says Tang. 'Throughout the entire interrogation, I only told them names I thought wouldn't matter. I kept all the secrets I needed to keep.'

By the end of Tang's interrogation, twelve thick books had been filled, each 'full of sheer rubbish. They will take down whatever you say, and attempt to put it together. In the case of students like myself, they were attempting to paint a larger picture of the movement so they could see who the key figures were, and what to do with these people.' Tang adds: 'It is impossible for an individual to reform his thoughts in the way they want. They begin by building on the foundation of your past, and asking you to recount everything that has happened to you. The only thing they can do with these methods is to destroy your self-confidence. It can be very emotionally damaging. It's as if you are asking someone to crawl on the ground for 24 hours a day. When that person attempts to stand up, he will be destroyed.'

The Public Security Bureau also tried simple 'thug tactics' to extort a confession from Tang, by ordering his cellmates to gang up against him. 'On one occasion, seven or eight of the toughest inmates – two of whom were murderers famed throughout Changsha – turned on me,' says Tang. 'I was so badly beaten up I could scarcely move for a week. Even to this day, I shudder to recall the incident.' Throughout the interrogation and physical torture, Tang fell ill several times. In another attempt to undermine his resolve, he was still denied medical treatment. Yet still Tang's conscience would not allow him to give his interrogators the information they wanted.

On 29 December 1989, Tang was formally placed under arrest, after serving just over five months as a detainee. Until his trial on 17 July 1990, Tang was left alone. He spent his time making matchboxes, sleeping and eating a diet of sour-pickle soup with a little winter melon, pumpkin and seaweed thrown in. The cramped living conditions in the 18-square-metre cell, crammed with twenty other prisoners, led to a rash of skin infections and diseases among the inmates.

At his 'public trial', Tang was sentenced to three years' imprisonment with two years' subsequent deprivation of political rights on charges of 'counter-revolutionary propaganda and incitement'. He was accused of 'plotting to hold a memorial meeting on 8 June for the counter-revolutionary thugs suppressed in Beijing', and drafting a speech that 'invented the story of our martial law troops having massacred students, workers and citizens and of having killed thousands of them . . . It was most pernicious.'

When Tang complained that his lawyer had not turned up at the trial and that his classmates were not present to testify as witnesses, the judges and procurators looked puzzled. 'Let your campus mates come? Why, that would never do!' they said. 'The sentence had nothing to do with the law,' Tang says now. 'A cadre told me afterwards that it had all been decided before the trial, which was nothing but a façade. The length of time they gave me was in accordance with the political needs of the time.'

Throughout his incarceration, Tang was imprisoned in a total of sixteen cells of seven jails and prisons in five different places, and interrogated by agents of at least ten different public security or screening organs. His case cost the government, he found out later, more than 140,000 yuan. Most of his sentence was served at Longxi prison (Provincial Number Six) in Hunan, a labour reform camp known publicly as the 'Shaoyang Marble Factory'. Prisoners were forced to work in the manufacture of marble products, often for export, from building slabs to lamp shades and paperweights. Many prisoners were injured by the tough physical work.

If prisoners did not meet their work quota, they were punished by solitary confinement, or by taking away points in a system which increased the prisoner's sentence. Tang was once punished by being thrown into the 'strict regime' – a prison within the prison – for holding a 'counter-revolutionary rally' (in reality, a chat between a group of seventeen of the political prisoners).

'For the first three days of this punishment, we had to sit motionless for an average of ten hours per day performing so-called "introspection",' says Tang. 'One is made to sit on a tiny stool less than 20 centimetres in height on a raised platform of about 90 square centimetres, with back held bolt upright, both feet flat on the floor and hands placed neatly on one's lap. Throughout, one has to look directly at the wall just ahead, and if for any reason such as a momentary lapse of attention one happens to slouch forward slightly or bend one's head, one will be hit by the guard with an iron rod or handcuffed to the door. At night, one is locked up alone in a small room less than two square metres in area, in which the only bed is a cement slab of about 30 centimetres in width – not long enough to lie down fully.'

Food was barely adequate at Longxi, although better than at the normal prisons. Again, Tang was fed pumpkin, cabbage, dried vegetables and occasionally a meat dish.

The worst ordeal for Tang throughout the whole experience, however, was the institutionalized violence. The prison was ruled by brutality, among both the inmates and the prison staff. 'It's not the same as Western prisons,' says Tang. 'Prisoners beating up other prisoners serves a purpose – it's all part of the system. Cell bosses terrorize other prisoners. Usually they are made responsible for a group of about ten people. If that group does not achieve its quotas, the prisoner or prisoners responsible will be beaten up by the cell boss. As a reward, the boss is given special treatment from the authorities.'

Tang faced more bullying when he refused to labour. 'I didn't see why they should force us to do hard labour – being a prisoner was one thing, but working for the state another,' he says, with a logic that must have infuriated prison officials. Punishment came in the form of a spell of solitary confinement – and Tang promptly went on hunger strike to protest. 'The more they oppressed me, the more I wanted to fight back,' he says. They let him go after seven days. 'There was a particularly strong attitude towards prisoners who refused to labour because labour camps have become so important to the economy,' says Tang. 'Thought reform has lost its power to control prisoners. Now violence is the only thing that works.'

The abuse by 'cell bosses' is one of the major factors in a system of internal terror and control. These prison thugs, who are basically the regime's unofficial hit men, are more intimidating than the prison staff. 'Cell bosses have numerous specific ways and means of tormenting other prisoners and making their lives intolerable,' says Tang. 'Clubbing the dreamer' is one of the most painful punishments inflicted upon prisoners who will not readily submit to their authority. It usually takes place late at night, when the prisoner is sound asleep. Several other inmates will be ordered to the cell to assault him. Some of them first wrap a cotton quilt tightly around his head and upper body, and the others then begin kicking him viciously, stamping on his body and battering him about the head. The victim's screams are completely inaudible, muffled by the quilt.

The punishment known as 'heroic martyrdom' often generates considerable psychological anxiety. The cell boss orders two of the other inmates to 'apply the leg fetters' (in reality these are just a piece of cloth tied to the victim's feet). The cell boss then pretends to be a judge and declares that the death sentence has been imposed. He orders the prisoner to be 'dragged out and executed', so two inmates drag him across the floor by his hands and make him stand near the cell wall. At the sound of 'gunfire' (a 'ping' sound by the cell boss), the prisoner has to fall directly backwards, landing flat on the cell floor. 'Prisoners who have experienced this punishment several times learn quite quickly how to fall backward without hurting themselves too much,' says Tang. 'But first-timers, especially if they are overly anxious, often crack the back of their heads hard against the stone floor, sometimes knocking themselves out.'[10]

Tang did receive some sympathy from cadres and other prisoners. 'They all knew why I was there, and most of the cadres who oversaw the prisons felt that what the students were doing was right. So most of them had a conscience when they were dealing with me.'

After serving eighteen months, Tang was finally released owing to a combination of international pressure and internal concern over his sentence. 'The main reason why I was released was because of internal pressure on officials in Hunan,' he says. 'There was a lot of sympathy with my case. Because I was the only student in Hunan who was publicly declared wanted on television and radio, when they wanted to release someone to satisfy this pressure, I was the first to come to mind.'

Tang's release is largely credited to the influence of an internal document that had just been issued by the central authorities requiring the local judicial authorities to review cases of certain prominent pro-democracy figures who had been sentenced too heavily. Wang Dan, the Tiananmen leader who had been declared the 'most wanted' student, had been given a relatively lenient sentence of four years in January 1991. This sentence was intended to deflect international pressure on China from the West in the wake of Tiananmen; however it also caused internal concern over the discrepancies in sentencing whereby provincial leaders such as Tang Boqiao could be given three years.

On release, Tang was told that he was only on parole, and that he could be back in prison at any time if his 'performance was poor'. He was forbidden to leave his home town, and to have any contact with 'turmoil elements'.

'One rainy day just before Chinese New Year's Eve, in February 1991, I appeared before my family again at last, shaven-headed and drenched from head to foot,' recalls Tang. His mother, who looked ten years older, greeted him with a mixture of joy and sadness. Tang was devastated to hear that his father had died while he had been in prison. The pain still runs deep today when he remembers hearing that his father had been killed in a road accident, the day after he received his copy of the arrest warrant for his son. 'The copy of the arrest warrant, with its charges of "counter-revolution" and "treason" was still in his pocket at the time,' recalls Tang. 'My father was only 54 years old when he died. He worked diligently for China in the field of education all his life. He underwent innumerable hardships and scored remarkable achievements. A man of strong integrity, he was much respected by the people in my town. But he left the world in despair.'

Tang discovered that his whole family – his father, mother and two sisters, as well as people from the households who had sheltered him while he was on the run – had suffered in his absence from the Public

Security Bureau: they had all been branded as suspects. His mother had travelled hundreds of kilometres a month to visit him in prison – only to be forbidden to see him each time she arrived. Now Tang was the only male in his family. How could he leave them now?

Yet the oath which Tang had made after the Tiananmen massacre – to dedicate his life to the pursuit of democracy and justice – haunted him. Ultimately, he had to choose between his duty to his family and duty to his cause. Perhaps only a Chinese, who understands the importance of blood ties and kinship in Chinese society, can comprehend the agonizing nature of this choice.

Finally Tang made the decision. 'Seeing my mother's face growing thinner day by day, I could only say this in my heart: "I'm sorry, my good mother. Your son cannot be loyal to his cause and filial to you at the same time." I left home with my head bent low.'

Tang made contact with other pro-democracy activists in Changsha, and applied to start a business partnership in order to support himself. As with so many other democracy activists, the authorities constantly obstructed his progress. Tang and other colleagues formed an underground organization: 'This time we were more experienced, and were able to be totally secretive,' says Tang. 'Our aim was to start a magazine to disseminate democracy propaganda, and eventually to form a political party.' Tang was forced to watch his back constantly: 'I had been released, but I was still not free,' he says now.

More than two years since the last time Tang had gone underground, he was finally forced to go into exile. The Public Security Bureau had become convinced that Tang was involved with a protest rally in Changsha commemorating the 4 June massacre. When officials went to his mother's home and told her that they were going to make him 'repeat' what he had gone through before, Tang knew it was time to leave.

Supporters from Hong Kong and China helped him to leave, smuggled on board a boat. Nine months after reaching Hong Kong, Tang was granted political asylum in the USA. He began work with Human Rights Watch in New York. Now he works in business, dealing in stocks and shares. He shares a neat and subtly furnished apartment with his girlfriend Felicity Lung, a delicately beautiful American-Chinese woman, and a brown and white cat. In Felicity, who is a trainee lawyer, he has found his soulmate. When asked when they met, Tang says: 'We have been together since before we were born.'

Tang has found American society baffling compared to China. 'Human nature is the same everywhere, but still I don't understand American culture yet. I hope to learn more about it as I stay here.' He still feels a retributive anger about his experiences in prison. 'I'll always remember it:

just like I'll always remember those people who helped me afterwards, and the way my father died with my arrest warrant in his pocket.' Tang often thinks about the peasant who risked his own life to help him escape. Soon after Tang's own arrest, the peasant was imprisoned for three months. Tang attempted to track him down after his release, but without success. No one knew where he was.

Tang continues his human rights work in exile. He says: 'I can only live with these experiences in my mind if I am doing something about it.'

Notes

1. Asia Watch, *Anthems of Defeat*, p. 193.

2. Market Partners International, *Publishing Trends* (September 1995).

3. Asia Watch, *Anthems of Defeat*.

4. Andrew J. Nathan, *Chinese Democracy*, p. 3.

5. Orville Schell, *Mandate of Heaven*, p. 35.

6. *Ibid.*

7. Schell, *Mandate of Heaven*, p. 99.

8. Fan Zhong was arrested on 29 June for taking such an active part in the democracy movement. He was held until December 1991 in Changsha Number One jail, and more than once during his sentence he was manacled to the 'shackleboard' for several months. He was also subject to electric shocks. Fan was later accused of the crime of 'disrupting social order'.

9. Harry Wu reported the existence of a similar underground passage on his journey to the lakeside villa in Wuhan where he was held prisoner in summer 1995 (see Chapter 7). Underground passages also exist in Beijing between various sites of strategic importance (see Zhisui Li, *The Private Life of Chairman Mao*, pp. 23–4).

10. Asia Watch, *Anthems of Defeat* (Human Rights Watch, 1992).

CHAPTER 12

Getting Used to Surviving
Zhang Xianliang

Some devil hides behind every kind of beauty.

One should not ask what is more terrifying than death, but rather what is more important than life.

Zhang Xianliang[1]

Zhang Xianliang writes about a loneliness so deep that lice infesting the bodies of prisoners are 'lovable dependants', alleviating feelings of solitude and destitution. He tells us about a hunger which deconstructs the soul and causes people to consider scabs on their lips as edible 'meat'. And, perhaps most movingly, he writes about falling in love, sexual intimacy and the neuroses of the psyche after experiences of trauma.

Grass Soup is a harrowing autobiographical chronicle of life in the labour camps in the 1960s, based on Zhang's own 22-year sentence in prisons, labour camps and state farms in north-west China. He bases his book around prosaic fragments of his camp diaries. The first entry reads: '11 July, 1960. Capital construction: hauled dirt clods.' From these remnants of past experience, Zhang constructs a novel of extraordinary lyrical power in which we confront a world of famine, suffering and death. It is a world in which the family of a prisoner is simply regarded as a source of supply: the emotions of love and compassion have no place in the bestial struggle to survive. Zhang is frightened about this in himself: he believes that truly unthinkable, terrifying behaviour comes not from a loss of reason but from loss of the ability to feel emotion. 'Labour reform does not make a man lose all human feeling,' he writes. 'Hunger does.'

Zhang describes the effects of hunger on the body in awful detail. Just as we would know what salad dressing to use or how long to microwave a ready meal, he knows the importance of the secretions of the body; that urine and saliva had their uses in an emergency, and that, if you did not allow yourself to shit for a long time, you could make believe that there was actually something of substance in your stomach.

One of the most haunting accounts in his memoirs is of a woman who came to the camp with her small child to see her husband, who was one of the convicts. As the prisoners watched from a distance, they saw that the Troop Leader had given permission for her husband to see her. He walked towards her, 'like a man with rickets, his head nodded downward at every step'. Every muscle in the woman's body was concentrated on watching her husband approach. When he reached his family, the man did not touch her; he did not hug his daughter. Instead, he grabbed the cotton bag she held in her hands, and crawled to the top of the canal bank to devour its contents. His wife stayed at the bottom of the canal, crying quietly, her child cradled in her arms. Zhang took up his sickle again to begin work, saddened by what he had witnessed. Forty minutes later the air was wrenched with a blood-curdling scream. The convict had eaten the flatbread and eggs. After he had done so, he had cut his wrists with a sickle. His wife did not see him do so; but when she climbed up to the top of the canal bank, she found her husband upside down with his head facing downward on the canal slope, and blood flowing from his veins into the water from the Yellow River, dyeing the brown water a dark red. She let out the scream that Zhang Xianliang has not forgotten to this day.[2]

In his novels *Half of Man Is Woman* (1984) and *Getting Used to Dying* (1991), Zhang explores ideas about relationships both in the camps and later in exile, as his narrator attempts to live with the 'terror that lives inside all Chinese'. While revealing in itself, his writing about love and sex has a political subtext. In *Half of Man Is Woman*, the narrator's sexual experiences are a metaphor for the emasculation of China during the Cultural Revolution. In *Grass Soup* (1994), Zhang recalls how a fruitless attempt to milk a cow during the years of starvation in the camps resulted in a fantasy about a cow's udders; even today, whenever he sees a woman with full breasts, he thinks first of eating, then sex. In the same book, a woman's attempted kiss becomes a symbol of everything that is pure and natural in a false world.

Many years later, when a woman expertly thrust her tongue into Zhang's mouth for the first time, he was not aroused:

> *The woman was sleeping beside me that night, but I had lost interest in her. Tears filled my eyes as I fiercely remembered that female convict. In the summer of 1960, when many Chinese had either died of hunger or were on the verge of dying, in a dilapidated little room that had been used for storing grain in a remote labour reform camp in the north-west, she had played out a scene that was both beautiful and terribly human. The pink tip of her tongue now turned into a true, red flag, beckoning me not to a*

Communist paradise but to a true paradise on earth. She had been so brave, so liberated, supernaturally un-vulgar, completely oblivious to the false, defeated, tragic world around her, that it shocked me into understanding. Her actions revealed another, natural world, to me.

I not only don't know her name, I have even forgotten her face. The passage of time, none the less, has brought the fact of her into ever sharper focus. Her face and body seem perfect to me, and the vibrations, the aura she gave off, have defined 'feminine' for me ever since. Actions that I could not understand at the time have now become classic and elegant in my mind. She has already become a song that lingers when I am lonely, that tells me to believe in people. They may be trying to 'express themselves' to 'put in a performance' in the political sense, but their true selves are stubbornly holding on. Later, when I was being struggled against, when I was being criticised, I did not feel antipathy towards those who criticised, for I believed there was also a true self within them.

The difference between the public self and the true self is an enduring theme in Zhang's work. He says:

We have been pushed onto the stage too many times, to be criticised and struggled against, not to know that acting has become the most important part of a political movement. Lowering the head, trembling with fear, curving your back as you bow down, demeaning yourself, pretending to be absolutely blank – I have had more than enough experience of that.[3]

In *Grass Soup*, he refers to the false responses Chinese have been forced to adopt when faced with new political movements:

Experience taught people to be hypocritical. As political movements started rolling over the country, gathering in ever more people, the experience became general, to the point that dishonesty became a common practice among all Chinese. Dishonesty not only permeated our daily lives, it affected our standard of ethics and culture – not just then but also later.

Chinese people have learnt to adopt a series of masks to hide their private, inner selves – masks decreed by tradition, society and most importantly the Party.[4] Each Chinese has an armoury of these masks which he or she can use to take part in charades. But ultimately there is a price to be paid. Zhang writes:

For me, the worst thing is when you can't say what you feel. When people get up in the morning, they put on their underwear, then their clothes, then a padded coat and finally they wrap themselves up in an invisible suit of armour before going out. Everyone's huddled inside their own suit of

armour, so even though there might be a lot of people working in a camp,
they never really get to know one another.[5]

So is Zhang's writing also a mask, a beautiful artifice hiding the truth?
And what does Zhang Xianliang see when his own mask falls away and
he gazes into the mirror?

In September 1995, Zhang Xianliang made a rare visit to Britain. At the
Swansea Literary Festival, he was guest of honour together with Chinese
poet Bei Dao and American-Chinese writer Maxine Hong Kingston. In
London, he gave a talk to assorted China-watchers, writers and other
admirers of his work at the Great Britain–China Centre.

Dressed in a smart navy suit with fashionable light framed glasses, 59-
year-old Zhang could have been a Hong Kong businessman in
appearance but for the koala bear print on his burgundy tie. He is slim
and tall, with grey sideburns and a dull pallor to his skin. ('There are two
good ways to stay in shape,' he wrote in *Getting Used to Dying.* '. . . [to]
endure starvation when you are young, and fear when you are middle
aged.') He is escorted by his literary agent and a cultural attaché from the
Chinese embassy. The presence of the latter indicates that Zhang may not
be departing from the official line on the Chinese system. Zhang's
responses to questions from the audience confirm this.

When one of the questioners, who introduces himself as the governor
of Brixton prison, asks whether the West should interfere in the human
rights affairs of another country, Zhang gives a small, dry laugh. 'Today,
the prisoner and the jailer sit together,' he says, and goes on: 'Everywhere
in the world prison is a dark place. After all, if it was like heaven, it would
not serve the function of punishment. From the human rights point of
view, the system has changed in China for the better. In the past innocent
people were sent to prison. Nowadays this doesn't really happen. I
haven't been to prison for ten years, but I understand that conditions in
Chinese prisons are now much better.'

Zhang now feels that, by its insistence on the importance of human
rights, the West is playing out the role of the imperial emperor,
demanding that China kowtows to its will. 'About two hundred years
ago the British sent an ambassador to China,' he says. 'According to their
usual custom, the Chinese demanded that the ambassador kowtowed to
their Emperor. The British, according to their custom of imperial
superiority, refused. A good opportunity for cultural exchange and
dialogue was wasted due to the obstinacy of both powers. But now China
has abandoned these old concepts and customs, and has learnt a great deal
from the West. The number of Chinese who are learning English in

China now outnumbers the population in Britain, for instance!

'For years, the Chinese have been locked in an insular concept of the West. Now they are the opposite, and we want to embrace the world. The West has become the Chinese Emperor two hundred years ago – demanding human rights standards and applying them to China. I fear that a historic opportunity will be lost.'

Zhang's opinions echo the views of officialdom in China regarding the so-called 'interference' of the West in its 'internal affairs'. This is the argument used by China when the Western world expresses, for instance, its concern for the rights of prisoners of conscience or labour camp inmates. Li Peng's address to the National People's Congress in March 1994 explicitly laid down this policy with the announcement that 'China will never allow anyone to interfere in its internal affairs'. The idea is supported by some in the West, who believe that, just as our cultures and societies are governed by different rules, so should our judgement of 'human rights' issues be. However as sinologist Andrew Nathan points out,[6]cultural relativism itself is a Western concept. The Chinese them-selves have always taken a stance of cultural universalism in condemning other countries and systems: the 'bourgeois democracy of the West', for instance. Mao's idea of world revolution was also universalist in content. Hence China's criticism of other countries when they attempt to 'interfere' in its internal affairs is inconsistent with its own world view.[7]

Zhang's other comments about the human rights system in China changing for the better would be refuted by human rights groups such as Amnesty International, and by the contents of this book. The number of political prisoners may have decreased from about ninety per cent of the prison population in the late 1950s to around ten per cent now,[8] but the machinery of repression that makes up the entire system is still in place, and Chinese who express a point of view contrary to the government continue to be imprisoned. Ex-prisoners including Han Dongfang and Liu Shanqing would also disagree with Zhang's contention that prison conditions have improved in the last ten years.

Zhang spent more than twenty years pitted against the system he now defends. He was born to a wealthy family in Nanjing in 1936, but was not allowed to go to university because of his 'bad' class origin. So, in 1955, he went to Ningxia, a province bisected by the Yellow River which lies to the south of Mongolia. At the time, the area was being opened up, and Zhang was allocated a job as a teacher in a cadre school. In the 1950s, during the Anti-Rightist movement, he wrote a poem which branded him a Rightist, and he was sent for reform through labour. Zhang was held in prisons, labour camps and state farms in the north-west of China for 22 years. He was repeatedly a target for struggle sessions and self-criticisms. The Ningxia labour reform camp and the state farm Zhang worked on during the Cultural Revolution are described in his story *Half of Man Is Woman*. (The novel begins in 1966 and ends in 1976, after Zhou Enlai's death in January but before Mao's death in September.)

In 1979, Zhang received a formal recognition of the 'mistake' involved in sending him to the gulag for two decades in the form of official rehabilitation. In the usual official jargon, he was informed that he had been 'wrongly dealt with'.

When *Half of Man Is Woman* was published in China in 1985, it caused a sensation owing to its frank depiction of sexuality. Zhang says that his account of sexual impotence is a metaphor for the emasculation of the Chinese intellectual during the Mao years. However, though many of Zhang's descriptions of life in the labour camps and the language of politics could still apply to China today, Zhang does not seem to intend any criticism to the regime. He is not using the common pretence of 'using the past to criticize the present'. Whereas his spoken language is of the present and the future, Zhang describes his writing as fixed in history. This genre of writing has been described as 'scar literature', or 'the literature of the wounded' (*shangwen wenxue*). The genre consists of accounts, sometimes fictionalized and often real, of people's experiences during the Cultural Revolution.

While Zhang was travelling overseas in 1985, his novel was the subject of much debate on the mainland. As with any book, the surrounding controversy was a marketing person's dream, and *Half of Man Is Woman* became one of the bestselling novels of the year. The *Literary Gazette* claimed that sales of the novel even rivalled those of 'kung-fu fiction'. 'The talk one hears about town is that it is a novel all about "sex",' wrote a Gazette correspondent sniffily:

> *I am not saying that the writer's sole intention was to cater to vulgar tastes. Nor would I go so far as to say that this is a pornographic or dirty book. However, it is a novel that contains too many naturalistic descriptions of the relations between men and women . . . As a female reader I must admit I find the author's naturalistic descriptions [of sex] quite unacceptable. I'm sure many young girls would feel the same.*[9]

When Zhang returned home, claiming to have refused the offers of Guomindang agents to grant him asylum in Taiwan, he was hailed as a patriotic hero.[10] Zhang's current status as President of the Writers' Union in Ningxia and a representative to the People's Consultative Conference indicates that his rehabilitation is complete.

He has participated enthusiastically in China's economic transition. In Ningxia, where he has made his home, Zhang is an entrepreneur and director of various cultural enterprises and a film studio. In 1993, he set up a trading company to assist the local community in developing a market economy: floppy disks are now being manufactured near the state farm where he was once imprisoned, tending livestock. Zhang has also written a novel, *Reform Fiction*, about a movement in the 1980s that promoted not only economic reforms but the reform of Chinese society. The movement had the full blessing of the authorities. Now Zhang is writing another novel, this time about contemporary China.

'Since 1979, Chinese writers have begun to raise their voices for the first time in society,' says Zhang. 'Some are overjoyed with their new freedom, others are worried about the new directions in society. Some feel lost and confused at the great changes taking place. In the past there was a unified criterion for writers; whatever they said had to be the voice of the government. For twenty or thirty years there was only one voice in China – the voice of Mao. Only money could break this framework, and destroy the previous structure of the Chinese government.

'I'll tell you a true story, which happened recently. In a muddy street in a Chinese city, various small businessmen set up stalls. One young, very pretty woman had a stall which sold only underwear, and she used to hold the underwear up to show passers by. She would shout out to people that this was not common underwear, it had special medical effects. If women wore this type of underwear, it would cure a type of women's disease. The Premier himself had even vouched for this sort of underwear. A policeman standing next to the stall didn't take any notice of the woman.'

Zhang continues: 'To me, this story indicates the extraordinary transformation of China. In the past, if anyone dared to say that underwear was promoted by the Premier, they would definitely be sent to prison, for at least ten years because of their contempt for leaders of the Chinese government. But now you just saw people passing by the stall and not taking any notice, and a policeman also standing by with no interest. This indicates that the political structure has been changed by money. The market economy has provided a basis for equality.'

Zhang points out that the story also shows an important cultural shift with regard to underwear. 'For thousands of years throughout Chinese history, women's underwear could not be shown in public, even hanging on a washing line. It always had to be dried in a hidden place so it wasn't seen by others – that was a taboo of Chinese society. Women also had to buy underwear from a special desk in shops or stalls. Now the separation between males and females has been eliminated. These taboos are being destroyed by the Chinese market economy. If there is any opposition to these changes, I haven't seen it.'[11]

Zhang's enthusiasm for the transforming power of materialism sits uneasily with his previous concerns for human spirituality and literature, as expressed in his novels and stories. His literary exploration of the nature of love and sex has also undergone a metamorphosis. 'I now feel that the topic of sex cannot be truly explored in the form of fiction,' he says. 'It's better to discover it through science. Recently I've been reading the US writer Shere Hite, who has given me a good insight into women. Writers who cover the subject of sex are usually just expressing the feelings of the writer.'

Bearing in mind the psychological terrain Zhang covered in his previous novels – from psychosis to love, death and sexuality – this idea, and his new preference for exploring love and sex in science rather than literature, seems to have its imaginative limits. One of the characters in Zhang's story *Mimosa* survives his sentence in a labour camp by driving all ambitions and romantic longings from his mind and dreaming of only 'a wife and a big beef and cabbage stew'. Is Zhang confining himself to the literary equivalent by dispeling more uncomfortable thoughts in favour of the new materialism?

Many intellectuals in China today have taken the pragmatic step of accepting the regime without criticism, in order to live a normal life after the trauma and persecution of previous years. And certainly there have been many positive changes in China within the last decade. But it is still hard to accept that someone can endure 22 years of virtual starvation, beatings and hard labour in a state system and then concede that this same regime has changed entirely within a decade, and that human rights problems simply do not exist in today's China.

Perhaps the answers lie in Zhang Xianliang's own writing: in his distinctions between the 'true self' and the 'public self', between that which remains silent, and what is expressed in public. And maybe we should also consider the reassessment of values made by Zhang during his incarceration in the camps. As one of his characters discovers: 'He had long known the value of a piece of bread, a length of rope, a torn blanket. All man's scholarship talks of the inner life and extols ideals, but in reality everything confirms that the important things are what a man can physically hold in his hand.'[12]

Notes

1. Zhang Xianling, *Grass Soup* and *Getting Used to Dying*.

2. Zhang recalls how a female friend once pretended to be his fiancée in order to gain permission to see him at the camp. 'Her big eyes looked resolutely into mine, searching in them for some sign of hope. In return, I stared at the package she had brought, estimating how much food was packed inside. Twenty-five years later, a critic wrote that I was a "writer of the school of realism". That hurt. I alone knew how many beautiful things my "realism" had destroyed, how it had never accurately measured the enormous weight of weightless feeling' (*Getting Used to Dying*).

3. Zhang, *Getting Used to Dying*, pp. 115–16.

4. Bette Bao Lord, *Legacies*.

5. Zhang, *Mimosa*.

6. 'Sources of Human Rights Thinking', in *Human Rights in Contemporary China: A Study of the East Asian Institute and of the Centre for the Study of Human Rights* (New York: Columbia University Press, 1986), p. 163.

7. A high official in the Party told the British Foreign Secretary in 1994 that 'it is not fair to force the developed nations' view of human rights onto developing countries. China will certainly not accept America's concept of human rights' (Xinhua News Agency, 12 March 1994). Professor Xu Liangying, an intellectual who experienced denial of his rights firsthand when he was placed under house arrest, says: 'It is difficult to suppress laughter when officials make such enlightening remarks, since they are obviously in contradiction with the facts of the development of world civilisation and of the history of China, and furthermore, clearly violate the fundamental spirit and principles of the United Nations' Universal Declaration of Human Rights' (quoted in *China Rights Forum*, summer 1994). Professor Xu points out that, in 1945, China promised to 'put into practice Sun Yatsen's Three People's Principles, Abraham Lincoln's principle of "to the people, by the people and for the people" and Roosevelt's "four great freedoms". Sun Yatsen's principles stated that the people enjoyed even types of rights of freedoms, including "freedoms of expression, writing, publication and of assembly and association". Mao's declaration meant that after 1949, in essence, the Party accepted the world's universal human rights principles' (*ibid.*, p. 11).

8. Chinese government documents, quoted in Harry Wu, *Laogai*.

9. *The Literary Gazette* (28 December 1985), quoted in Geremie Barme and John Minford (eds), *Seeds of Fire: Chinese Voices of Conscience*, p. 218.

10. *Ibid.*

11. Another interesting cultural shift in the lingerie world is the recent emergence of padded bras in China. Twenty years ago, it wasn't considered 'socialist' for a woman to emphasize her breasts, but today a curvaceous figure is heralded as the 'new shape' (Debbie Taylor, *My Children, My Gold*, p. 34).

12. *Getting Used to Dying*.

CHAPTER 13

The Fatigue of Supporting Freedom

Palden Gyatso and China's Siberia

A time when the living are envious of the dead.

Resident of Sarajevo, June 1995

'Those who expect to reap the blessings of freedom,' the political philosopher Thomas Paine once said, 'must undergo the fatigue of supporting it.' Palden Gyatso, a Tibetan Buddhist monk, has borne more of that fatigue than most. For demonstrating against Chinese rule, he was imprisoned for 33 years in Chinese prisons and labour camps in his country.[1] A sentence of this length is indicative of a prisoner whose thoughts remain stubbornly his own and who refuses to break under torture and 'thought reform'.

Palden Gyatso is now 63 and living in Dharamsala, India, home of the exiled spiritual and political leader the Dalai Lama (Plate 13). He doesn't have a house of his own, but is looked after by friends. He regards Dharamsala, in his own words, as 'a temporary rent'; his real home is Tibet, which has been occupied by China since the invasion of the People's Liberation Army in 1949-50. The 'temporary rent' will probably last at least the rest of his lifetime; but Tibetan Buddhists have an expansive concept of time.

Palden is a tiny man with clear watery eyes and a shaven skull that pokes out of his monk's robes like a tortoise. His arms are still misshapen after torture in the 'aeroplane' position. He became known in the West after visiting Britain, Italy, Portugal and America in spring 1995, bringing with him a collection of torture implements, still stained with blood and bodily fluids, that he smuggled from Tibet after bribing a Chinese prison official. Officials at Edinburgh airport were not as easily pacified when he travelled from Scotland to London, carrying electric shock batons, handcuffs and knives (with a hook at the end of the blade for gouging out

163

flesh) in his monk's pouch. They detained him until anxious representatives of the Dalai Lama in London could explain who he was.

In the UK, Palden's presence made an emotional impact on hundreds of volunteers and supporters of the host group, Tibet Support. 'When I look at Geshe-la, I feel as though I am on the edge of comprehension,' said Adrian Abbas. 'I can understand the deep reserves of strength utilized by Tibetans to endure torture without giving in.'

During his British tour, Palden stayed at Adrian's and Maria Salak's house in Leicester. Each morning he woke at 4.30 a.m. to say his prayers and click his mala beads. After five hours of prayer, he ate several croissants with blackcurrant jam, cut carefully and delicately into small pieces: his teeth were knocked out during torture in prison, and he has difficulty in chewing solid food.[2]

There is an old Tibetan saying, he says, roughly translated as: 'One cannot eat and at the same time blow your own trumpet.' For many *laogai* prisoners who watched friends starve to death, food has become of symbolic importance, signifying life and freedom. If given too much food, Palden will eat it all rather than see it go to waste. Yet years of virtual starvation leading to a shrunken stomach and distended belly have given him a small appetite. Once he has finished his croissants, however, Palden is happy to talk for as long as is required.

Palden, whose extraordinary story is soon to be told in an auto-biography,[3] is a living witness to one of the most turbulent eras in Tibetan history, which may end with its extinction. He endured the eradication of his family, virtual starvation during the three-year famine, and torture during the Cultural Revolution for his refusal to reform and to give up the Buddhist faith. He speaks of his suffering in universal and religious terms, ascribing to Tibetans like himself a role of sacrifice: 'If you work hard for the benefit of the greater good with enough conviction, and if you are on the right side you might find that you are somewhat rewarded, even if you die. The greatest example in the West is Jesus Christ, who died in great pain when he was nailed on the cross and sacrificed himself for the benefit of the people. His conviction and determination became a source of inspiration and an example to many believers. As for myself, my studies of Buddhism have shown me that, compared to the Buddha, I have suffered very little. The Buddha offered his eyes and flesh for the benefit of others.'

Palden was born in Panam, Tsang district, Tibet, and he lived together with an extended family of cousins, aunts and uncles – 29 altogether – in a large house. On Palden's release from prison in 1992, most of his family were dead – killed by executions, starvation or torture. None of them had ever been able to visit him during his 33-year sentence.

In Tibet almost every family has a child or relative in a monastery or nunnery from an early age. Celibacy and spirituality are valued by society, and monasteries are also centres of learning and education. Palden's family was no exception, and, at the age of 10, Palden became a monk at Gadrng Gompa in Shigatse. He studied at Gadrng until he was 16, and then moved to Drepung monastery, close to Lhasa, the capital city of Tibet, which for several centuries had been one of the great cultural and trading centres of ancient Asia.

Although many parents in Tibet today are too frightened to talk to their children about the real history of independent Tibet, Palden had become politicized from an early age. He says: 'My father was a devout Buddhist, and he told me about Tibet before the Chinese invasion when I was a small child. I felt very strongly about the suffering of people in my country.' (Palden's mother died a month after his birth.)

On 10 March 1959, at the age of 28, Palden went to Lhasa on private business. He found that a large crowd had gathered outside the Norbulingka (summer palace) of the Dalai Lama. The young leader known in the West as a 'god-king' had been attempting wary conciliations with the new Chinese rulers of Lhasa since the invasion. Tension had increased and fears grew that the Chinese would attempt to kidnap the Tibetans' beloved leader. When Palden arrived, virtually the entire population of Lhasa was out in the streets in an attempt to stop the Chinese kidnapping His Holiness. Thousands of people were lying on the ground and on vehicles to form a mass blockade outside the palace.

Palden decided that he had to summon other monks to help and to fight if necessary. 'His only thought was for the safety of the Dalai Lama,' says his interpreter. He returned to the monastery to discuss with other monks what to do – but their small army never had a chance to fight. They fired some shots in the direction of the Chinese army but were overwhelmed by shelling.

None of the thousands of Tibetan who died in the March Uprising knew that the leader they had been trying to save had made the agonizing decision to leave his people and flee to safety in India. By the time the Chinese were firing shells into the crowd, the Dalai Lama was crossing the mountain by mule into safety. There was no one in the summer palace to protect.

All the fighting was over within two days, and Palden returned to his monastery on 21 March. Drepung was occupied by Chinese forces and most of the monks had fled. When Palden crept into the monastery through a back door, he found only his 72-year-old teacher, Rigzin Tenpa. Palden took his teacher on his back and began the fourteen-day walk to Palden's home county, Panam. They didn't know where else to go. The main road was blocked by Chinese soldiers, so they travelled through the countryside. As soon as they reached Panam, Rigzin Tenpa was arrested. But he managed to avoid being flung into prison by pretending he was Indian and showing Chinese police a picture of himself with Jawaharlal Nehru. The Chinese sent him to India, accusing him of being an Indian spy.

Palden was not so fortunate. He was manacled in 'self-tightening' handcuffs, which gradually increase pressure on the wrist, causing blood to spurt out of the thumbs and often the loss of a hand. He was taken to Drepung for interrogation and was kicked and beaten with a wooden stick studded with nails. He says: 'I was arrested because of my actions in the uprising. The Chinese claim they invaded Tibet to "liberate" the country from feudal serfdom and foreign imperialism. But this is not true. Tibet wants independence and freedom. When we rose up against the Chinese on that night in March 1959 the Tibetans made a statement requesting that the Chinese leave Lhasa. I made up my mind from the beginning that as long as I lived I would fight for my country, and for what I believe in.'

Palden was branded a 'reactionary counter-revolutionary', and his first sentence was seven years. For the first eight months he was assigned to work in a carpet factory. Although his hands were free, his legs were still in chains, making it difficult to move. He dug a hole in the ground, put his legs in it, and was finally able to weave. After two years his leg-irons were removed.

For all of his 33 years in prison, Palden had to endure 'study sessions' – virtually every night – in which Chinese officials attempted to reform his thinking. 'Since 1959, the interrogation and propaganda was continuous,' says Palden. 'But instead of diminishing our resolve, the endless propaganda only increased the determination of most of us. Some people of course caved in. One lama, who is now in Dharamsala, told the Chinese what they wanted to hear and his sentence was reduced to three years. If I had changed like him, I wouldn't have stayed in prison for so long.' Palden has an uncompromising approach to those who gave in during *thamzing* (struggle sessions) and study sessions. 'This lama, who is now free and enjoying his life in India, betrayed his people and many other prisoners.'

Violence was used to maintain the power structure of the prisons, and brutality within the system is also a result of the endemic Chinese perception of Tibetans as inferior. Tibetan prisoners are often dragged from their cells at night so that drunken jailers can use them as objects for practising their martial arts skills. Although Tibetans occasionally report a feeling of solidarity with Chinese prisoners,[4] others report random acts of violence – for instance that Chinese prisoners routinely step on the faces and bodies of Tibetan prisoners when they get up in the night to go to the toilet.[5]

A Chinese intellectual, Su Xiaokang, summed up the Chinese attitude of racial superiority over the Tibetans when he said recently: 'It is as if when we hear a Tibetan has been killed, we don't really think that a human life has been lost.'[6] In Chinese prisons in Tibet, many Chinese consider the questioning and interrogation of Tibetans a kind of entertainment, or a game. 'Sometimes I saw torture sessions which were put on as a show to entertain the Chinese prison personnel, or which were used as exemplary events,' a former prisoner reported to Tibet Information Network. The supposed aims of interrogation are to extract 'confessions', to intimidate prisoners, to gain information about other possible participants outside jail and to attempt to convince Tibetans of the futility of independence.

The same prisoner recalled that Chinese prisoners are generally not tortured as much as Tibetans. He recalled the case of a Chinese who stole a gun and killed someone. The prison guards simply hit him on the cheek. 'They told him: "There are so many things which you can steal. Why did you steal a gun?" He was almost treated like a joke.'

Beating up by prison officials was also continuous throughout Palden Gyatso's sentence. 'During a beating session two doctors would often be standing by,' he says. 'If the guards knocked you unconscious, they would revive you with an injection. Then if the doctor believed you were not too badly hurt, they would tell the guards to continue. If they thought you were on the brink of death they would tell them to stop. Often I wished I could die during these beatings.'

During the Cultural Revolution in the mid-1960s, Palden would often see smoke rising from the fields beyond the prison walls and know that monasteries were being burnt down. During this period, Palden was being held at Drapchi prison, Lhasa. All prisoners were forced to work for at least nine hours a day, digging, growing vegetables, cultivating wheat and carrying out building work. Palden was frequently harnessed in a yoke together with three other prisoners and made to plough the land surrounding the prison. If they stopped to rest they were whipped, with the flesh often torn. 'The Chinese used people as human ploughs as a method of punishing them, but mainly it was because they wanted to increase production,' says Palden. 'We were being used as labour to boost the Chinese economy. What we produced was mainly exported back to China.'

Prisoners in Drapchi and other prisons and labour camps throughout Tibet were virtually starving, and hunger became the cruellest punishment. 'Each day we were given just one bowl of cooked peas or rotting vegetables floating in a watery soup,' says Palden. 'We couldn't stop working, otherwise we would be beaten almost to death. Even if we were ill we had to carry on.' In the mornings, prisoners didn't have the strength to raise their heads without pushing them up with their hands.

When Palden wakes, sweating, in the night, it is often with indelible images of those years in Drapchi in his mind. He says: 'Every day the Chinese would come into the jail with a cart pulled by three horses. They would load the cart with people who had died overnight, or others who had collapsed in the plough harness. You could see heads rolling about over the edge. They would take the bodies and burn them or bury them. Many were monks. Many of them were my friends.'

The famine in Tibet in the 1960s led to the deaths of thousands of Tibetans outside prison as well as inside. The famine was a result of the intransigence of the Chinese Communist Party and its mismanagement of agriculture in the territory they occupied. Tibetans mostly eat barley, a high-altitude staple crop. A small ball of barley mixed with tea is a high-energy food suitable for inhabitants of an elevated plateau who make their living from manual labour. The Chinese, however, mainly eat wheat – which can be grown only in limited quantities in Tibet owing to the altitude.[7] In the 1960s, Chinese government directives forced Tibetans to plant wheat. The result was the first famine Tibet had experienced in a two-thousand-year history.[8] Even today the Communist regime enforces silence over the truth of those years.

Palden recalls: 'We were driven by hunger. We thought of nothing else. Some prisoners would eat the bones of dead rats or insects they found in the fields. I soaked my leather boots in water and began to chew on them. Soon there was nothing left. The lack of food was frequently used as a method of punishment.' As he talks, he twists and untwists the wrapper of a Murray mint in his hands. He has also pulled a flannel from the folds of his robe to wipe his eyes. 'In our study sessions we would occasionally be shown an official film about the visit of some high delegation to Tibet. This would usually show them enjoying a feast of food and alcohol. This made our hunger even harder to bear.'

Millions of Tibetans suffered during the 'three lean years', even those outside the prison camps. Palden remembers peasants from the fields and nomads even approaching the *laogai* officials for food. Their precarious way of life did not even guarantee them one bowl of watery vegetables a day, like the prisoners. Like Palden, other Tibetan prisoners began to consume whatever they could. Dr Choedrak, a Tibetan doctor who was imprisoned in the camps at the same time, was sustained for a short time by eating his fur-lined jacket, roasted over a fire made with stolen brush. Dr Choedrak also caught a Chinese inmate holding a long red worm in his cup. The man told him he had defecated the worm in his stool.[9] He had picked it out, washed it and brought it back from the toilet to mix in with his food and eat.

Prisoners and non-prisoners alike were governed by a hunger so consuming that nothing else seemed important. The mind was entirely focused on the body's cravings. In spring 1960, rations were cut dramatically at Jiuzhen prison, where Dr Choedrak was being held. To save grain, the authorities had instigated a mixing of indigestible roots and bark with the food. The first type was rotten bark, which left dumplings tinged red when it was mixed with the dough. The dumplings left an unpleasant, heavy feeling in the stomach. If ingested for too long, the bark produced bleeding sores inside the stomach, and after only a few days the prisoners found blood in their stools. Chaff was mixed in with the dough too, and, later on, a waste material from soy beans.[10]

By summer, most of the prisoners were in an advanced state of starvation. Their stomachs swelled out, their teeth were loose, their hair fell out and their eyes bulged. Many of them resembled barely living skeletons, and were confined to their *kangs* (raised sleeping platforms), unable to move. A Chinese inmate in this condition developed large bedsores, which became infested by maggots. There were reports of cannibalism outside the prison.[11]

Despite his own state of debilitation, Dr Choedrak noted that many prisoners suffered from an inability to sleep, difficulty with their vision and a constant loud rushing noise in the ear. According to Tibetan medicine, this is caused by the rising of *lung* or wind, which is produced by starvation. Many prisoners died from dysfunctions of the digestive tracts: the excess roughage of chaff and bark in the food could scrape away the interior lining of the stomach. Once worn through, the intestine then burst. When water was drunk, it passed direct into the abdomen, causing intense pain. Deaths were also caused when prisoners' sphincters cracked apart owing to the hard indigestible objects lodged in their intestines.

In 1966, the famine had eased. The ideological struggle of the Cultural Revolution could begin with renewed fervour. Prisoners had to hand in every Tibetan item they had: cups, clothes and rosary beads. One day in Drapchi prison officials gave all the political prisoners a speech about progress in Communist countries. Palden remembers that the official emphasized how democracy was dying, and Communism becoming more powerful. He told them that the Indian government would soon hand over the Dalai Lama to the Chinese government. After the lecture, the prisoners were divided into groups of about fifteen, and were told they were free to agree or disagree with the views expressed by the

official. Palden joined a group which supported Tibetan independence
and attacked Communism. Each prisoner wrote down his views and
handed it into the officials as a signed statement. The debate then began,
and about half of the political prisoners spoke out for the freedom and
independence of their country. The entire debate lasted seven days, and at
the end prison officials declared that the Tibetans supporting
independence had won the argument – but that they were not sure
whether it could be realized.

Palden believed at the time that the officials were sincere. But later he
realized that the debate's real purpose was for Chinese officials to learn
more about the culture, history and politics of Tibet – in order to be able
to distort the facts later. The Chinese finally used the arguments to
demonstrate that neither group believed in independence any more.
They gave the names of independence supporters and 'proved' they were
pro-Chinese. The 'free and open' debate had become another
opportunity by the prison officials to divide the Tibetans among
themselves.

Palden witnessed many executions during the Cultural Revolution. In
1966, while imprisoned in Outitru prison, he and other monks were
urged to speak out against the Dalai Lama and traditional Tibetan society
during struggle sessions. They were told to step on to his picture. Those
who were too outspoken against this were forced to sign a 'confession'
which stated that they had behaved badly and so should be executed.
Those who refused to sign had a pen placed in their hand and pulled arose
the page by officials.

On the eve of their execution, the prisoners who were scheduled to
die by a bullet in the back of the head were forced to sing and dance
before the other prisoners. 'We all cried when we saw this,' says Palden.
'They were even denied the dignity of dying in their own way.'

On the day of the execution, wooden blocks with Chinese characters
were hung around the necks of the prisoners, and they were thrown into
trucks and driven to Drapchi. 'Some died of fear before the execution
took place,' remembers Palden. Palden and the other prisoners were
taken there in separate trucks and forced to watch from a distance.

'The condemned men were made to kneel down close to an open pit
and listen to their "crimes",' says Palden. 'After the crimes were
announced, the men were shot, one by one. I can remember a monk
from Ganden who didn't die even after seven shots had been fired at him.
The executioners dragged him to the pit and buried him alive.' Prisoners
were forced to lift up their hands after each execution to signify that they
approved. They were forced to remain completely silent and to show no

signs of grief. After the executions the prisoners' families were sent an invoice for the bullets.

Executions were routine in the Tibetan *laogai*. During the Cultural Revolution, charges were usually unspecified. Names of those who were about to be shot were nailed to the prison walls, with judgements such as 'suffers from old brains'. A red mark would be made beside the names of those who had been executed.

Cases have also been recorded of Tibetans being buried alive, beheaded, disembowelled, stoned and even crucified.[12] Most of these executions took place after the 1959 uprising; however, they occurred in later years, too. On 9 June 1968, the bodies of two men were dumped in the street in front of Ngyentseshar (the old Lhasa jail). Their corpses were pocked by nail marks, not only through the hands but also in the head and major joints of the torso.[13]

In Leicester, Palden Gyatso wants to walk everywhere to 'feed his eyes'. As he walks along terraced streets, he gazes up at houses and pats and strokes red brick walls beneath privet hedges. 'These are much better quality than in Tibet,' he says. 'These bricks last hundreds of years.'

Palden spent several years making bricks during his nine-year sentence in a labour camp about 15 miles out of Lhasa, where he was interned after being released from prison in 1975. While in the labour camp, he had to 'wear a black cap' to show he was a reactionary element – a term of abuse for an 'ex-'prisoner. The quantity and quality of food in the camp was scarcely better than in prison, and the prisoners had to purchase all their food – salt, wheat, flour and vegetables – from a tiny wage, which also had to cover clothing and costs of electricity. Discipline was fierce, and, if prisoners didn't obey orders immediately, they would be beaten.

During Palden's sentence, eighteen people committed suicide, some of them by throwing themselves under the wheels of a truck. Others died from weakness after hard labour or from illness. There was a special graveyard for the 'black caps' called Fulo Dhotoe (*fulo* means 'black cap').[14]

Palden was also assigned to work in a carpet factory. Lost in contemplation, he occasionally runs his hands over radiators or armchairs, carefully examining the texture. 'Making carpets was more bearable than all the other hard labour,' he says. 'My drawing was quite good and so I was allowed to create patterns for the carpets. I was also involved in spinning and dyeing. Some of the officials used my carpets to furnish their accommodation and they brought me small gifts.' Palden was paid a small salary of 16 yuan, which had to cover his own salt, wheat, flour and clothes as well as the cost of electricity. It was always a temptation to spend most of the money on food at the beginning of the month, but prisoners who did this ended up starving at the end of the month before their next payment.

During his sentence Palden suffered regular physical beatings and mental torture. He was also punished for trying to escape, and for continuing to defy Chinese rule in Tibet. On one occasion he was suspended above an open fire with another prisoner. 'We were suspended from the ceiling by our arms, which were tied behind our backs,' says Palden. He puts his hands behind his back and attempts to contort himself into this position to demonstrate. 'We were left like this for a few hours and beaten. A fire was lit underneath us which scorched our skin. The worst torture was when they beat me with an electric baton, sticking it into my mouth so that I lost my teeth. The pain was like someone pumping you inside out. It was unbearable. I blacked out, and fell down. I was lying in a pool of blood, broken teeth and shit. I still remember the name of the man who tortured me. He was called Pancho, and he was Tibetan. This method of making Tibetans torture other Tibetans is a Chinese policy. I feel no grudge towards this man. He was doing it because he had to do so.' Palden wipes his eyes, this time with a red napkin from the table. 'To survive these things, your mind has to be like an iron column, and your thinking ability as big as a mountain.'

A younger generation of Tibetans is now making similar sacrifices for the sake of their religious and cultural identity. The prison population includes those who have spoken out or demonstrated in favour of Tibetan independence, monks arrested for rebuilding their monasteries, and nuns who have been imprisoned for singing nationalist or Buddhist songs. There are currently more than seven hundred known political prisoners in Tibet: 1995 saw the most arrests for five years.[15] This figure also includes children and teenagers, some of them as young as 12 years, who have been detained and imprisoned for taking part in demonstrations. Tibetan children accused of political offences have been tortured or ill-treated, held with adult prisoners, and forced to do hard labour.[16]

Punishments of Tibetan political prisoners are often more severe than punishments of Chinese dissidents; they often receive longer sentences for 'counter-revolutionary crimes' which would not merit the same in China. There are also reports that Tibetan prisoners are often allocated to repetitive, demanding hard labour in the camps while Chinese prisoners are channelled into skilled work with better conditions.

A slight-looking 29-year-old monk called Bagdro was once one of those young monks who sacrificed his freedom for his political cause.

Bagdro is now living in Dharamsala, following his release from Drapchi prison in April 1991. He had escaped across the mountains to India 'with the help of Palden Lhamo', Divine Protectress of Tibet. He still suffers from tuberculosis, and is still scarred and in pain after torture with electric prods and handcuffs so tight that they caused the blood vessels in his fingers to burst.[17]

Bagdro is one of a generation of young Tibetans who gained political awareness by joining a monastery, and, later, in prison. He said: 'I grew up in an environment in which people did not dare to tell their children the true history of Tibet. The most profound difference wearing monastic robes made for me was that for the first time I became aware of what was happening in Tibet.'

In 1986, Bagdro pulled a curtain across the window of his room at Ganden monastery, made sure the door was double-locked and, by the light of a candle, read the Dalai Lama's autobiography, *My Land and My People*. If he had been found with the book, he would have been sent to prison. He says: 'From this book and from the scriptures, I realized that Tibet has no human rights. I also realized that having no responsibility for a wife or children it was my time now to do something for Tibet even if this meant sacrificing my life.'

Monks and nuns in Tibet have a tradition of political activism: their vows of celibacy enable them to sacrifice their lives without fear of abandoning parental or family responsibility. It is also believed that dying in the selfless act of campaigning for independence ensures rebirth in the next life as a human being, rather than as a lower form of life such as an animal. A young Drepung monk once told Tibetologist and sociologist Ronald Schwartz:

> The Chinese are saying that we have freedom of religious faith and so on . . . But we need real freedom. Through freedom we can make preparations not only for this life, but work for the future lives to come. As the Chinese reject the existence of future lives, that is a difficult point. If one is only talking of freedom to eat and drink, it doesn't have much significance. That can be done by any animal such as a dog or a cat . . . To be human has a deeper meaning.[18]

The expression of freedom carries a constant risk to Tibetan monks' and nuns' earthly existence. Monasteries are peopled by security police, often posing as monks, and there are often intensive 're-education' campaigns.[19] A common pattern in monasteries, nunneries, and the wider Tibetan community is for suspected activists to be watched for several weeks, months or even years, evidence collated, and an arrest made. In this way Chinese security police build up a picture of independence activities and the network of participants.

For Bagdro, an opportunity to express his dissent against Chinese rule arose during the Monlam prayer festival in March 1988. Bagdro led a group of monks starting to chant pro-independence slogans as they came into the Barkor (heart of old Lhasa). Bagdro also flung stones at Chinese taking video film from above, and using ordinary cameras at street level. Around two to four thousand monks were involved, and later in the day several thousand lay Tibetans joined the protests. The main movers behind the demonstrations were the Ganden monks.

Bagdro recalls: 'The Chinese opened fire. I had lost all fear. I was very angry. Bullets were coming very close to me. A Khampa [eastern Tibetan] right beside me was shot in the head. We broke into Chinese businesses and burned their products. We chased the Chinese away and told them to go home . . . Some monks were seized . . . I saw Chinese beating and kicking them with sticks and metal bars. They tied them up and threw them into trucks like stones.'

Bagdro was hit on the head by a stone thrown by a Chinese soldier, and he ran for cover between two buildings. A group of soldiers on the buildings above him rolled a boulder from the roof. 'This came straight down on to me and would have crushed me, but a very strong woman suddenly caught hold of me and pulled me back so that the boulder just missed me,' says Bagdro. When he turned around to see who the woman was, there was no one in sight. He believes she was Palden Lhamo, the spiritual deity reputed to protect Tibet and its people.

When he discovered that the Chinese were looking for him, Bagdro went on the run. He slept under a stall at Lhasa market; traders helped him to disguise himself as a woman, with earrings, lipstick and a dress. All of his friends had been arrested and imprisoned. Bagdro was on his own. It was only when he heard that the police were closing in on his family that he decided to go home. He could not bear his family suffering for his actions. 'Early on 17 April, I went home. I met my family and the villagers; all my family were crying. I got there at 6 a.m. on the 17th. At 8.30 a.m. on the 18th the Chinese came.'

Bagdro was arrested, clamped into self-tightening handcuffs and taken to Gutsa detention centre. The interrogation began the next morning. During interrogation, Bagdro was tortured by one Tibetan and one Chinese. 'The questioning was very aggressive,' he says. 'The gun was slammed on the table . . . They wanted to know if I was part of a pro-independence organization in the monastery, and if I had any connections outside Tibet . . . When I said I hadn't, the Chinese stuck the electric baton in my mouth. It made my mouth bleed. He also shoved it on my face and down my chest. Both the Tibetan and Chinese man kicked me several times. The Tibetan was a bit less brutal. The Chinese man stuck cigarette ends in my face.'

When Bagdro refused to reveal names of other monks involved in the demonstration, he was pressed against a wall and kicked in the stomach so hard that he began to vomit and bleed from his mouth and nose. When he lost consciousness, they poured water over him, then picked him up and smashed his head against the wall. When he still wouldn't give the information his interrogators wanted, he was left hanging by his wrists for twelve hours. Electric prods were applied to his neck, below his ears, and he was beaten with rods. Bagdro begged his torturers to kill him. He lost consciousness and, when he revived, could not walk.

On the seventh day after his arrest, he was so hungry owing to deprivation of food as a punishment that he took his vest off, tore it and began to eat it. He also ate a *tin momo* (a small Tibetan dumpling) which had been excreted whole in a toilet bowl.

Bagdro's recollections of his torture are excruciating in their detail. He remembers the types of metalled boots worn by his interrogators; the feelings he experienced while hanging by his wrists all through the night until sunrise; the type of pain produced by an electric prod. ('A vibration goes through your body. It gets very hot inside and you feel that you are losing consciousness. It is also very painful.') He remembers the day he was given some potatoes from fellow prisoners because he was being given nothing to eat by prison guards. And he remembers screaming for his mother when the Tibetan and the Chinese interrogator crushed his hands underneath their metalled boots.

After a month Bagdro could not cope with the torture any longer, so he confessed to hitting a policeman with an iron bar. His captors wrote out this confession, and Bagdro and five other Tibetans were accused of being the leaders of the demonstration and being responsible for killing the policeman. Only three days before the court appearance, Bagdro and his co-defendants were given the charge sheet. They were told they could appoint a representative each, but they feared that any representative would come under undue pressure from the Chinese, so did not ask for one. There was no mention of any lawyers. Bagdro says: '[During the hearing] my confession was mentioned and I said right away that it was taken under torture. However, I was prevented from speaking further. We all managed to get out that our statements were under torture . . . Before we had been taken from the prison to the court, just before we left, we had been told not to say anything about the beating . . . We were taken out by a side entrance to the outside. There we were heavily beaten [by soldiers] . . . I was convicted of killing a policeman, throwing stones at the police and taking part in a demonstration . . . When we went back to prison we were told that we had ten days to write down our complaints.' Bagdro did not do so; he knew it would be useless. The rejection of the others' complaints came back twenty days later in writing.[20]

As the most junior of the six Tibetans accused of involvement in the murder, Bagdro was sentenced to three years, first in Gutsa detention centre and then in Drapchi prison, from 14 April 1988. He was greeted with respect from other prisoners, who called him *kusho*, a respectful way of addressing monks. Bagdro was put to labour, which was mainly splitting rocks and laying bricks. The ordinary Tibetan prisoners were so proud of him that they would not let him work. Local people in Lhasa brought meat, butter and *tsampa* (roasted barley) for the political prisoners, which they shared out with the rest of the prisoners. The authorities told the other prisoners that they were eating 'the food of the undesirables'. By 1989, 85 political prisoners had been moved in, and they were moved to a new block after officials decided they were 'infecting' the other inmates. Every month, during political study sessions, Bagdro and other counter-revolutionaries were forced to endure haranguing by officials on their 'splittist' activities.[21] All the political prisoners had to go for a run around a playing field from 6 to 8.30 a.m. The elderly and the ill had to run, too, and if they couldn't keep up the pace guards used the electric prod on their anus.

Just before Bagdro's release from prison on 9 April 1991, some of the political prisoners were preparing for a demonstration after the visit of an American delegation. 'I wanted to join,' says Bagdro. 'I said that we were all in this together, and we should win or lose together. However, the other political prisoners said that I should not do this as my prison term was nearly over. I should go out and make known to the world what was happening at the prisons. Everybody was crying when we discussed this. They told me that my job was to try and escape to India or otherwise do my best to make known what was happening. I was released ten days later.' Bagdro did escape to India, again, disguised as a woman ('Women have played a very special role in my life,' he says).

Prisoners like Bagdro who are allowed to leave at the end of their sentence are in a minority in Tibet. Most inmates of China's 'Siberia', Qinghai, are forced to remain in the camps after the completion of the sentence. Qinghai is the Chinese name for the former Tibetan province of Amdo. Before the Chinese invasion, Tibet – which is about as big as western Europe and roughly a quarter of the size of China – was made up of three vast regions: U-Tsang, Kham in the north-east and Amdo in the north, bordering Xinjiang and Gansu. Under the Chinese, U-Tsang became the Tibet Autonomous Region (TAR), known to the Chinese as simply Tibet. Kham became absorbed into the province of Sichuan. The area the Tibetans call Tibet is more than three times the size of the TAR at 3.8 million square kilometres.

Since 1952, forced labour prisoners have been sent to Qinghai, where about sixty per cent of them stay on after their release.[22] Tibetans are still sent today to the Qinghai camps from Lhasa and other parts of Tibet. Although a Qinghai official has said that the province has not accepted prisoners from other provinces since 1985, former prisoners, Chinese officials and other sources state the opposite. One prisoner interviewed by the International Campaign for Tibet, Thapgey Gyamtso, was transferred to the hydroelectric brick factory outside the capital, Xining, in 1988. Xining is a city that is essentially built around labour camps, and prison labour has become a mainstay of the region's economy.[23] Members of an Eisenhower Foundation delegation to China and Tibet were told by officials that 'Some serious repeaters are sent to Qinghai'.[24] Wei Jingsheng was held at Tangkarmo in Qinghai for seven years.

Prisoners in Qinghai work in brick factories, in massive agricultural enterprises and on the development of an infrastructure of roads and railways. There is also worrying evidence that they are used as labourers in China's nuclear development programme.[25] Nuclear missiles are stationed on the Tibetan plateau on at least three sites: Delingha, Da Qaidam and Xiao Qaidam.[26] Prisoners in Qinghai, Xinjiang and Jiangxi provinces excavate radioactive ore, and there are also reports that prisoners are forced to enter nuclear test sites to perform dangerous work.[27]

Tibet is known as the 'treasure-house' in China because of its rich natural and mineral resources. Since 1959, more than a quarter of Tibet's mineral resources have been extracted.[28] According to the official Chinese news agency, Xinhua, 126 types of minerals, with major deposits of uranium, lithium, bauxite, borax, chromite, copper, gold, iron and silver have been identified in Tibet by the Chinese. China is already short of natural resources, and within the next decade seven of the fifteen key staple minerals essential to its economy will run out. This indicates that the plunder of Tibet's natural riches will continue.

Both Tibetan and Chinese prisoners are forced to work in gold mines across the country. Tsering Dorje, a 31-year-old Tibetan farmer who escaped to India after working in a gold mine called Gatha, 30 kilometres east of Kanze on the road to Chengdu in Sichuan, testified to miserable and bleak working conditions in the mines, with little concern for safety.[29] Tsering was sent to the gold mines in eastern Tibet in April 1992, after being arrested for putting up posters advocating independence for Tibet in his home village. Every day, each man had a certain quota of earth and ore to dig, and all the earth and rock extracted had to be carried to the surface in baskets on the back. There were no machines, and no one could stop work until the quota was fulfilled. Those who could not work quickly had to go on digging until 11 p.m. or even midnight.

Food for all the prisoners was extremely poor: Tsering and his colleagues were given one piece of steamed bread and some boiled vegetables for lunch and even more meagre quantities for the rest of the day. They were beaten frequently, and guards used electric prods on prisoners if they complained or didn't work. When the guards had been drinking, they would sometimes beat the prisoners just for fun.

Many Tibetans were allowed extra food, brought in by relatives. But some of those without friends or family nearby – particularly the Chinese prisoners – attempted to kill themselves by swallowing nails or stabbing themselves in the stomach. Tsering recalls: 'Many Chinese cut off their fingers to avoid work. Tibetans tried to give the Chinese a little food secretly but didn't have much to give. Some prisoners, both Tibetans and Chinese, became so desperate that they deliberately broke their own legs or even smashed their heads open with their picks or shovels.'

Tsering also claims that the guards, who were mostly Chinese with a few Tibetans, helped to hasten the end of those who were on their last legs by brutal beatings. Sometimes they would even break the limbs or poke out an eye of those prisoners who could no longer work fast enough and were holding up production.

Political prisoners attempting to escape the mines were liable for the death penalty. However, this did not stop many of them making a bid for freedom, and it did not stop Tsering. He seized his chance one afternoon, when he asked a new guard on duty for permission to go and fetch some coal from the power house to boil up some tea. The new guard did not know he was a 'political' and so had to be watched. He allowed him to go outside the wire to the power house, and Tsering knew this was his chance. Behind the power house was a mountain covered in forest; Tsering had spied out the lie of the land from the truck when they were being taken off to work in the gold mines, and decided that the forest was the best route of escape. Tsering crossed the stream and entered the trees. With nothing but a ball of *tsampa* dough in each pocket, he began to climb the mountain through the trees, often knee-deep in snow. He escaped into India after an arduous trek of nearly two thousand miles through the highest mountains in the world. The complete story of Tsering's journey has to remain untold. He explains: 'It has to be passed over almost in silence, for nobody escapes entirely without help and the monster is as ready as ever for fresh victims.'

Most prisoners in Qinghai serve their entire sentences without the opportunity of escape. And when they are released, many prisoners settle in the province with their families,[30] thus causing concern among human rights groups about the numbers of the immigrant Chinese population on the northern Tibetan plateau.[31]

Bagdro now lives in a simple room in a compound attached to the Buddhist Institute of Dialectics in Dharamsala. He keeps a cardboard box full of pictures of his recent visit to Europe beside his bed. There are photos of him with Danielle Mitterrand, wife of the former French President and a keen supporter of the Tibetan cause in Paris, and with supporters all over Europe. He has several Sony Walkmans and expensive watches sent to him by people he met in Britain and France. The enthusiastic reception he received during his travels in Europe (there were press conferences, addresses to the House of Commons, throngs of people who wanted to hear his story, and gifts showered on him), and his frequent Western visitors set him slightly apart from other monks at the Institute. The contrast between his life in prison, his new role as a spokesperson on human rights in Tibet and the simple monk's life expected of him now could hardly be greater. It has been hard for him to retain a sense of perspective.

Like that of many Tibetan monks, both in exile and in their home country, Bagdro's study of Buddhism is being neglected in favour of a greater struggle. This struggle has become the focus of his life and his rage, and Buddhism a method of healing. 'In my mind,' he says, 'Political struggle and religious practice became the same thing because they are about the welfare of the people. Buddhism is a very strong element of Tibet − it is interdependent with the culture. We have a Buddhist identity. And if we don't care about the political struggle in Tibet, there will be no religion, and so our culture will disappear.'

Robert Ford, an Englishman who has been accepted as an 'honorary Tibetan' by the Dalai Lama, knows that young Tibetans, like Bagdro, will continue their struggle for independence, even in exile, and at immense personal cost within Tibet. To prove it, Ford has first-hand experience of imprisonment by the Chinese after working with Tibetans.

When the 'people's army' 'liberated' Tibet in 1949-50, Ford was working as a radio officer for the government of Tibet. He was captured when the People's Liberation Army invaded Kham, where he was working, and held in prison for five years, accused of espionage, anti-Communist propaganda and murder. His book *Captured in Tibet* gives a graphic description of the methods of repression, both mental and physical, used in Chinese prisons.[32] Ford says: 'The Chinese just don't realize the strength of Tibetan religious imperviousness. I remember the

Dalai Lama once saying that he pitied the poor Church of the Western world because we only have one lifetime in which to work on our spirituality. The comment was made as a joke, but there's a lot of truth in it. The commitment of the Tibetans to their cause is, to say the least, long-term.'

Notes

1. The longest sentence in the Soviet gulag is believed to be 35 years; this miserable record is held by Balys Gajauskas, who was imprisoned for taking part in the Lithuanian resistance to the absorption of his country in the Soviet Union, and then later for 'planning to translate Solzhenitsyn's *The Gulag Archipelago*'.

2. By the end of his visit, Palden had a full set of false teeth after several visits to a London dentist.

3. Written with Tsering Shakya and to be published by Harvill in 1997.

4. 'The Chinese prisoners must have been Buddhist,' one lama said, referring to the comradeship between both Chinese and Tibetan prisoners in the cell during his recent imprisonment (Tibet Information Network, testimony of the lama 'MM').

5. Tibet Information Network.

6. Susan Whitfield (ed.), *After the Event, Human Rights and Their Future in China*. It is worth remembering that we in the West are not above this form of dehumanization, particularly when engaged in warfare. The language of dehumanization was particularly evident in some sections of the national media when referring to Iraqis during the Gulf War or Argentinians during the Falklands conflict. A US soldier typified this attitude when he said: 'I enjoyed the shooting and killing. I was literally turned on when I saw a gook get shot. When a GI got shot, even if I didn't know him . . . that would bother me. A GI was real. But if a gook got killed, it was like me going out here and stepping on a roach' (Mark Baker, quoted in Sam Keen, *Faces of the Enemy: Reflections of the Hostile Imagination*).

7. John Ackerly, Director, International Campaign for Tibet. Also see 'The Reforms Revisited: The Implementation of Chinese Economic Policy and the Future of Rural Producers in Tibet', a paper presented to the International Association for Tibetan Studies held in Austria in June 1995, written by Tibetologist and sociologist Ronald Schwartz.

8. John Ackerly, interview.

9. John Avedon, *Exile from the Land of the Snows*.

10. *Ibid.*, p. 251.

11. Cannibalism was reported in other areas of China during this period and also during the Cultural Revolution. Some evidence has only just come to light: for a harrowing account of cannibalism in south-west China during the Cultural Revolution, see Zheng Yi's book *Red Monument*. Dissident Zheng Yi unearthed secret but official documents, which list the 'different forms of eating human flesh'. These included: 'Killing and then having a feast, cutting up together but eating separately, baking human liver to make medicine, etc.' In one instance, a raiding party seized three brothers and knifed them to death. Their bodies were then carried down to the river, where the gang removed their livers and cut off their penises to eat them. The bodies were then thrown into the river. This was called 'the great victory of the people's proletarian dictatorship'. Harry Wu also recalls an incident of cannibalism in his memoirs, *Bitter Winds*. After the execution of a prisoner, Yang, for 'stubbornness and refusing to reform', the executioner had scooped out Yang's brains and given them to one of the mine captains called Li,

whose 70-year-old father had eaten them for their medicinal qualities.

12. The International Commission of Jurists, quoted in Avedon, *Exile from the Land of the Snows*. A 23-year-old nun, Zimpa Pharmo, reported a recent incidence of 'crucifixion'. Zimpa, who is now living in exile in Dharamsala, was arrested for taking part in a pro-independence demonstration in Lhasa. During her interrogation, her captors showed her a film of a young monk being crucified. 'He was shouting for freedom while they were doing it. Then they poured kerosene on him and set him alight. The soldiers clapped when he died and the film ended . . . I was forced to watch the film every day for the next three days' (interview with Vanessa Baird, *The New Internationalist*, no. 274, December 1995).

13. Avedon, *Exile from the Land of the Snows*, p. 291.

14. Another prisoner, who was imprisoned from 1978 until 1990, recalled that the Chinese were pleased when one of the 'black caps' died: 'I remember that the Chinese used to comment when a prisoner died: "This is very good! Ha! Ha! One of the black hats is dead! We shouldn't let these prisoners out. They would be like a black spot in the white milk. All the milk would be spoilt."' The prisoner, Tsewang (not his real name), who was interviewed by Dalha Tsering and Louise Fournier in Dharamsala in 1994, said that dead prisoners were carried to an area called Miro Lhungpa (land of the corpses) and were left there for the birds to eat. When many Tibetans were released from prison, they lost everything – not only their families but also their livelihood. When Tsewang returned to his village after his release to reclaim his field and his house, he got only a wall. 'I was told that as I am "fourth stage of black hat" I could not have my land. I went to the bank for a loan, but they said I was a criminal and refused to give me a loan.' Tsewang finally escaped to Nepal across the border.

15. Robbie Barnett, Tibet Information Network.

16. A juvenile section reportedly exists in Gutsa detention centre in Lhasa. However, juvenile political detainees held there for investigation, or with an administrative sentence, are reportedly never kept in this section. Instead, they are mixed with adult political prisoners. Juveniles at Drapchi are reportedly held with adult political prisoners (Amnesty International, *Persistent Human Rights Violations in Tibet*, ASA 17/18/95, p. 23). Sherab Ngawang was 12 at the time of her arrest on 3 February 1992 duing a peaceful demonstration in Lhasa. A novice from Michungri nunnery, Sherab was taken to Gutsa detention centre, where she stayed for at least 2 months awaiting trial. She was reported to have been beaten during detention. Sherab was reportedly sentenced to three years' 're-education through labour' in May 1992 (*ibid.*).

17. Bagdro's story is compiled from an interview with the author and a Tibet Information Network testimony, *Account by Bagdro of Torture and Imprisonment, 1989–91*.

18. Quoted in *The New Internationalist* special issue on Tibet (December 1995).

19. Two monks formerly of Tashilunpo monastery who recently escaped to India bore testimony to China's interference in Tibetan religious life. They claimed that the Chinese authorities have placed the monks of Tashilunpo monastery under heavy surveillance, with 'work teams' moving into the monastery to start a campaign of denunciation of the Dalai Lama and 're-education' of the monks (Department of Information and International Relations, the Tibetan government in exile, *World Tibet News*, 9 January 1996).

20. Amnesty International, *Persistent Human Rights Violations in Tibet*, ASA 17/18/95, p. 13.

21. That is, their counter-revolutionary belief that Tibet should be 'split' from the Motherland.

22. Tibet Information Network, *Labour Camps in China: Notes on Qinghai Prison Economy* (source reference: 1KT/FX). Two

prisoners, Ama Adhi and Rinchen Samdup, said they were made to stay on after their sentences because they were 'fourth stage of black hat' and should not be allowed to mix with the 'white' (pure) public outside.

23. Harry Wu has reported that one of the city's main streets, Nandajie, or South Avenue, is full of distribution outlet offices for all the factories and agricultural-processing enterprises that are attached to these prisons.

24. Eisenhower Delegation, 1987, p. 37.

25. For further information on China's nuclear programme in Tibet, see the International Campaign for Tibet's 1993 report, *Nuclear Tibet*.

26. See the International Campaign for Tibet, *Environment and Development News*, November 1995.

27. Harry Wu, *Laogai*, p. 35.

28. UNIDO, 1994.

29. This testimony was given to Tibet Information Network.

30. It is extremely difficult in the People's Republic of China to have a rural household registration changed to an urban one. However, when prisoners are sent to remote wasteland areas such as Qinghai province, officials will actively facilitate the influx of families with rural household registration in order to encourage immigration into such areas.

31. An independent survey claims that there are now more Chinese in Tibet than Tibetans: 5.0 to 5.5 million Chinese compared with 4.2 million Tibetans (Mike Wills, Anders Hojmark Anderson and Sarah Cooke, *The New Majority* (London: Tibet Support Group, 1995). The Dalai Lama has described this worrying phenomenon as 'intentional or unintentional genocide' on the part of the Chinese.

32. Robert Ford, *Captured in Tibet*. Subsequent quotations from author interview.

CHAPTER 14

Sexual Reform and Pseudo-Boys
Women in the *Laogai*

A woman's virginity is more important than her life.

Survey on women's status, 1990[1]

A string quartet plays delicately in the background as elegant waiters bearing cocktails glide as if on coasters through the coffee lobby of the Peninsula Hotel in Hong Kong. 'Of course, every new prisoner in a Chinese jail is given a body check for sexual diseases,' Miss Zhang is saying. 'And women are usually tested for pregnancy.' Miss Zhang is a pale, pretty woman, elegantly dressed in a cheesecloth blouse, silk skirt and spiky pearl earrings, who looks younger than her 37 years. She sits with her arms folded across her stomach, clutching her handbag. Because of the insecurity of her position in Hong Kong, she does not want her identity to be revealed. The government is giving her temporary shelter, although, as a former political prisoner and writer on an anti-Communist magazine, Zhang fears that she will be arrested again when the Chinese take over the colony in 1997.

She is telling the story of a fellow prisoner held in the same jail during her six-year sentence from 1984 to 1990. 'In 1986, we were labouring on a prison farm,' says Zhang. 'One of the women was very fat, and seemed to be getting fatter every day. We were puzzled because the environment was very harsh, and we had very little food. We thought the woman had a disease, because she was always hungrier than the rest of us, the whole time. One day we heard a loud scream from the toilet, which was basically just a large hole in the ground. One of the women had found a baby in the toilet. The fat woman was lying unconscious beside the baby, which was curled up in the dirt, kicking its legs.'

The guard who was responsible for managing the jail was summoned immediately by the troop leader. When the guard saw the baby lying in a prisoner's arms, she ordered her to kill it immediately. Zhang was furious. 'I told the official that, if the baby was killed, it would be an illegal act and

I would report her to the authorities. I told her that if she killed the baby, the baby's mother would kill her and all her family members.' The guard finally conceded to her point of view. The baby was wrapped in a cloth and sent to hospital, together with its mother. 'When the mother came back to the prison, she liked me very much,' says Zhang. After this incident, the prison management called a conference in order to establish who was responsible for the body check of prisoners. The mother of the baby had slipped through the net; generally pregnancy tests were given to new prisoners.

Although the Chinese Procedure Law stipulates that medical body checks of prisoners should be carried out by a woman or a doctor, medical examinations are sometimes used to abuse and humiliate women detainees.[2] Amnesty International reports on such an examination of eighteen female members of the Jesus Family while they were detained at Weishan County detention centre, Shandong province, from July to September 1992. Each woman was forced to undergo an intimate medical examination in the presence of male police officers. One of them reported:

> Since most of us women were unmarried and young, we cried with indignation and anger. After undergoing the forced physical examinations we were sent back to the detention centre. Several sisters felt very humiliated and angry and became suicidal. For a few days they did not eat anything at all. What is worse, the head of the County Public Security Bureau humiliated us further by saying that if any of us were found pregnant, we would be sent to the hospital and forced to have an abortion.[3]

Although regulations specifically prohibit the detention of pregnant women, practice in China proves otherwise. In 1990, prisoners in Huanghua prison in Guangzhou reported sharing a cell with a woman who was at least six months pregnant. In Tibet, Damchoe Pemo miscarried a week after she had been made to stand for twelve hours, tortured with electric batons and deprived of food and sleep in Seitru prison in 1993.[4]

Chinese population control policies state that, in most regions, urban couples may have only one child unless their child is disabled, while rural couples are allowed to have two babies if the first is a girl. A third child is 'prohibited' in most available regulations. Regulations covering migrant women indicate that abortion is mandatory if the woman does not return to her home region. Unmarried women are also required to have abortions if they become pregnant.

If a prisoner is found to be pregnant 'illegally' (above the quota), Zhang reports that they will be sent for an abortion, or the child will be put out for adoption. In the tea plantation where she was held for five years, official policy allowed many male prisoners who were 'reforming well' to return to their towns and villages for home visits once a year. 'Female prisoners did not have this privilege,' says Zhang. 'The authorities were too afraid that they would get pregnant. For the same reason, female prisoners were kept away from the men.'

There were other opportunities for pregnancy, however, the main one being sexual relations with male guards. Former prisoner Mo Lihua, who was imprisoned in Changsha for nearly two years, recalls how one woman was being held in detention, and told that she would be charged with prostitution. A male guard made a deal with her: if she slept with him, she would be released. The woman decided to do so, but another prisoner found out about it. The police officer was sacked, and the woman was kept in detention. From then on, the policeman's friends used her for sex when they wanted.

For many women presented with such a choice, the element of free will is decidedly absent. Zhang recalls how some women prisoners used to seduce male guards with the intention of earning merit points and gaining an early release or better treatment. 'They wouldn't necessarily give sexual favours, but they would do things like washing a guard's clothes or other personal things,' she says. 'If they did this and the guard liked them, they would be looked after and nothing bad would happen to them.'

Zhang was not aware of any cases of rape or sexual assault in the prison or detention centre where she was held. Throughout China, few cases of rape are reported involving prison officials and women in detention – although the authorities are aware that sexual abuse within prisons does exist.[5] In some local detention centres and 'shelter and investigation' units, however, rape appears to be a serious problem. Amnesty International has received reports from female political prisoners that cellmates have been raped and abused by male inmates in pre-trial detention centres in the southern provinces. One woman reported being raped in 1985, when she was 13, by an official at a repatriation centre for migrants in Fujian province.[6]

Many reports of sexual torture come from Chinese-occupied Tibet. In the early years following the 'peaceful liberation', rape and other forms of abuse were common in Tibetan prisons. Former prisoner Adhi Tapey, who now lives in exile in Dharamsala, India, says: 'Young and attractive women prisoners were often called by the warden to clean his own rooms and do the laundry. They were also repeatedly raped. I was one of these women . . . We used to be called in rotation and raped. As a precaution against getting pregnant, we were forced to drink musk water immediately after the intercourse. If we resisted, we were threatened with harsh punishments, even death. There was no way other than to obey and keep silent.'[7]

Today, female prisoners in prisons, labour camps and detention centres in Tibet and China report the use of electric prods on breasts, thighs and genitals. They recall beatings with sticks, rifle butts and leather belts, and, sometimes, dogs being set upon naked women. One Tibetan woman, Dawa Langzom, reported having her nipple cut and her toe stabbed with a pair of sharp scissors after being arrested for demonstrating in Tibet seven years previously.[8] Zhang recalls seeing female prisoners made to stand in a line, then being beaten by male inmates with their belts.

Often, the more accepted aspects of prison life are traumatic. Zhang recalls her discomfort at the lack of privacy during the early months of her detention. 'I wasn't allowed to close my window, and there was a small window in the door too, so I was constantly watched,' she says. 'I was watched even when I changed my clothes or took a bath.'

Zhang was born in the province of Guizhou, in the southern heart of China, and later moved to the Portuguese enclave of Macau, which is less than an hour from Hong Kong by jetfoil or high-speed ferry. Her parents were both fiercely Communist and proud of the Party. But Zhang began to see cracks in the ideology when she was growing up, and in 1979 she went to her first democracy demonstration on the mainland. Her political awareness grew, and she soon began to write articles about the 'Beijing spring' movement.

Zhang was arrested in 1983, while returning to Guizhou from Macau to see relatives. Customs officials confiscated a tape she had in her possession: a Cantonese opera cassette sung by Deng Lijun. Possession of this tape was later quoted as one of the reasons for her imprisonment. During Zhang's sentence, to encourage her to reform her thoughts, officials used both 'hard' and 'soft' tactics. They offered her fruit and sweets, and, if this didn't work, they put her in handcuffs and leg shackles and tortured her with electric batons. But the most painful and unpleasant part of her prison experience was undertaken in the name of 'medical tests'. Zhang claims it was merely torture.

'They told me I had a disease of the brains, and that they wanted to do some tests,' she recalls. Zhang had been suffering from diarrhoea, and had asked for some medicine. She also suffered from high blood pressure. She was taken into hospital, and she remembers waking up one morning lying on her side surrounded by medical staff with masks. Previous nursing training gave Zhang an idea what was happening as she watched. 'One of them was holding a large syringe and expelling the air from it,' she says. 'In the syringe was a transparent colourless liquid. I felt behind me and found a swab attached to my back. I tried to call out but I couldn't. My right hand was handcuffed to the bed, and two male uniformed Public Security guards were sitting at the door. I guessed that they had extracted spinal fluid, since normal treatment and medicine cannot reduce pressure inside the skull, which is what they intended to do.'

Zhang had no choice but to lie there, waiting for her cranial pressure to return to normal. She felt too intimidated by the guards to ask to go to the toilet or to move. 'I was sustained by my faith,' says Zhang, who became a Catholic in 1981. 'I lay there, singing a psalm and praying.' Zhang knew that removal of spinal fluid can cause long-lasting splitting headaches, loss of memory, insomnia and other symptoms. It is difficult to ascertain whether prison doctors were carrying out a routine tissue sample by removing spinal fluid for medical reasons or whether they deliberately intended to create more discomfort for Zhang. She believes the latter. Certainly, her treatment in hospital amounts to a form of torture: she was handcuffed to the bed, intimidated by male guards, isolated and given no choice about her treatment.

Further reference to suspicious 'medical tests' is made in a recent official brochure produced by Shanghai Number One prison which is a glowing testimony to the 'transformation and reform' of individual prisoners in the prison's 'Ninth Brigade'. The document boasts of a medical treatment unit which has recently been set up specially for female 'sex criminals'. In this centre, doctors and prison police can help to reform sex criminals by both 'medical and educational methods'. Their targets are women who are 'very sexually active or too sexually inclined'; hence they need medical, rather than simply spiritual, treatment. Many of these women will have been arrested for prostitution, or may have been caught engaging in lesbian activities within the prison. According to the document, prison doctors have reached some surprising conclusions:

Results of the test showed that the mental state of the women sex criminals was not healthy, due to the sex hormones (ji su) . . . These hormones make a person sexually more active and more vulnerable to commit crime . . . The women being studied secreted more of these hormones than other women.

An example is given of a woman called Mao Meifen who had been sentenced to eight years in 1983 on charges of robbery and prostitution. Because of Mao Meifen's 'frequent lesbian activities', she was sentenced to an additional year in prison in 1988. However, with the help of the sex correction centre, Mao Meifen was soon on the right path. She happily consented to treatment, according to the document, and was given various pills to control her 'sex hormones'. After half a year doctors concluded that the physical abnormalities had been straightened out, and her physical condition was 'normal'. Mao Meifen proved her return to 'normality' by writing a series of frank self-confessions, admitting that her whole life had been a series of criminal activities.

Another prisoner, Li Shuzhen, had been sentenced to eleven years on charges of prostitution and for inducing women to prostitution. After a period in the correction centre, she began to confess her crimes, and she also revealed that her stepfather had sexually assaulted her when she was young and that this was the reason for her behaviour.

'These reforms are a great achievement,' boasts the document. The success of the centre was infectious: in April 1990 new groups were apparently set up for the prisoners to study painting, literary appreciation and knitting, in order to 'cultivate their characters'. Figures showed that seventeen women prisoners gained a reduction of their sentence, and 97 per cent of the women prisoners gained a 'recorded appraisal of their labour activities'.

The fragments of information given in this brochure do not give a clear picture of the real nature of the 'Sexual Crimes Correction Centre'. However the 'scientific' conclusions seem flimsy at best, and testimonies of former prisoners and other evidence indicate that prisoners probably have little choice about undergoing the treatment. In the words of a famous Chinese saying, this official account 'takes all the weeds out and leaves the flowers'.

The humourless propaganda in this document also indicates a discriminatory approach to the 'abnormalities' of female sexuality which is reflected in the wider Chinese society. One official survey estimated that 90 per cent of crimes committed by juvenile females are 'sex crimes'.[9] These can range from prostitution of a professional kind to a woman sentenced to four years for sleeping with two men and telling each of them that she loved him.[10] Other sex crimes include adultery, bigamy, 'hooliganism' (which can include having sexual relations with foreigners when the effect on society is judged to be damaging) and 'destroying a soldier's marriage'. Many women are the victims of their husband's actions: Zhang recalls meeting a prisoner who had been sentenced after her husband forced her to have sex with another man for money. Often, if a man is arrested for political reasons, his wife, mother, girlfriend or colleague will be imprisoned too. Tong Yi, assistant to Wei Jingsheng, was sentenced to two and a half years of re-education through labour without being charged or tried. She had already spent eight months in detention following her arrest on 4 April 1994 after informing journalists of Wei's arrest, which she had witnessed.

When the Communist Party took over in 1949, it outlawed footbinding and the purchase of child brides and concubines, and Mao declared that 'women hold up half the sky'. Young women in China today no longer hobble around with 'lotus feet' but they still suffer an inferior status which has led to the murder of thousands of baby girls every year. (This attitude is reflected in the recent description of a woman who did so well in her work that she is regarded as a 'pseudo-boy'.)[11]

A 1990 survey on women's status revealed that nearly 70 per cent of all respondents agreed with the statement that 'a woman's virginity is more important than her life'. Just as ideology came before humanity in the Mao years, so this ideal of perceived purity is now judged to be superior to women's lives. This widespread attitude, prevalent among women as well as men, has led to a stigma which has discouraged women from reporting rape and sexual assault: often women who have done so have been driven out of their homes (particularly in rural areas), while others fear they will lose their jobs. One woman who accompanied a rape victim to the police station was charged with 'false accusations and charges' and sentenced to three years' imprisonment.[12]

The pressures on women to give birth to boys rather than girls are intense: often they suffer brutality and beatings from husbands and family members as a punishment for infertility or for the birth of a girl. Often the authorities refuse to take domestic violence seriously.

Despite Mao's stand against trafficking in women and children, the ugly practice has again reared its head in contemporary China, and looks likely to increase together with the decline in the female population.[13] Women are often transported long distances to be sold as wives, slaves or prostitutes, and there are reports that local officials are either involved in the practice or turn a blind eye.[14]

The increasing imprisonment of women for 'sex crimes and hooliganism' reflects an entrenched feudalism in Chinese society explicit in the Party judgement of such offences. Describing the tendencies of juvenile delinquents, Shao Daosheng wrote:

> Some young women, having once lost their virginity, will abandon all sense of honour or shame and hanker after the male sex unscrupulously. They even regard it as 'honourable' to have sexual relations with several men . . . [Others] view illicit sexual activities as 'the happiest moments in life'.[15]

These attitudes, apparently, lead to anti-social tendencies, 'lopsided development' and crime.

It is not, of course, the Party hacks, policemen and businessmen who visit brothels who end up in labour camps. Similarly, it is not the wealthiest prostitutes or those with connections in high places who languish in the gulag. Just as in every aspect of Chinese society, money and *guanxi* (connections) count.

The Chinese *laogai* today is not populated by women like the beautiful Shanghai seductress with top-drawer clients. Those who serve the longest sentences, and who are sometimes even executed, are women like the desperate migrant worker who comes to the city in a box train to find work and who turns to prostitution to buy food to keep herself alive; or the middle-aged peasant woman who sells her body to pay for treatment for her sick husband and four children. These are also the women who are said to poison Chinese society by their 'lack of morality'.

Notes

1. Response of 70 per cent of all respondents in a 1990 survey on women's status, Chinese Academy of Social Sciences, Demography Department, 1993, quoted in the Amnesty International report *Women in China*, ASA/17/29/95.

2. *Women in China*.

3. *Ibid.*, p. 19.

4. *Ibid.*, p. 20.

5. Amnesty International draws attention to an article in the *Supreme People's Procuratorate National Gazette* in March 1992, replying to one such case raised by the Hubei Provincial Procuracy in 1991, although no details were given (*ibid.*, p. 19).

6. *Ibid.*

7. Adhi Tapey's full story is told in David Patt's powerful book *A Strange Liberation*.

8. *Women in China*, p. 16.

9. *Women in China*, p. 2.

10. Reported by Mark Baber.

11. Shao Daosheng, *Preliminary Study of China's Juvenile Delinquency*, p. ii.

12. *Women in China*, p. 2. The woman was released one year later after a successful appeal, but received no compensation.

13. The female population in China is on a dangerous slide owing to the one-child policy and the preference among Chinese for male children. There are fears that this will lead to a nation of spoiled 'little emperors' and dissatisfied young men unable to find wives.

14. Amnesty International reports that in Shanxi province in January 1995 some village-level cadres 'have gone so far as to stir up the masses to besiege and beat up police trying to rescue the women' (*Women in China*, p. 3).

15. Director of the Criminal Remoulding Psychological Professional Committee of the Chinese Law of Reform Through Labour Society, *ibid.*, p. 31.

CHAPTER 15

The Biggest Player in the History of Man

China's Economic Miracle

The whole experience of Chinese capitalism is like a film directed by Fellini, with a set by Ceausescu, from an original idea by Adam Smith.[1]

In Beijing, a rich businessman invited some Cantonese magnates to dinner. The final bill for their banquet came to $3,500 (approximately 20,000 yuan). The Cantonese guests returned the favour by inviting the Beijing group to a dinner at 60,000 yuan per table. And, so as not to lose face by being outdone, the Beijing host arranged another meal for the Cantonese. Before the beef and bean curd cooked in a subtle sauce, layers of spicy prawns and mountains of vegetables even appeared on the table, the Beijing host pulled out 350,000 yuan ($61,000) and announced, 'Today we'll be eating this amount of money!'[2]

In Guangzhou, a restaurant began offering meals dusted with gold – to be able to eat gold is a sign of good fortune.[3]

Mao once said that a revolution is not a dinner party. But it's a different story for the new *dakuan* (fat cats) in China who are heralding a commercial and communications revolution on the cutting edge of Deng Xiaoping's 'socialist market reform' programme.

China is taking the plunge into capitalism like a Peking duck into hot oil. It is a revolution in which people have money to burn – sometimes literally. To demonstrate their wealth, two rich businessmen in Hangzhou recently had a contest to decide who was richer than the other by burning real paper currency. At least 2,000 yuan of each man's money went up in flames.[4]

Despite its surreal elements, however, this explosive transition from entrenched Communism, based on the dismantling of material and spiritual structures and replacement with ideology, could lead to China becoming, in the words of the former Singaporean prime minister Lee Kuan Yew, the 'biggest player in the history of man'. Lee Kuan Yew, who was speaking in 1993, added: 'The size of China's displacement of the world balance is such that the world must find a new balance in thirty to forty years.'

Many believe that China will rock the world balance by becoming an over-sized fourth pillar to the tripolar economy revolving around the United States, Japan and the European Community. According to World Bank projections, Greater China's net imports in the year 2002 may be $639 billion, compared with $521 billion for Japan (Greater China includes the mainland, Hong Kong and Taiwan). Using comparable international prices, Greater China in the year 2002 is projected to have a gross domestic product of $9.8 trillion, compared with $9.7 trillion for the United States. If these forecasts are correct, then so would be Lee Kuan Yew's analysis. China would not just be the fourth pole to the world economy, it would be the biggest of all.[5]

The economic prognosis and outward trappings of wealth and opportunity have inspired a feeding frenzy by Western business people, who travel to China expecting the streets of Shenzhen and other Special Economic Zones to be paved with gold. By the end of 1992, the total number of newly signed foreign investment projects topped forty thousand, an almost hundred per cent increase over 1991 and more than the combined total of all such pledges since 1979.[6] Trade had risen $30 billion over 1991 to $165 billion, an increase of 22.1 per cent. The International Monetary Fund concluded that China's national income of $1.7 trillion was third in the world (behind the United States and Japan) in terms of actual purchasing power.

Chinese investment in the West also soared to record levels. Mainland investors bought businesses, Porsches, restaurants and luxury apartments in the USA, Europe and Hong Kong. One Chinese reputedly spent $517,000 for a parking space to accompany his new home in Hong Kong's swish mid-levels district.[7] In 1994, the number of Chinese *kuanye* ('cash god') millionaires was put at four to five million – and rising fast.[8] About a quarter of a million Chinese now own cars, compared with almost none before the economic boom. At the lower end of the scale, the number of people living in absolute poverty, unable to feed themselves adequately, has fallen to below a hundred million from a population of 1.2 billion – about one in twelve. Although this sounds high, it is worth remembering that in 1978 the proportion was more than one in four.[9]

The commercial revolution has swept through every one of China's thirty provinces or regions, each large enough to be considered a separate country anywhere else. The fastest-growing area has been the Chinese coast: in particular Guangdong province, inland from Hong Kong, and Fujian, across the sea from Taiwan. Three hundred million people live along these strips of coast, and their incomes in the next decade are set to grow by 11 per cent a year. 'Never in human history have so many grown so rich so fast,' wrote Will Hutton.[10]

Guangdong was once a cluster of fishing villages; now it is a sprawl of skyscrapers, expensive hotels, karaoke bars and department stores on the wild frontier of 'capitalism with Chinese characteristics'. Youngsters on the street listen to Nirvana or Canton techno-pop on their portable CDs instead of chanting 'The East is Red'. By the end of 1991 some three hundred thousand people in southern Guangdong alone were reported to have acquired electronic pagers, while another thirty thousand had bought cellular phones (*dageda*).[11] Less than ten years ago, there were few public phones even in major cities.

In *Mandate of Heaven*, China-watcher Orville Schell describes the rapid change in the southern landscape:

> In the early eighties the outskirts of Canton had been a weave of flat green rice paddies and vegetable fields, now the land was so honeycombed with construction projects that the few fields remaining looked like part of a wool garment that was in the terminal stages of being devoured by moths. Whereas the city itself had previously boasted only a few tall buildings, before me was an imposing skyline of high-rises stabbing up into a penumbra of smog . . . Young women were dressed to the nines, their bright red lips and gaudy clothes the only relief from the surrounding smoky drabness. Just two years earlier Chinese youth had been so possessed with the urgency of political reform that almost everything else had seemed irrelevant. Now they appeared just as intent on making money, shopping, hanging out, and enjoying the good life.

Later Schell was told by a Chinese friend working for a foreign company in Beijing that people want to forget the past and politics and get on with their lives:

> They're . . . hoping that after all these years of being deprived they can get something for themselves. And I say, 'Good for them!' Even if it's just fashion, food, and karaoke, the point is that at last they are thinking about themselves rather than the Party. In a curious way, this may be their first step forward to independence and individualism − a real break with the past.[12]

The five counties between Shenzhen and Canton − Zhongshen, Dongguan, Shunde, Nanhai and Bao'an − have been called the Five Small Dragons of South Guangdong, alluding to the so-called Four Dragons of Asia − South Korea, Taiwan, Hong Kong and Singapore − also famous for their high growth rates. Incredibly, the growth rates in these Guangdong counties actually surpassed those of the Four Dragons during their own boom years.

The main engine driving the immense growth rate of Guangdong is the presence of Hong Kong across the border. Increasingly the economic fortunes of the two regions have been intertwined: virtually the entire manufacturing industry of Hong Kong has moved its factories across the border, taking advantage of lower labour costs and cheap rents in China. The manufacturing base in Hong Kong has been seriously undermined by this move, causing serious unemployment in the colony and a greater divide between rich and poor. In 1982, for instance, 3200 toy factories were open for business in Hong Kong. By 1992, 98 per cent of them had moved across the border to Guangdong.[13] Three million labourers in Guangdong province work for Hong Kong companies.[14]

When photographs of Deng Xiaoping – grinning into the camera lens against a background of loading cranes at a new dock area or beside a towering skyscraper in Shenzhen – appeared as front-page news in 1992, the world knew that China's senior statesman was giving the green light to a new form of aggressive commercialism in his country. Deng chose to visit the Special Economic Zones and surrounding cities of the south in January 1992. The man whose role as the Butcher of Beijing appeared to be forgotten spent his visit posing at various construction or commercial sites during endless photo opportunities, and preaching the gospel of market reform and 'opening up'. He told local officials that, without the implementation of these new policies, the demonstrations at Tiananmen Square might have led to civil war.

'Without the achievements of reform and opening up to the outside world, we might not have been able to pass the test of the June 4 incident,' he said. 'And if we had failed to pass the test, there would have been a chaotic situation that might have led to civil war, as was the case during the Cultural Revolution. The reason our country remained stable after the June 4 incident was that reform and opening up had already promoted economic development and improved the people's livelihood. Therefore both the army and the state government must continue to safeguard this line, this system, and these policies.'[15]

Deng added that 'Reform and opening up require boldness and courageous experiments . . . They must not proceed like a woman with bound feet . . . In this sense, making revolution means liberating the productive forces.' In the generous spirit of socialism, he concluded that economic development was important for the whole of China, not just the Special Economic Zones: 'Areas that have developed first should bring along the less developed areas to achieve the final goal of common affluence.'

Deng's tour of the south and enthusiastic support for economic, if not political, reform gave additional encouragement to Western investors. At the end of the year, Deng was on the cover of *Time* magazine, and was also the *Financial Times* Man of the Year. Sino–US trade hit a record $40 billion; China enjoyed a trade surplus with the USA of more than $22 billion, second only to that of Japan.[16] When applied to China, the phrase 'economic miracle' was fast becoming a cliché.

The statistics are dazzling. But, in the furnace of the money-making machine, people burn. There is a dark side to China's economic growth. There was a similar darkness in the cotton mills, factories and textile mills of nineteenth-century England: conditions of squalor, suffering and exploitation. In China today, these conditions are not only suffered by prisoners in labour camps; they are endured by millions of migrant workers and children.

The darkness is also in the environmental legacy the Chinese are bequeathing to a younger generation. China burns billions of tons of coal without any proper pollution control devices. In some cities, people's lungs are literally black. One of the most polluted places in the country, Benxi, a Manchurian city, completely disappeared from satellite photographs at times during the 1980s because of the haze of soot.

Many experts believe that China will become the world's largest source of acid rain by the year 2010. The acid rain is produced by the sulphur in the coal: most of China's huge amounts of coal is of poor quality and contains large amount of sulphur. Acid rain produced by China's coal industry is already affecting the great forests of Siberia and Korea. By 1991, China was the world's largest user of coal, consuming more than a billion tons a year and emitting over 16 million metric tons of ash.

The thickness of the fog which hangs over Chongqing, close to Sichuan's border and near Guizhou, is equivalent to the great smog of London in the 1950s. The fog and rain in the city are virtually as acidic as vinegar. When *New York Times* correspondent Sheryl WuDunn travelled to the city to write about air pollution there, the smog was so bad that the plane couldn't take off for her return to Beijing, and the air was so polluted that her photographs looked as if they had been taken under water.[17] Respiratory disease is the leading cause of death in China, accounting for 26 per cent of deaths.[18]

In Tibet, the Chinese have perpetrated a series of environmental disasters: timber is being removed from the forests of the Himalaya at a rapid rate, causing soil erosion and climatic changes in low-lying areas. Half of Tibet's forests are estimated to have been felled since 1959, providing the Chinese with $50 billion worth of timber. The floods in Bangladesh have been linked to environmental degradation in Tibet.[19] As industrial activity increases, the rate of environmental degradation worsens.

Global warming is caused by the release of carbon dioxide by burning coal. Carbon dioxide is the most important of the greenhouse gases that are suspected of trapping heat around the earth's surface. A continued rise in the earth's temperature would probably have far-reaching effects on the earth's climate and raise sea levels so as to flood many coastal cities, islands and entire countries around the world. Although China's contribution to global warming is immense, it is still not as large as that of the Western world or the former Soviet Union. Every American is responsible for nine times as much greenhouse gas as one Chinese.[20] However, China is undergoing a continuing, and rapid, industrialization, so levels look likely to increase. Also, while the West is making an effort — as late in the day as it is — to curb greenhouse gases, China is unresponsive to anti-pollution moves internationally.

China is also facing serious threats in being able to feed its population because of both land use and the pressures of a growing population beginning to outstrip grain production. The rapidly growing use of chemical pesticides is weakening the land and helping to reduce the country's annual grain harvest by approximately 3 billion kilograms. At the same time, millions of acres of arable land are being lost to property and commercial development. In suburban areas, new factories and industrial development zones are not only encroaching upon farmland, they are also polluting the air and water. In 1993, approximately four million acres of cropland were consumed by industrial development, forcing some sixteen million peasants out of agriculture.[21] This has a knock-on effect in the urban developed areas, as peasants leave the land and seek work elsewhere. Lester Brown, president of the Worldwatch Institute, believes that soon the world won't be able to grow enough food to satisfy China's pressing needs. When China turns to the world market on a large scale, as it soon must, its food scarcity will become that of the whole world. Brown warns that, once this happens, the grain-exporting capacity of the United States and other countries will simply be overwhelmed.[22]

China's quest to be *fu-qiang*, or rich and powerful, has fragmented the country. On one side are the businessmen from Hangzhou who burn paper currency and the Beijing fat cats who spend $61,000 on one meal. On the other are the dispossessed, the tens of millions of migrant workers and the rural poor who roam the country in search of work. The criminal gangs, the kidnap rings who gang-rape women before selling them off as wives and prostitutes, the drug dealers who, when caught, are dispatched with a bullet at the back of the head, and the bent police officers who tip off crooks about police busts in advance — all of these are as much a part of the new China as the men with money to burn, the frantic development and the stocks and shares.

This is a China with 25 per cent inflation, with workers often unpaid by their state employers or, if they are peasants, by the government. The estimated hundred thousand state-owned companies in China – the backbone of China's socialist tradition – are one of the biggest drains on the new and dynamic national economy. These companies are being allowed by the government to go on consuming money unproductively on a huge scale. In 1994, around forty per cent of state-owned firms lost money.[23] It is impossible to predict how long China will allow the unproductive state-owned companies to be a drag on the wider, expanding economy. If China's banks operated on commercial principles they would have stopped lending to state-owned firms years ago. The Party's reluctance to bankrupt these businesses, however, does not only lie in a desire to cling to socialist values. It is also because their dissolution would worsen the unemployment statistics; and because the government would then end up paying for the housing, education and health-care currently provided to workers in these businesses.

One of the greatest sources of anxiety regarding the Chinese economy for those who wait in Hong Kong is the tangled web of business, official crime and corruption that proliferates on the mainland. As the Chinese saying has it, 'cops and robbers are of the same tribe'. A senior anti-narcotics expert in Hong Kong says: 'China is notoriously corrupt. There are occasional crackdowns. But for the most part, we've found from informants, traffickers and defendants that China's wide open. The right amount of money to the right official can fix anything.'[24] Li Mingxian, for instance, is an ethnic Chinese former commander of the Communist Party of Burma; his party was once beholden to Beijing, and he has enjoyed close contacts with Chinese military intelligence. Today he heads a thirteen-man committee running a patch of 5,000 square kilometres north of Kengtung in Shan state (across the border from Yunnan), overseeing the production of several heroin factories.[25]

Co-operation between the police and criminals has become so acute that in September 1993 the Public Security Ministry issued a list of ten 'No-Nos' for Chinese cops on the beat. These included: no selling of protection services to dance halls, massage parlours, smuggling rings and so on; no tipping off crooks about police busts in advance; no helping yourself to food or merchandise from people without paying. 'Next thing you know, you'll have to remind the police "no killing, no stealing,"' complained a disgruntled factory manager to the *Far Eastern Economic Review* in June 1994.

Corruption is present at the highest levels of Chinese society. The Hong Kong community was shocked to hear that Deng Xiaoping was advocating official crime in the form of the involvement of the notorious

Triads gangs: the 14K, the Chaozhou mob, the Wo Hop To. 'The Triads are not all bad, and some of them are patriotic,' said Deng in 1984. 'Most of them still consider themselves descendants of the Yellow Emperor and still retain Chinese dignity. Most of them have shown a good attitude. Of course we need to do some work on them to persuade them to control their hands and feet. So Triads are not all bad, most are good.'

Since then, the message has stuck. It has undermined any hopes Hong Kong may have had of creating with China a system that fights official and unofficial corruption. It also undermines the rule of law, and indicates a lack of desire to clean up the security services from within. As Emily Lau, of the Legislative Council in the colony, commented: 'When we have the authorities joining forces with criminals, then there's no doubt that we can kiss goodbye to the rule of law.'

The *laogai* system is caught between the two Chinas, embodying the country's split personality. The separation between rich and poor, foreigner and Chinese, privilege and non-privilege, is acute in the prison system, mirroring the outside world. Party officials or policemen who have been arrested for corruption enjoy privileges which set them apart from the other prisoners. Political prisoner Liu Shanqing recalls the story of two 'prisoner bosses' who enjoyed such privileges. One of them had been the political officer of the Migration Bureau in Shantou, and the other was a department head in the Bureau. They had been convicted along with the Shantou police chief. 'They were allowed out of the prison to stroll around the streets at night,' recalls Liu. 'Because they had no money, they couldn't find much to do, so they were always trying to borrow money from other prisoners. They tried to borrow some from me once. I told them I didn't have any.'

Liu also recalls that three former high-ranking cadres serving long sentences enjoyed private rooms and servants within the jail. 'It's just the same as in China's feudal era,' says Liu. 'There's no equality on the outside, and no equality in the prison cells.'

Prisoners with high-ranking families or parents in the security services can also earn these privileges. 'If your father is a police cadre and you yourself a criminal sentenced to five years on a robbery charge, on Family Visit Day a car will be sent for you,' says Harry Wu. 'Similarly, if your father is a mayor, things inside are very different for you than for others.'

The new breed of 'economic criminals' with experience of cutting deals and making money are much in demand with *laogai* personnel who want to make money through production. According to Harry Wu, these 'criminals' are often treated better than most policemen.

In certain cases, money can also buy freedom. Wu reports that, in Hunan province's Number Seven Labour Reform Detachment, three public security cadres accepted 200,000 yuan from the family of Chen Wenxiong, who was sentenced to death by Hunan province's Hengyang Municipal People's Court for counterfeit and robbery. On 14 April 1989, Chen was released from his handcuffs and given a police uniform. He was smuggled out of his cell and helped to escape from prison. Eventually Chen's luck ran out. He was later recaptured and executed.[26] This sort of incident would have been unthinkable in the early days of labour reform.

Liu Shanqing remembers cadres dreaming up crazy ideas to make money in prison. 'I don't know which cadre first proposed the idea, but it was suggested that they run a hotel in the prison. It was to be called the "Meizhou Grand Hotel." They even thought of renting out cells. Who knows, maybe there even would been guests who might have been interested in trying them out.'

Notes

1. Boris Johnson, writing in the *The Telegraph* magazine (October 1995).

2. *The Beijing Evening News* (9 May 1993), quoted in Nicholas Kristof and Sheryl WuDunn, *China Wakes.*

3. *Ibid.*, p. 342.

4. *Ibid.*

5. Projections are from *International Economic Insights* (May–June 1993), pp. 2–7 and 50. However, it is wise to treat all projections as to China's future wealth or otherwise with caution. They are generally based around high inflation rates, volatile exchange rates, past guesses and national statistics of variable reliability. Together, these could produce a figure for China's gross domestic product per head in 1994 of as little as $425 or more than $3,500. At the low end, this would make China's economy the ninth largest in the world or, at the highest, China would be competing with Japan for the number two position, behind the USA.

6. Orville Schell, *Mandate of Heaven*, p. 404.

7. 'Government's Pledge to Lower Prices Seems to Damp Property Market Slightly', *Asian Wall Street Journal Weekly* (25 April 1994), p. 2.

8. Schell, *Mandate of Heaven*.

9. *The Economist* (18 March 1995).

10. *The Guardian* (21 December 1993).

11. Schell, *Mandate of Heaven*, p. 333.

12. Schell, *Mandate of Heaven*, p. 339.

13. *Ibid.*

14. Kristof and Wudunn, *China Wakes*, p. 372.

15. In fact, the soaring inflation and disparity in people's income caused by the sudden transition is thought to have contributed to the unrest expressed at Tiananmen.

16. Schell, *Mandate of Heaven*, p. 405.

17. Kristof and WuDunn, *China Wakes*, p. 389.

18. H. Keith Florig, 'The Benefits of Air Pollution Reduction in China', quoted in *ibid.*, p. 389.

19. Further information from Tibet Information Network.

20. Philip M. Boffey, 'Editorial Notebook: China and Global Warming', *New York Times* (8 December 1993), p. A16.

21. Schell, *Mandate of Heaven*, p. 424.

22. Graham Hutchings, 'Why They Could Devour the World', *Daily Telegraph* (2 June 1995).

23. Zhu Rongji, China's senior vice-premier in charge of the economy, reported this figure. It is only a small improvement on the figure of 60 per cent in 1993. Little of the money channelled into state-owned businesses returns to the state.

24. 'Inside Story: Law and Disorder', *Asiaweek* (25 August 1995).

25. *Ibid.*

26. Harry Wu, *Laogai*.

CHAPTER 16

The Dream of Gold
Gulag Capitalism

Labour reform departments [in China] are not allowed to engage in foreign economic and trade activities, and China has never granted any labour reform department a permit to engage in foreign trade. No products made in prison are exported.

Chen Defu, Press Counsellor, Embassy of China, Washington, DC[1]

Do you think Labour-Reform units are afraid of deaths? If one dies, we bury one. If two die, we bury two!

Prison official, the Lingyuan Number Two
Labour Reform Detachment

In the early years after the Communist revolution many labour-intensive large-scale projects were completed using *laogai* labour. In the 1950s, a hydroelectric dam was built on the Huai river, a drainage canal and hydroelectric plant were created in northern Jiangsu province, the Chengdu to Chongqing railway was built, and the Lanzhou to Qinghai railway completed.

A former inmate who worked on the Chengdu to Chongqing railway from January 1950 to June 1951 recalled how official directives urged prisoners to work with 'the violence of the rain and the madness of the storm'. Prisoners were forced to work for at least ten hours a day on a diet that was barely sufficient to keep a human being alive. The rice they ate daily was dark yellow, smelt bad and was full of sand. The vegetables were of a quality that Sichuan peasants would give to their pigs, and soup was a boiling cauldron of salted water. Prisoners often died during labour,

[Some] grew dizzy, fell to the ground and died. Others foamed at the mouth, fell to the ground, tore at themselves, and, after long suffering, died, with their flesh torn to shreds. Others were wracked with pains in

201

their stomach. They begged our chiefs, 'Shoot me, shoot me.' The troop
chiefs had a slogan that ran: 'One may not treat sickness perhaps, one may
not have a funeral for the dead, but one cannot stop work.'[2]

In the 1960s, the administration continued to focus on major projects such as the development of state farms and roads in Xinjiang, Qinghai and Tibet. Tens of thousands of prisoners in immense military convoys were sent into the desert at the westernmost limit of the Great Wall of China and past the point known as Demon Gate Pass, a land of howling wind and wasteland which traditionally evokes the terror of eternal banishment to the Chinese. Thousands of ageing 'historical counter-revolutionaries', bureaucrats and Rightists imprisoned during Mao's purges in the 1950s and 1960s still languish here today beside Red Guards, supporters of the Gang of Four, Roman Catholic priests and democracy activists. They are labouring still in the fields, in zinc or copper mines and in factories.

During the 1950s and 1960s, prisoners in Xinjiang often slept in the open, in pits of their own digging, even when temperatures plunged to minus 30 degrees or lower. Prisoners in the Stalinist gulag at least slept in tents and barracks. In Xinjiang, inmates were forced to labour whatever the weather, even when it was hard and painful to breathe and their rations of steamed bread were frozen solid. Work was brought to a standstill only during the great Gobi blizzards: blinding snowstorms which submerged the land and sky in darkness.

Large-scale projects using forced labour are still very much in evidence today in this bleak wasteland. In October 1995, Harry Wu's Laogai Research Foundation reported that a World Bank project in Xinjiang province is supporting cotton and grain production in at least 21 forced labour camps as well as 30 special farms controlled by the People's Liberation Army. Known as the Tarim Basin Project, the *laogai* network in the area is seeking to improve irrigation and drainage for cotton and grain production in areas bordering the Taklimakan desert. The project is scheduled for completion in 1996.[3]

A massive work force has also been recruited for the prospecting and production of oil in Xinjiang, particularly in Junggar, Tarim and Turpan-Hami. This area is now China's leading oil production base: Chinese specialists say that the Tarim basin alone could have oil reserves approaching 20.5 billion tons, equivalent to the oil found so far in the North Sea.[4]

In the urban areas of China, forced labour was also used to build a number of relatively modern factories known as 'special state enterprises', including the Liangxiang Elevator Factory in Beijing, the Huadong

Electric Welder Factory in Shanghai, the Zhaoyang Lead Plant in Guizhou province, and the Chengdu Machine Tool Factory in Sichuan.

These enterprises were on a huge scale, requiring considerable discipline and a steady input of prisoners – readily supplied by purges, anti-Rightist movements and later the Cultural Revolution. An indication of the scale is given by Harry Wu, who quotes the example of the reclamation of farmland in the Bao'anzao reclamation area in Jalaid Banner, Inner Mongolia Autonomous Region, involving the transfer of 150,000 prisoners from a labour reform camp in Shanghai municipality and Jiangsu, Fujian and Zhejiang provinces. The reclamation of one million mu of farmland (1 mu = 0.0667 hectares) in Heilongjiang province required the transfer of three hundred thousand prisoners from labour camps in Beijing and Tianjin.[5] A Party document states:

> Over the past forty years, laogai production using unskilled labour has included hydroelectric dams, roads, wasteland reclamation, bringing new land under cultivation, and building construction. In the area of skilled labour, [laogai production] includes many different kinds of both light and heavy industry. In these enterprises the level of mechanisation and automation has risen steadily. Some enterprises have received national medals of honour and the laogai system also contributes to the international market.[6]

In 1956, Liu Shaoqi declared that, despite the heavy emphasis on production, 'the primary object of labour reform work is reform; production is of secondary importance'. This analysis followed Party concern over uprisings begun by prisoners owing to excessive work load, lack of food and insufficient medical care between 1955 and 1965.[7] One of these protests against conditions occurred at the Zhihuai engineering project in Anhui province. More than two thousand prisoners had died from infectious disease in only two months during the project. The survivors plotted to escape, for which they were all executed.

The Party's declared intention of 'reform first, production second' was carried out throughout the 1960s and 1970s, but came to an end in practice if not in theory during Deng Xiaoping's era. Some products of laogai enterprises had found a market overseas before the 1980s – but the opening of China to the West, and the Party's emphasis on export earnings, led the administration to step up its efforts to encourage foreign trade. There was also an increased willingness to enter into joint ventures with foreign firms.

'Judge the hour, size up the situation, and seize the opportunity,' enthused cadet He Liang, from the Reform through Labour Police Academy of Sichuan province, in his article 'The Path Is under Our

Feet'. 'The reform-through-labour units now face intensified competition from enterprises run by villages and towns and those run by the military and others,' says He breathily:

> In this competition, we suffer from our own weaknesses. It is, therefore, necessary for us to judge the hour, size up the situation, adjust our orientation in a timely manner, and find a path that suits us, in view of our own conditions and the external environment.

He adds that, thankfully, reform through labour units do have some advantages – namely, cheap labour under military organization:

> Comparatively speaking, we have greater manpower at our disposal, and our workers are young, concentrated; they cost less and they follow a military routine . . . Our advantage lies in the full utilisation of the rich convict labour resources for the development of labour-intensive products.[8]

Yu Guoqiang, head of the Judicial Department of Zhejiang province, wrote:

> Developing export products increased the effective supply for the society and promoted the production development of the reform and re-education through labour system . . . In recent years, the export products production of the reform and re-education through labour enterprises in our province has developed quickly . . . In our province, the factories of the reform and re-education through labour system have all adapted international standards as their goal.

Guoqiang goes on to say that the production of the *laogai* system is organized according to the number of detained criminals and those whose cases are under investigation:

> Due to the turnover, the labour force is unpredictable and the equipment is old. In addition, the sites usually are located in remote ill-informed places, where the managing is backward and the price for raw materials has gone up often. All those conditions affected the development of export production.

> However, the labour is cheap and this is good for developing labour-intensive production. Our province is near the coast, so that it is easy to go in and out. The export trading of the reform and re-education through labour system in our province has certain foundations and we have some products in great demand. These are the advantages of developing the exporting production of the reform and re-education through labour system in our province. Through this analysis, we decided to concentrate on developing export production.[9]

The first joint-venture enterprise in Zhejiang province, according to Guoqiang, was with the Japanese Sanming Zhushi Huishe company and the Zhejiang Tea Import and Export Company, to produce steam-processed green tea to export to Japan. The authorities went ahead with this joint venture after they discovered that the dark dust tea being produced by Nanhu farm (a labour reform camp) was not only wasteful but also created little foreign currency. The joint venture was an unqualified success: in the first year of production, the farm created $300,000 of foreign currency. Guoqiang also announced proudly that 'we also cordially receive the invited foreign businessmen to visit our factories and to negotiate business', and that they also send observation and sales groups to Britain, the USA, France, Germany, Japan, Canada, Spain and Asian countries to observe trade and make sales.[10]

An example of a production-oriented labour reform camp is the Lingyuan Motor Vehicle Industrial Corporation, otherwise known as the Lingyuan Labour Reform Sub-Bureau. This large, sprawling complex, consisting of six labour-reform detachments with more than 160,000 square metres of factory floor space, fixed assets of nearly $30 million and manufacturing units producing everything from tractor-trailers to trucks and engine parts, is in Manchuria's Liaoning province. After the 4 June crackdown in 1989, so many political prisoners were housed here that in 1990 the Ministry of Justice gave it the honorific title of 'Outstanding Collective in Curbing Turmoil and Suppressing the Counter-Revolutionary Rebellion'.

Amnesty International has received numerous reports of torture at the Lingyuan detachment, particularly about a group of political prisoners arrested in connection with the 1989 democracy movement. The prisoners have been assaulted with electric batons, have been beaten up by prison guards and criminal prisoners, and have been taken away for punishment either to the correction unit or to the strict regime unit. The six prisoners in the correction unit were locked in tiny solitary confinement cells which measured one metre by two metres. They were stripped naked, held down on the floor and repeatedly given shocks with high-voltage electric batons administered to various parts of their bodies, including the head, neck, shoulders, armpits, stomach and inside of the legs. One of the prisoners, Li Jie, went into spasms and became unconscious. When the electric baton used against one of them ran out of power, he was kicked by a guard wearing leather boots and two of his ribs were broken.[11]

One of the prisoners, Liu Gang, was made to wear leg-irons weighing about 9 kilograms for the entire time he was under 'strict regime' and then forced to sit on a bench without moving for as long as twelve hours a day. Two others, Leng Wanbao and Kong Xianfeng, went on hunger strike to protest against their conditions. On the second day they were force-fed through tubes pushed down their throats while they were held by guards. Leng Wanbao's left arm was pulled so hard by the guards that it was dislocated. Zhang Ming, who also went on hunger strike to demand family visits for the prisoners, was kicked and beaten as he was told by a prison official: 'It is my job to beat you. It is to reform you. You want to go on hunger strike? Go right ahead! Do you think Labour-Reform units are afraid of deaths? If one dies, we bury one. If two die, we bury two!'[12]

Laogai officials are under orders to diversify operations and develop the market where production is concerned. 'The majority of reform through labour enterprises suffer from the fact that they are single-product concerns and have difficulty adapting themselves to market changes in a commodity economy,' writes He Liang of the Cadet School. 'Diversification means more ways are opened up for breathing life into the reform through labour economy.'

One of the methods of diversification became the contracting out of large groups of prisoners to state- and foreign-owned enterprises. These contract-labour battalions are called 'special schools'. In the first six months of 1988, more than 710,000 labour reform prisoners had received an 'education' in the new 'special schools'.[13]

Many labour reform units were unashamedly honest about their source of labour when dealing with foreign companies. One *laogai* official assured Harry Wu, who was posing as a businessman, that workers in his factory are beaten severely if they fail to meet production quotas. And in 1989, Charles Chi, chairman of the consulting firm Chinter in Brussels, Belgium, was quoted as saying that the Chinese government had authorized him to offer prisoners to any Western firm willing to open a factory in China. He wrote the following letter to Volvo, the Swedish car manufacturer:

> *Dear Sirs,*
> *We are representing Chinese Reform of Criminals (labour reform) Bureaux of all the provinces along the coast of China. We heard that your esteemed firm has intention to establish factories in Asia.*
> *All the Bureaux can provide many existing factories for your choice on rent basis. They have also many lands to rent. Besides they can provide large numbers of criminals, who received already basic technical training as very cheap labour[er]s on lease basis. The number of labour[er]s and the security are fully guaranteed. We are ready to show you all the relevant*

information. If you are interested in our proposal, please don't hesitate to call upon us.

Looking forward to hear from you, we remain,
Truly yours,

Charles H. J. Chi
General Manager[14]

Volvo turned down the offer; company spokesman Hans Rehnstrom said the deal did not conform to Swedish ideas of business ethics, and that the overtones of slave labour were revolting.

According to Chinese documents, labour costs in forced labour factories are 'ten to twenty per cent lower' than in other factories.[15] In a series of articles obtained by Asia Watch,[16] prison officials or officials of provincial Bureaux of Labour Reform make it clear that the use of forced labour is a central government policy, not merely one adopted on an *ad hoc* basis by units in the coastal provinces, where much of the production is concentrated.

Other articles published in the same journal confirm that it is normal practice to confine labour reform camp prisoners to the camps after their sentence is finished, with the payment of a small wage. This means that export-oriented productivity will not be diminished by their departure from the system. 'Time-served prisoners retained for in-camp employment . . . cannot join labour unions, do not enjoy retirement benefits when they become old, and their wages and living standards are low.'[17] The policy of 'forcible retention of time-served prisoners for in-camp employment' is most commonly used for those prisoners who have allegedly remained 'unrepentant' during their sentences, and its main purpose is to remove such people from society permanently. Political prisoners are often included in this category.

The overall productivity of the *laogai* system and its importance to the Chinese economy is difficult to establish. Harry Wu believes the labour camps to be a vital prop to the economy. He says:

> *Labour reform camps' armies of low-paid, forced, highly efficient workers play a very important role in the Communist government's 'socialist construction.' The production of labour reform industries constitutes a large proportion of the PRC's national economy . . . Never before has there been a nation with a prison system so extensive that it pervades all aspects of national production, has such careful planning and organisation, and composes such an integral part of a people's economic and productive system.*[18]

Jean-Luc Domenache, author of *Chine: L'Archipel Oublié*, argues that claims of the profitability of the labour camps are made without taking into full account the costs of running the labour reform system. The 'Labour Reform Economic System' Study Group under the Ministry of Justice Research Institute traced the development of the labour reform economy from the 1950s up to 1990. While noting the success of some units, the group found that, throughout the system, profits fell in each year of the Seventh Five Year Plan except for 1988.[19] According to the Group,

> From the 1980s though 1989, aside from the six or seven coastal provinces and cities and Yunnan, which made a profit, the majority of provinces, cities and districts could not but depend on special financial allocations to survive. Many provinces and cities even suffered the heavy burden of years of losses.

According to the Group, these money-losing units in the central and western parts of the country, many of them agricultural, acted as a drag on the labour reform economy as a whole.[20]

Prior to 1983, all income from production in the labour camps went to the state, and the state allocated funds to cover all expenses associated with operation of the system. However in this year, finances were 'contracted' to the individual labour reform unit. This meant that, while units could keep their profits, the state no longer provided for their expenses and running costs. The anti-crime campaign in August 1983 coincided with this transition. The laogai system was thrown into upheaval by what was probably the greatest structural change in Chinese prisons since 1949, and the doubling of the prison population after the anti-crime campaign.

Democracy activist Liu Shanqing, who was being held in Meizhou prison at the time, recalls the sea change in attitudes:

> There were fundamental changes in the distribution of power within the prison, in the supervision and education of prisoners, and in the prisoners' daily lives. The best overall description of these changes is that from this time on, the prison abandoned the enterprise of political thought reform, and 'looked towards money', just like all sectors of society were by then doing . . . I don't think there has ever been another society at any time in history in which the dream of gold burned so intently that it was able to penetrate even into the prisons, and effect such a total transformation of the prisons' atmosphere.

The contract system meant that the prison competed in the open market for contracts within the labour market. For the prisoners, the change was dramatic and unwelcome. At Meizhou, Liu relates that the cadres did away with the old work system, and in its place instituted a

THE DREAM OF GOLD

work system 'approximating modern slavery'. The original eight-hour
working day was lengthened suddenly to twelve hours, and sometimes
there was overtime as well. However there were compensations. Political
study was dropped in the fervour of production, and prisoners' food
rations increased. 'There was more meat, and at night there was
"overtime congee", even with strips of meat in it, to restore the prisoners'
strength,' says Liu.[21] The same increase in hours occurred in prisons
throughout China, and, if prisoners refused to co-operate, they were
punished by 'strict regime' or beatings.

Meizhou prison also instituted a system of contracts between
production brigades and individual prisoners, and bonuses were given for
completion of production quotas. Prison officials were horrified when
some prisoners working on contract began to earn more than 100 yuan a
month, and they withheld the wages, throwing a banquet to quell the
inmates' anger. Despite the withholding of high wages, prisoners still
threw themselves into their work because, just as with thought reform
previously, they could earn reductions in their sentences. Some even took
vitamin pills to keep going.

Testimonies from former prisoners indicate that corruption within the
system contributes to the losses sustained in labour reform units. Mark
Baber, a former prisoner at Shanghai Number One municipal prison,
recalls that the production materials were usually controlled by prisoners.
This led to less wastage than if prison officials were involved – as they had
been known to filch goods for their own purposes.

Mark Baber also recalled an example of an increasingly common
phenomenon: the system of contracts between the prison and outside
companies. One particularly rude and obnoxious prisoner at Shanghai
Number One was known as Big Boss because his father brought a
contract into the prison for making clothing. Big Boss was promoted, and
became head of his work detachment. By demonstrating his faith in
Communist Party policies of economic reform, Big Boss had shown
initiative and a good attitude. He was also a candidate for early release.

Prisoners can sometimes buy their way out of prison by encouraging
their families to arrange sales contracts. According to human rights activist
Tang Boqiao, a sale which nets a profit of 8,000 yuan (around £900)
earns the prisoner a minor merit point. Larger sales earn more merit
points. Tang remembers one prisoner who had worked for a Chinese
corporation in Shenzhen. Although he had been sentenced to ten years
for corruption, he arranged such impressive contracts for the labour camp
that he was technically due for release very soon after his imprisonment.

Often foreign companies are involved in contract deals with the *laogai*.
Their involvement, however, does not imply an opening up of the

system to foreign inspection – or an improvement in conditions for prisoners. Instead, the screws are often tightened. He Liang writes:

> Faced with a serious task of foreign trade production, our mill has insisted on instilling into our cadre of police a sense of dictatorship and a sense of hardship, so that they are constantly on the alert. As a result of our successful development of a foreign-oriented economy, our mill has become well-known and our interaction with society has increased . . . Under these new circumstances, we began by tightening control, revised and perfected our system of supervision. For example, we stepped up the education of prisoners in foreign affairs discipline . . . Prisoners are not allowed to have direct contact or talks with foreign businessmen, etc. We have summed up and formulated a whole set of effective administrative measures such as 'preventive measures taken well ahead of time, prevention by means of regulations, prevention at key points, and timely prevention'. In this way, the 'three orders' have been effectively maintained in the prison, and no secret has ever been leaked, and other incidents involving foreign contact have been effectively prevented from happening.[22]

In 1988, for the first time, a national trade fair was held in Beijing displaying goods made by prison inmates. The fair, held from 15 to 19 August, displayed two thousand different kinds of products from more than a hundred *laogai* factories and farms. The fair was intended to attract foreign buyers rather than state-owned enterprises, which are already well aware of the kinds of goods available.

In 1989, Anhui province claimed to have earned $3.7 million in prison exports.[23] Products from the Xinsheng Dye Factory, also known as Jinzhou prison, Hubei province, reportedly earned more than $8.49 million in foreign currency in 1989.[24] In April 1986, the *People's Daily* reported on 1983 statistics of production by labour reform enterprises:

> In 1983, LRC [Labour Reform Camps] nationwide produced over 12 million tons of raw coal, over 6,000 machine tools of various sorts, over 6,000 agricultural irrigation pumps, 16,000 tons of zinc, over 200 tons of mercury (one-fifth of the total national production), 25,000 tons of asbestos (one-fourth of the total national production), over 16,000 tons of cast steel pipes, over a billion jin (about 500 million kilograms) of grain, and 24 million jin (about 12 million kilograms) of tea leaves (one-third of the total national production).[25]

Chinese internal government documents show that prisons and labour camps in China are exporting to more than thirty countries around the world, with export earnings of at least several hundred million dollars. Two of the countries actively importing *laogai*-made goods are forbidden by law to do so. These countries are the USA and Britain. The USA has legislatively banned the importation of products made by 'convict and/or forced labour'. In the first sixty years of the legislation, the USA took action twice – against products produced in the Soviet gulag and a Mexican prison. Since then, Harry Wu's research has prompted a snowballing of seizure orders and a number of prosecutions. 'It's the tip of the iceberg,' he says.

Harry Wu's ground-breaking work into the import of *laogai* goods to the USA and Europe has paved the way for other human rights organizations to undertake similar investigations. In 1994, Human Rights Watch/Asia revealed imports of around 100 tons of latex medical examination gloves made by the Beijing Latex Factory, a production facility that was at the time using dozens of political and other prisoners at Beijing Number Two prison to carry out quality-control checking of the gloves. The gloves were being imported to a small company in Roscoe, Illinois, called Technical Consulting Trade Co. Inc.[26] The company claimed that it was not aware that prison labour was used.

Former prisoners in Beijing Number Two, a recent building located in a rural suburban area to the south-east of the capital, report being forced to work ten to sixteen hours a day, seven days a week, at various production tasks. Food in the punishment block consists of five steamed buns per day with a little pickled vegetable. The complex includes a 'special prison' building where the prisoners check the gloves, which are mainly for export. Prisoners, who receive no pay, sometimes have to work through the night if they have a large order to fulfil. Many of them are said to have developed respiratory conditions and severe hand ailments as a result of the prolonged forced labour.

The British legislation consists of an 1897 Act forbidding the importation of foreign prison-made goods, aimed at protecting British workers from zero labour costs in prisons overseas. So far, the Act has never been enforced. A major difficulty with the legislation, which is due for a reassessment by Parliament, is that it was enacted at the end of the nineteenth century under a very different trading environment to the present day. And since the UK is now part of the European Customs Union, goods which have been imported via another European country cannot be seized by the British.[27]

The UK's cumulative investments in China amounted to $3.08 billion by the end of 1993, of which $1.99 billion was invested in 1993 alone. These figures put the UK first in the league of European investors, and indicate the rapidly growing volume of British investment in China.[28] Despite increasing evidence of *laogai* imports coming into Britain, there has been a distinct lack of political will to enforce the Act – linked perhaps to concern over the handover of Hong Kong to the Chinese in 1997.

Products likely to be coming into Britain from the camps include machinery, shoes, hand-tools, tea and toys. Christmas lights are also made in many labour reform camps and prisons; Mark Baber witnessed prisoners making them at the Shanghai Number One municipal prison. Researchers in London found evidence of chain-hoists and lever-lifts from a labour reform camp called Wulin being imported into Britain. A member of the group posed as a businesswoman and travelled to a company to buy the chain-hoists. The managing director of the company told her that the factory of origin was 'Wulin'. However, when he was told about the results of the research, he backtracked and said the goods in fact came from 'Hangzhou'. The Wulin Machinery Plant is also known as Zhejiang Province Number Four prison, and is situated on the outskirts of Hangzhou. (See Appendix 1.)

Further investigations in the UK revealed that the illegal trade with labour camps is harming British businesses, which are unable to compete with 'zero labour costs'. Companies spoke of being offered chain-hoists, for instance, from China for £6.50 – while the cheapest British-made equivalent was priced at more than £100.

Other businesses in the UK have faced severe difficulties owing to goods being imported at such low prices. China is now the world's biggest footwear manufacturer, swamping the export market with hundreds of millions of pairs of shoes and other footwear every year. The British Footwear Manufacturers Federation claims that the impact of Chinese imports is disastrous, not only on industry but also on jobs in the UK. Several Chinese *laogai* camps are known to operate footwear assembly plants, and some of these plants may be exporting their finished products to the European Community. *Laogai* factories are also involved in associated processes such as leather curing and tanning, plastics and glue manufacture, and metal mining and smelting.[29]

The British toy industry is similarly affected – about a third of the world's toys come from China, and 90 per cent of America's toys – leading to calls from the International Confederation of Free Trade Unions for a China 'toycott'. Many of the cheapest toys come from the southern province of Guangdong, which is responsible for 50 per cent of China's exports. When US President Bill Clinton was recently considering the renewal of China's Most Favoured Trading Nation status, it was rumoured that the USA would never cancel it because children across America would suffer a bleak Christmas – lower-income parents could only afford toys from China.

In America, too, businesses have been ground down by competition from cheap Chinese goods. Jeff Fielder, a director of the Laogai Research

Foundation, told two House subcommittees in Washington that the Chinese prison labour system has destroyed American jobs in the shoe, toy, garment, textile, hand-tool and electronics industries.

Many companies fight shy of unravelling the complex web of the Chinese production and supply system. How is it possible to distinguish between manufacturing units and labour camps, they say, when prisons are listed under a factory name, or when goods are sold through a Hong Kong intermediary with no reference to their source, or when company bosses change brand names so quickly? It is even possible for *laogai* officials to change the status of prisoners in response to Western concern over exports made in prisons – from ordinary inmates to forced job placement prisoners for instance, being paid a small wage. Some company directors also claim that they visited factories which are known by human rights researchers to be prisons, and said they couldn't tell whether they were prisons or not. Their confusion is hardly surprising: many Western companies are tricked by the Chinese practice of *yi jian liang zhi* – 'one prison, two systems' – in which convict labour is technically 'contracted out' to a separate internal organization charged with turning out the goods. A show workshop inside the labour camp is often installed, staffed by non-prisoners, to fool visitors.

The answer is that companies have to utilize information already available from the Laogai Research Foundation, Asia Watch and other independent researchers and advisers on the camps and factories involved, as well as carrying out independent investigation themselves, and being aware of questions that should be asked to suppliers.

Ignorance was not an excuse for Columbus McKinnon, a company based in Buffalo, USA, when customs impounded machinery the firm was importing from factories Harry Wu had shown to be *laogai* camps. When interviewed by the author about photographs showing the company president among gaunt, shaven-headed men in prison uniforms, Vice-president Robert L. Montgomery Jr said: 'There were absolutely no uniforms. We got back and looked at the pictures and still couldn't find anything [that indicated they were prisoners]. If it [prison labour] was going on at all it was well-hidden.'

Unbranded goods, such as tea or coal, are often the most difficult for Western companies to source. Twinings tea company admits that it relies upon the 'corporations through whom we purchase our Chinese teas' for assurances that all of these teas come only from commercial plantations producing specialist teas and do not include any tea from prison farms.[30] According to the *Chinese Law Journal*, up to a third of the 580,000 tonnes of tea annually produced in China comes from prison farms. Several of the *laogai* survivors featured in this book, including Miss Zhang and

Harry Wu, worked on tea farms during their imprisonment. Wu claims that it is an industry which needs to be fuelled by a constant, reliable source of labour, and so prisoners are ideal. Because tea produced and picked in prison farms is blended with other leaves plucked from ordinary farms before export, it is almost impossible for importers to discover the source. Britain is Europe's largest importer of tea from China: the British import about 7,000 tonnes a year, which is about 1 per cent of China's total production. Companies like Twining usually buy tea through agents and representatives; it is therefore up to individual companies to seek assurances from their Chinese suppliers about the origin of the tea. Because of the mixing of tea leaves at source, however, whenever a consumer buys a product labelled 'China Tea', there is a possibility that it may be from a *laogai* camp.

As the West joins the gold rush of investment in the Chinese mainland, the issue of *laogai* imports is marginalized or, worse, ignored. The effects of this disregard will ripple throughout the global market, as labour costs elsewhere drop in an attempt to compete, thus causing further competition for European and American businesses already undergoing a severe recession. It is in the interest of companies to abide by the legislation against labour camp products. Unfortunately most appear to think in terms of short-term profit, rather than long-term good sense. It is not a question of 'containing' or boycotting China; it is a question of engaging responsibly with a country which has the most spectacular growth rate in the world.

As a member of the UN's Security Council, China has a particular obligation to observe internationally approved standards of prison labour. These international standards are clear: prisoners convicted of criminal offences may be obliged to work. Other (untried) prisoners may be offered an opportunity to work, but should not be forced to do so. In both cases, work should be remunerated. The 1930 International Labour Organization Convention also prohibits government officials from imposing forced labour 'for the benefit of private individuals, companies or associations' (Article 4.2).[33]

The opportunity to work in prison is not necessarily abusive, nor is it prohibited by international law. Sometimes it is even a humane feature of prison systems, including Britain's own. The case of China is very different. Reform through labour and re-education camps require inmates to work in sometimes terrifyingly dangerous conditions: in nuclear installations for instance, uranium mines or in coal mines with little protection or safety procedures. Some work in asbestos mines, such as Xinqang mine, situated to the west of Chengdu. They work without protection: a short imprisonment in an asbestos mine is, effectively, a death sentence. 'If one dies, we bury one. If two die, we bury two,' is the attitude to the lives of prisoners. As we have seen, inmates are often forced to carry out procedures such as handling explosives and performing on-site blasting operations in open-cast mines.

Food rations are often cut as punishment for those who fail to meet work quotas. Torture is routine: prisoners are beaten up, handcuffed, shackled in leg-irons, jabbed with electric batons and confined in the 'dark cell' for infringements of discipline, resisting reform or failure to meet labour reform production quotas. Prisoners are rarely paid for their work: in some units or model prisons, a token payment of a few yuan per month is made. And political prisoners often have to endure solitary confinement for long periods, without daily contact with other prisoners, letters from home or visits from their loved ones.[34]

Companies who buy from the *laogai* are departing from civilized standards they would never dream of departing from in their own country, in their own workplaces. Buying from the *laogai* makes a mockery of free trade. 'We want China to develop economically, but we also want China to develop socially,' says Bill Jordan, International Secretary of the International Confederation of Free Trade Unions. 'The most spectacular economic growth in the world is currently taking place on the mainland alongside totalitarian methods of government. It's time for governments and companies to take a stand against forced labour. We are, after all, talking about minimum standards.'

The Massachusetts state legislature recently made a step in the right direction by voting to set strict human rights guidelines for companies in the state that do business with China.[35] Codes of conduct for businesses are another method of discouraging the use of forced labour, and acknowledging its existence. Some companies, such as Levi Strauss and Timberland, have pulled out of China altogether because of concern over human rights violations.[36] Reebok and Nike have also developed sourcing guidelines based on ethical standards when trading with China. One of the 'Business Partner Terms of Engagement' adopted by Levi Strauss addresses the *laogai* issue directly, stating: 'We will not knowingly utilize prison or forced labour in contracting or subcontracting relationships in the manufacture of our products. We will not knowingly utilize or purchase materials from a business partner utilizing prison or forced labour.'

Foreign firms are ideally placed to push for legal and even social reforms by showing that they are necessary for China's long-term growth – economically and socially. Lawyer Skip Kaltenheuser says:

They can use their time in China to help develop the infrastructure of a civil society that nurtures limitless economic growth and opportunities. Or

business can take the low-road of non-involvement, lighting up E
Corruptos while cultivating the world's largest banana republic.[37]

As Deng Xiaoping approaches death, Maoism is dying with him and
being replaced by a new form of nationalism. Amidst the economic
fervour of the karaoke bars, the businessmen with money to burn, the
$61,000 dinner and the fury of construction, China is struggling to
rediscover itself. There must now be a reckoning with the suffering of
millions of Chinese being sacrificed to the new gods of the fastest-
growing economic giant the world has ever seen.

Notes

1. Letter to the Editor, *New York Times* (5 October 1990), quoted in the Asia Watch report, *Prison Labour in China*, 1991.

2. Testimony of Ma Wenpiao, CICRC, *The White Book on Forced Labour in the People's Republic of China*, vol. 2: The Record, pp. 225-30.

3. Details in the Laogai Research Foundation report, *The World Bank and Forced Labour in China: Mistake or Moral Bankruptcy?*, 1995. A further report on World Bank involvement was released by the Laogai Research Foundation in February 1996.

4. Tibet Information Network News Review no. 23, *Reports from Tibet Nov. 1994–March 1995.*

5. Harry Wu, *Laogai*, p. 73.

6. Quoted in Stephen W. Mosher, *Made in the Chinese Laogai: China's Use of Prisoners to Produce Goods for Export*, A Strategic Study by the Asian Studies Centre published by the Claremont Institute, 1990.

7. Wu, *Laogai*, p. 73.

8. *Lu zai jiao xia* in *Laogai Laojiao Lilun Yanjiu*, no. 2 (1990), pp. 56–7 and p. 33, quoted in *News From Asia Watch*, 19 April 1991.

9. Yu Guoqiang, *Administrating and Rectifying Enterprises to Adjusting Product Structure in Order to Promote Foreign Economy Development*, vol. 2.

10. *Ibid.*

11. Amnesty International, *Torture in China* (December 1992), ASA 17/55/92.

12. *Ibid.*

13. Li Chao, 'New System and Schools Help Reform Prisoners', *China Daily* (4 August 1988).

14. Reprinted in the *Gothenburg Post* (9 August 1989), quoted in Mosher, *Made in the Chinese Laogai.*

15. Asia Watch report, *Prison Labour in China*, 19 April 1991.

16. *Ibid.*

17. A contributor to the confidential labour reform journal included in the Asia Watch report *Prison Labour in China*, in the April 1989 issue, p. 11.

18. For a detailed breakdown of the profitability of labour camps, see Wu, *Laogai*, pp. 41-9.

19. The conclusions of the Study Group are reported in Harold Tanner, 'The Theoretical Bases for Labour Reform', *China Information*, vol. 9, nos 2/3 (winter 1994-5).

20. From an article published in 1990 by the Group entitled 'Again, on Reforming of the Labour Reform Economic System'.

21. Liu Shanqing, 'Encounter with Legalised Illegality', *Chinese Sociology and Anthropology*, vol. 26, no. 4 (summer 1994), p. 64.

22. Harold Tanner article.

23. MacDougall, *US Law*, quoted in Mosher, *Made in the Chinese Laogai*.

24. The periodical *Legal Developments* (January 1989), quoted in Mosher, *Made in the Chinese Laogai*.

25. Full extract quoted in Wu, *Laogai*, pp. 48-9.

26. Human Rights Watch/Asia, *New Evidence of Chinese Forced Labour Imports to the US*, 24 May 1994.

27. There may be a reassessment and updating of the Act in 1996-7. Proposals have also been made to enforce the legislation throughout the European Community.

28. Information from the British Embassy, September 1994. An increasing number of companies are expanding their operations in China, and many of the largest British companies, including ICI, BP, Shell, Rolls-Royce, Jardines, Swires, Lucas Aerospace and Pilkington have set up joint venture companies.

29. International Society of Human Rights (ISHR).

30. Letter from Mr S. H. G. Twining, Director, to human rights campaigner Sue Byrne, 27 May 1994.

31. See Appendix 2.

32. *China Legal News* (28 May 1987), quoted in *News from Asia Watch* (19 April 1991).

33. *Ibid.*

34. In October 1995 the Massachusetts state legislature passed a bill which will require companies receiving state economic development aid to do all they can to ensure that their business with China does not include prison or forced labour, or discrimination based on ethnic, sexual, religious or political views. State governor William Weld vetoed the bill on 3 August, saying it was 'impossible to apply and enforce'. But the house overrode Weld's veto with a 123 to 26 vote – more than the two-thirds needed to reverse a veto. One representative, Daniel Bosley, said: 'I'm not trying to tell people they can't do business in the People's Republic of China, but we have a reasonable expectation that when we give state funds to a company, that they have reasonable standards.'

35. Levi Strauss acknowledged that the garment industry is the perfect first step to industrialization since the capital investment required is very low, it is highly labour-intensive and literacy is not a must. Among developing countries, Hong Kong is by far the most significant clothing producer together with South Korea and the Philippines; more than 60 per cent of all clothing exports by developing countries to the industrialized economies originate from Hong Kong and South Korea. (According to Levis, approximately 40 per cent of the clothing made in Hong Kong is processed partly in China.) In their Global Sourcing Guidelines, Levi Strauss criticize the low wages of workers and bad workplace conditions in many developing countries. However, the company was particularly concerned about conditions in China, and on 27 April 1993 announced that it would no longer manufacture jeans in China owing to the country's 'pervasive human rights violations'. A company document states: 'The decision to pull out of China was further complicated by the fact that China, famous for its trademark violations, could easily manufacture Levi's products illegally and capture the market. Levi's therefore, can still be bought in exclusive Chinese stores as a hedge against the counterfeiters.'

36. *Asian Wall Street Journal* (29 August 1995).

CHAPTER 17

The Earth on the Other Side of the World

Han Dongfang

I know that at each stride a puff of dust rises in the air, but unlike the tread of feet, my eyes leave no trace behind. No, the earth that holds my footprints is on the other side of the world.

Zhang Xianliang[1]

In the middle of the night on 3 June 1989, Han Dongfang was lying in a tent in Tiananmen Square, dozing. Students camped out at the perimeter of the square began to hear the squeak and crunch of the tracks of approaching People's Liberation Army tanks. In the distance there was the occasional rattle of gunfire and crackle of a burning bus forming a primitive barricade against the massed ranks of 'the people's' troops. Han was exhausted; as leader of the labour movement during the democracy demonstrations that had rocked the whole of China, he had spent weeks making speeches and maintaining unity amongst the workers. 'Wake me up when it's all over,' he mumbled to his wife. Knowing there would be no possibility of ever waking him up if he stayed, three burly *qi gong* masters picked up Han and carried him to safety. 'We need you,' they told him. 'You're China's Lech Walesa.'[2]

As leader of the Beijing Autonomous Workers' Federation, Han had played out a solitary role during the Tiananmen Square democracy movement. The students, wary of the civil unrest they felt could result from the involvement of workers in the movement, did not at first take Han seriously. And when he stood up to speak to the workers, with his measured, rich voice and careful command of his subject, they felt he belonged on the side of the intellectuals. When asked whether the demonstrations might have had a different result if workers were involved earlier, Han says calmly, 'There are no "ifs" in history, only facts.' (Plate 13.)

After Tiananmen, Han went on the run, and later, typically, handed himself in to the police when his face appeared on television screens throughout the country as 'Number One Most Wanted Worker'. Guards at the gate of the local police station failed to recognize him because of his dishevelled appearance, and almost turned him away. However as soon as they realized he was telling the truth, Ministry of Public Security officials sat him down for tea and cakes. Their glee in bagging one of the country's most wanted men soon dissipated. The appearance of Han before them belied the more complex reality. 'We're glad you've come to confess your crimes,' they told him, locking him in a cell. It was the beginning of a 22-month ordeal in prison for Han. 'Oh, but I haven't,' said Han simply. 'I haven't come to admit anything. I'm not a criminal. I've just come here to set the record straight.'

When Han was later held in a 'shelter and investigation' centre at 21 Paoju Lane, Beijing, he gained the reputation of someone who could not be broken.[3] His interrogators made little progress. When they informed him that he was to be charged with 'counter-revolutionary propaganda and incitement', Han interrupted: 'Let me make two things clear before we start. First, forget all the talk about lenience for those who repent. I'm not here to look for lenience. I'm here to question and if I say "I don't know," then please drop that subject. You will never get a different answer. If you already have evidence, go ahead and use it. Please don't bother me with it.' His Public Security Bureau interrogators could scarcely believe what they were hearing from this mild-mannered, gentle-looking prisoner. 'But soon they began to understand my temperament well,' he says.

During Han's twelve-month sentence, he went on hunger strike until the prison authorities agreed to give him proper medical care when he was suffering from tuberculosis. When he refused to give in, the prison warden arrived in his cell with a group of criminal prisoners. They pinned him down to the bed and a rubber feeding tube was rammed up his nose. After about a foot of the feeding tube had disappeared, Han could feel that the tube had jammed somewhere inside his nasal passages. It was not sliding down as it should. All Han could focus on was the dirt-encrusted fingers of the medical orderly shoving the tube down his throat and the excruciating pain. Suddenly a jet of liquid food squelched into his insides. 'There seemed to be an explosion in my skull, I choked, and then everything went black,' says Han. 'When I came round, they asked me if I was now ready to give up the hunger strike. I said no, never.'[4] The warden looked at him. 'OK, you can see the prison doctor in a week,' he said. Han had won. But it was a short-lived victory, and the warden continued to torment the weakened Han.

Later, when he was being held in a cell underneath a courtroom, the judge of his trial came down from his office to see him. 'He came down and said to the guards, "Where's Han Dongfang? I want to see him." He came into the room and asked me if I was Han Dongfang. I said yes, and he opened the door and told me to sit down. I said no. Then the judge kicked me in the belly with such force that I went flying backwards and landed in a heap against the wall. He said to me, "You are Han Dongfang – now I understand you. Just don't think you're strong. This is a government machine, and it is stronger than you."'

The fury of the judge, and his complete inability to deal with Han on any level other than violence, is indicative of the threat he represents to officialdom and the Party. Han speaks with the voice of someone independent of, and separate from, the Party. This solitary voice – which could belong only to a member of his generation – threatens the deep structure of the Party, which appears to be based on collective action but is in fact controlled by an inflexible and centralized hierarchy.

Han's attitude of personal responsibility and independence continues to infuriate Party lackeys – often because it is beyond their understanding. His strong sense of identity emerged in his adulthood after suffering a childhood in which he was constantly made to feel 'different' from his classmates. In 1966, when Han was just 5, his uncle was denounced as a 'capitalist roader' and sent to a remote province to do hard labour. When people in the poor farming village of Nanweiquan ('Delicate South Spring'), where Han lived, heard of his uncle, neighbourhood children hung a heavy slate around the boy's neck, scrawled slogans on it and jeered at him. Han's mother, a strong, determined woman, decided a few years later that she had had enough of scratching a living in this rural community. Leaving her husband to tend the fields, she took Han to Beijing, where she found work on a construction gang.

Han had an unhappy school life in the city. Higher standards in education meant that Han, from a poor village, found it difficult to keep up. He was mocked by the teachers for his slowness. Instead of allowing the criticism to grind him down, Han developed a defiance against authority and an independent sense of his own worth which is even stronger today. He needs it: in his continued attempts to improve the conditions of workers in China and to seek justice, he has pitted himself against not only an entire country but a entire value system.

'I always listen carefully to my friends and colleagues and my family,' he says. 'And then I make my decision, based on the information I have and my own feelings. After that no one can change my mind. I have always been stubborn in this way.' It is all the more extraordinary that this attitude of defiance has emerged in someone who was once a part of this system of repression. Han served for three years in the Gong An Bing, the Public Security Soldiers Corps – a predecessor of the modern People's Armed Police.

Encouraged by his mother, Han joined the Gong An Bing after leaving school in 1980.[5] His basic training took place over three months at Qinghe prison labour camp, near Tianjin in Hebei province. The soldiers underwent a punishing schedule of physical fitness and training in how to fight, and how to use weapons. They also had weekly ideological study. 'It was a very terrible time,' says Han. 'I can still remember it very vividly. We were educated about the history of the Public Security Corps. All the time we were told that we always had to serve the people. You must remember that we served the people.' Han gives one of his deep, rich laughs. 'Ideological study was important because the PLA is controlled by the Communist Party. They always say that the Communist Party represents the people in China, so it follows from this that the army has to serve the people – although of course our first duty was always to serve the ruling party.'

Most of the recruits were only 17 or 18 years old, and from the countryside. Their lack of education due to poverty made them particularly receptive to the ideological training. 'For most of them, being in the army was much better than living at home,' says Han. 'The army changed their lives, and so naturally they found it easy to take in the propaganda of our political study.'

Han's easy way with people and natural leadership qualities were soon noticed by division leaders, who put him in charge of a squad of eight men. The authorities' hopes for him were soon to be dashed, however, as he gradually became disillusioned with the system. Their first shock came at the time of the annual review, when squadron leaders were expected to give a report full of the satisfactory achievements of their team during the year. Han didn't come out with the usual platitudes – instead, his speech pulled no punches. First he criticized the amount of food his squadron were given compared to the officers, who he claimed were stealing a third of their food allowance. 'This is in direct contravention of Chairman Mao's line that officers and men are equal and must share both sufferings and good times,' announced Han, to the delight and surprise of his squadron and the fury of the officers. Han's second complaint was about the treatment of his men by officers: he told the assembled audience that his men were beaten and abused at will by their superiors.

The next day his battalion commandant tore up Han's application for Party membership and shredded it into tiny pieces. 'Through being in the army, I understood how to struggle against the leaders,' says Han. 'I was beginning to realize how the Party works from the inside. But even though I was struggling against the leaders of the hierarchy, I still believed in Marxism. I told my colleagues in the squadron to keep up their work – because while there were bad guys in the Communist Party, the philosophy behind the Party was good.' Han believes that his colleagues were not tormented by the same doubts about political philosophy and the consequences of their actions. 'They didn't think too much about it, but just got on with their work,' he says. 'Now, I just think I do my work for myself, for what is inside my heart and my beliefs. I don't care if the leaders are bad or good.'

Han was disturbed by the atmosphere of brutality which existed within the security services. 'I heard, and saw, many terrible things,' he says. For a year, Han was on guard duty at Qinghe. 'Electric shock batons were used to torture prisoners, and many were beaten up by several men at once,' he says. 'There were other forms of punishment too. Once I watched some of the security police telling two prisoners not to talk to each other, but to think about their crimes instead. Then they kept watch through a small window in the door. One of the prisoners muttered something quietly to the other – I think it was a comment about what they were having for dinner. The policeman watching through the window told the prisoner who had spoken to stand up. At dinner-time he was not allowed to eat, and at night-time he was not allowed to sleep, although he begged the policeman to let him rest. He was made to stand all through the night until the next day.'

Although a prison law forbade inmates to smoke cigarettes, this ruling was generally ignored. One of the most precious possessions for a prisoner was a handful of scavenged cigarette butts. However prisoners found smoking were generally punished. 'One inmate who was found puffing on a cigarette end had his hands bound behind his back by self-tightening handcuffs,' says Han. 'After about thirty minutes of this treatment, the pain is excruciating. If anyone touches your fingers, you experience intense pain. After twelve hours, the policeman came back. He held the prisoner's hands up in the air – I saw the prisoner's face, it was a terrible face. He said, "Oh, please, stop." But by then the policeman couldn't stop, he could not keep himself from torturing this man. The prisoner kept saying, "Oh please, you are my grandfather, you are my father, please stop and I'll never do this again." Then he'd say: "Oh please, you are my grandfather, you are my father, oh fuck your mother, stop it!"'

Sometimes prisoners would be locked into tight handcuffs for up to two months at a time. After they were released, they sometimes lost all use of their hands; very occasionally the hands would simply break off at the wrist. Han goes on: 'Usually the policemen used prisoners to do the work of beating up other prisoners. I remember one case of a mentally ill man who was in prison because he killed a girl – he had beaten her to death because she wouldn't make love with him. The guards would always make other inmates beat him up, and then they would say that he couldn't be a fool because he understood pain.'

Although Han's application for Party membership was refused, he still survived three years in the army. His loyalty and concern for his men won him admiration, and, when he left in September 1983, his squad members nominated him for a commendation as an 'advanced individual in building socialist spiritual civilization'.

Han is a rare example of an individual who stands out against the system by rejecting the culture of routine brutality instilled during army training in China. His story may also reflect the increasing cynicism of young soldiers for the propaganda they are force-fed during their 'education'.

Army training also failed to immunize Han against the shock, and therefore acceptance, of violence later on in life. An acceptance of violence, based on corporate obeying of orders, prepares the mental ground for an army to carry out the massacre of civilians and students, for instance in Tiananmen Square in 1989 – a grim refutation of Mao's dictum that the people's army should be like fish swimming in the sea of the people.

Three years after leaving the army, Han still remembers his horror and disillusionment on witnessing an attack by the Public Security Bureau on student demonstrators in late 1986. University students had made an organized protest march into Tiananmen Square, and their route passed near his house. 'I was able to watch as about a hundred policemen rushed out of the compound and began beating student marchers ferociously with clubs. If the students had been chanting "Down with the Communist Party!" that would have been one thing. Even I would have opposed them. But their slogans could hardly be counted as opposition, and yet they were beaten to the ground! And then some of them were dragged off toward police vans and thrown inside as if they were pigs being sent to market! As I went home that night, I felt terribly upset.'

Han has consistently adopted a stance of non-violent resistance against the authorities, and he has made no secret of his opposition to the regime. When he spoke to an audience during Tiananmen, he always identified himself by displaying his worker's ID and residency pass. And when journalist Nicholas Kristof interviewed him, despite having taken the security precaution of hiding on the floorboard of a Chinese friend's car to travel to his house, to Kristof's amazement Han greeted him in full view of the security officer, and carried out the interview with the doors to his apartment wide open. 'Everything I do, I do openly,' he told Kristof.[6] For these reasons Han has a genuine incomprehension of arbitrary cruelty. It is not that he does not understand the brutalization process. It is more that he hates to accept that it exists. The memory of one night in a police cell several years ago has become the focus of his anger about what human beings can do to each other.

'The police pushed me into a cell after beating me up,' recalls Han. 'At the time I had TB and I was still very weak. They bashed my head against the floor and said, "Oh Han Dongfang, don't think we are afraid of you. And don't think you're stronger than anyone else." Then the judge came into the room and sat on my back. It seemed to go on for ever. I was choking. When he got up I managed to struggle to the door, and said to the guard, "I need some fresh air." I was gasping for breath and felt my lungs were about to collapse. But the guard reached through the bars with an electric shock baton and stuck it in my neck. It was like two metal points boring into my skin. I just hung onto the bars with my hands clenched tight. I felt as though my whole body was on fire.'

Han's reputation had clearly reached this guard too. 'He finally said, "Now I believe what people have said about you – you are strong. I just had to test it."' It was soon after this that the judge returned to Han's cell and sent him flying with a kick in his lower belly – again, he claimed, to show Han who was 'boss'.

'I'm a Christian now,' says Han. 'And if you asked me if there is anyone I hate, I can only think of one person – the judge who did this to me. After he kicked me, I couldn't breathe. I had to go to hospital, and they told me the whole right side of my lung was full of water, because the judge had been sitting on my back for such a long time. The lung was filled with blood and water. The doctors put a long needle in my lung and drained a litre of fluid from it. I have feelings of hate towards this man more than anyone else because I can't understand why he could do this to another human being. Just to come into my cell when I was sick and to do this. And he was a judge! I still think about it now.'

Han Dongfang doesn't go to discos much in Hong Kong. He prefers to enjoy a quiet pint of Guinness in a waterfront bar near his home. More than a pint, however, or a cup of strong coffee, causes him heart palpitations. And although he has recovered from tuberculosis, he still sometimes suffers from breathlessness due to his lung complaint. Mainly Han prefers not to go to discos in his home city because of the attention he attracts. 'People often recognize me; they come up to me and say "Are you Mr Han Dongfang?" And I can see their eyes looking at me, so it's difficult to relax,' he explains. 'It's not that I don't like dancing.'

Although Han's name is recognized in the USA, where his wife lives with their two sons Nathan and Jonathan, he enjoys a pleasant anonymity. 'In America, I can walk into town and buy food without being noticed,' he says. 'This is much better than being in Hong Kong.' Han noticed other differences in America too. 'When I first went there, I was taking some exercise outside in the morning. Another person was running towards me, and as he passed he said "Good morning!" In China this wouldn't happen! Or if it did, the person would think, "Why is he saying good morning to me? What's the problem? Is there something wrong with me?"'[7]

In Hong Kong, Han 'turns his face towards China'. Although he is in enforced exile, he spends his days researching and writing about labour rights in his country, and attending conferences all over the world. His publication, the *China Labour Bulletin*,[8] is distributed internationally and to workers inside China. It is aimed at giving workers a voice which is denied in their workplaces and silenced in the wider community.

Rising unemployment and inflation, and increased industrialization leading to the displacement of peasants to the cities, are all factors which have contributed to the desperation of workers in China today. Workers have suffered from the withdrawal of state subsidies for welfare and essentials, privatization and restructuring of enterprises, and the determination to provide a cheap and compliant labour force to attract foreign capital.[9]

From 1992 onwards, inflation shot from about fifteen to about thirty per cent, and growing deficits left the treasury unable to support the still predominant state sector in the cities or the agricultural sector. Hence both urban workers and farmers have suffered a sharp downturn in their living standards. Not only have their incomings decreased but they have also had to pay more for housing, medical care, their children's education and other living costs. Increasing numbers of workers receive incomes below the poverty line: the official Chinese trade union ACFTU (All China Federation of Trade Unions) admitted that seven million workers in state enterprises suffered poverty. (Taking into account their families, the *China Labour Bulletin* claims that this translates into fifteen million people.)

Although government statistics claim only four million unemployed in China, the real figure again is probably far higher. A report published by the Pacific Economic Co-operation Commission in early 1994 named China as the country with the highest ratio of surplus labour in the world. Official statistics give an estimate of 140 million surplus rural labourers. This statistic, taken together with the estimate that more than half of the state-owned enterprises are operating at a loss, indicates that some 160 to

200 million people in China face unemployment, with a state increasingly unable to support them. Loss-making state enterprises are no longer able to function as the 'iron rice bowl' (*tie woanfan*) for their workers.[10] And *China Labour Bulletin* figures show that only 21 per cent of the official unemployed – in effect this means 7 per cent of the urban unemployed and a mere 0.5 per cent of the total – received unemployment relief in the first three-quarters of 1993.

Han Dongfang's concerns are to protect workers' rights to speak out against exploitation, to organize themselves and, in a fundamental sense, to exist. He believes that the official trade union ACFTU, which represents a monopoly in the representation of workers, has shown itself unable to defend the rights, even the lives, of its workers.

Deadly industrial fires and accidents have increased steadily in both number and severity in the last few years, he points out. The *China Labour Bulletin* lists many examples of these horrific, and preventable, 'accidents'. In 1991, eighty people were killed in a fire at the Guangdong Dongwan Rainwear Factory; in 1994 at least ten workers died in the huge factory fire in Bao'an prefecture; and 84 workers' lives were lost in a fire at the Zhili Toy Factory in Shenzhen. Official statistics reveal that between 1990 and 1992 the number of deaths from industrial accidents reached 65,000. Again, the real figure is probably much higher.

Han points out that most of these disasters were preventable. For instance, workers' dormitories are often located directly above the factory floor, making them more likely to be trapped in the building when fire breaks out. They are usually locked from the outside. All of the fire escapes in these factories are usually blocked as a result of being used for storage areas. Highly flammable materials were also in use within the factories, but workers had not been given appropriate training in how to use them safely or the possible dangers in handling such materials. Again, when the fires broke out, fire-fighting equipment on the premises was seriously inadequate.

There are still many questions about the issue that puzzle Han. 'Why do workers tolerate being trapped inside their workshops and dormitories like prisoners without offering any resistance?' he wants to know. This indicates a way of thinking alien to Han's beliefs on personal responsibility. 'How would workers be treated if, before anything went wrong, they attempted to say something critical about the way fire escapes are blocked? Why are workers not allowed to organize and appoint their own representatives to monitor workplace safety? And why do the police prohibit surviving workers from having contact with outsiders by detaining them and depriving them of their personal freedom?'

Han knows there are no simple answers to these questions. The quiescent stance of the workers and their subservience to authority is of course often explained by their desperation for work to feed their families, and their awareness that they are as dispensable as the next man or woman. The situation of women workers is even worse than that of men. They are paid less than men, they are often sacked and replaced when they become pregnant, and they often suffer physical and sexual abuse, even rape, from their employers. In one enterprise in Fuzhou city, Fujian province, a woman worker took two pairs of shoes from the factory. The factory owner hung her up and had her beaten severely. He then put the two pairs of shoes around her neck and locked her in a cage together with a huge bulldog.[11]

Machinery in the factories poses other hazards for workers, and accidents often occur as a result of the extreme fatigue of workers operating them. A 14-year-old girl worker in a foreign-invested textile enterprise in Zhongshan city, Guangdong province, was so exhausted by her eighteen-hour working day that she fainted. Her hair was pulled into the machinery and she died instantly.[12] The lack of concern for the safety of Chinese workers also applies to factories run by foreign companies. Under the guise of protecting trade secrets, some foreign investors even bring to China dangerous production methods and chemicals that have been banned in other countries.[13]

Han says: 'All the indications are that Chinese workers have had to place even their own lives in the hands of others. The recent disastrous fires show that getting a job in China means giving up part of one's personal freedom . . . The sacrifice of personal freedom is the price one pays to find work. Even in a highly populated country like China, lost lives cannot be regarded lightly. After all, hasn't the right to exist been called the most basic right for all human beings in China? If this is so, workers should be allowed to fully exercise and protect their right to exist.'

Han Dongfang is fighting a lonely battle against a trade union which is part of the government system of repression. When asked about their position towards the support of independent labour activists such as Han Dongfang, an official spokesperson for ACFTU, Xue Zhaoyun, said:

> We strongly disapprove of any support for Han Dongfang. It would block the establishment of normal relations with the ACFTU. Han's efforts to support workers and free trade unions in China were unfriendly and unacceptable. This is our clear stance.[14]

Han is particularly concerned about the exploitation of the 'blind flow' (*mang liu*) of migrant workers. 'After Chinese New Year, millions of rural peasants and villagers leave their homes and board the "box train" supplied by the government to transport them to the coastal areas,' says Han. 'Every step of the way, they endure terrible conditions and exploitation. In our *Bulletin* we recorded cases of people coming from Sichwan province to Guangdong. On the trains, there are no benches or seats, and no windows. There may be one simple toilet, or hole in the floor, for several hundred people, and there are about 150 people in each "box". You just can't think about the conditions during the five-to-six-day train ride to Canton.' Workers from rural areas often have to pay double the cost for such a train ticket, because of the black market. Touts buy up all the tickets and sell them to make a profit. 'The police are fully involved in this form of corruption,' says Han.

Those in search of jobs in the promised land of the Special Economic Zones have little or no money for the journey. 'They are all expecting to find work but of course not all of them do,' says Han. 'They are left with nothing; they can't afford food or the train fare back home.' Periodically, gangs of migrants sleeping rough at stations around the province are rounded up by police. 'They use sticks to hit the people lying in the square,' says Han. 'Then they force them to move to a small yard, where they have to pay $5 per night. At 5 or 6 in the morning, the gates are opened and they are allowed to leave.'

Under these desperate circumstances, it is not surprising that people will group together, usually with people from their home village or province, to protect themselves. Gao Changwen, a supervisor in a kitchenware factory in Xiamen, says that virtually every day someone comes to him for help, looking for a job or money. He lends out thousands of yuan to people from his village who are in difficulty, and has introduced others into his factory for work. If he was sacked, he says, all his people would leave at once – so his boss treats him decently.[15]

The conditions in 'box trains', the herding of desperate job-seekers into the police compound, the casual violence on the streets are all indications of the state repression endured by the *mang liu* of China's new underclass. It is this group of Chinese who are suffering most in the *laogai* system today. In his paper 'Theoretical Bases for Labour Reform', Harold Tanner argues, 'Is not the incarceration of greater numbers of working-class Chinese in increasingly violent, and decreasingly effective, labour camps indicative of increasing social tensions, and increasng degrees of repression?'

The Beijing Workers' Autonomous Federation was the real 'cancer cell' the government sought to eliminate during the Tiananmen uprisings in 1989. 'The Goddess of Democracy represented the arrogant intrusion of decadent Western values into the symbolic heart of Chinese Communism, rupturing the sacred cosmology, the feng shui of the great square,' wrote Robin Munro and George Black in *Black Hands of Beijing*. 'But the crude red and black banner of the BWAF, less than a hundred yards away, signified the more terrifying power of the workers awakened' (p. 236).

Because of Deng Xiaoping's fears of an epidemic of 'the Polish disease' (in other words, a Chinese Solidarity in the making), the crackdown on the workers after Tiananmen was exceptionally harsh. After 4 June, they were the first targets. Any worker in any province of China who voiced criticism about the severity of the massacre was arrested immediately. On 6 June, six demonstrators blocking a railway track in protest were killed when police ordered an engineer to plough into them. Three of the remaining protesters, who were all workers, were sentenced to death and shot on 21 June. Countless others were shot by a bullet at the base of the skull; but details of their arrests were declared to be state secrets.

Workers attempting to organize unions or support for colleagues still face severe harassment, prison sentences or years in labour re-education camps. After Tiananmen, workers 'disappeared' across the country. Xiao Delong, a worker who was involved with the BAWF, was reportedly sentenced to a three-year prison term. Forty-five-year-old Xiao, who was arrested in September 1992 and tried in early 1993, apparently mutilated his face while on the run in an attempt to disguise his identity. Accurate figures are not available on the number of Workers' Autonomous Federation detainees still being held after the Tiananmen demonstrations in 1989.

Some of those released, or recent escapees, arrive in Hong Kong, like Han Dongfang did when he was expelled from China. Han is not an exile by choice: he tried to return to his homeland in August 1993, after he spending a year in the USA recovering from tuberculosis. A day after his arrival in China, Han was seized in Guangzhou by the Public Security Bureau, beaten up and forced back across the border to Hong Kong. Officials confiscated $1600 of Han's money and bought him an air ticket for Switzerland. Han insisted that he wished only to return to his country, that he had no intention of trying to overthrow its government but wanted to establish a free trade union to help ordinary workers bargain for their rights in China's new economic climate. On 21 August, the Chinese announced that Han's passport had been cancelled – effectively leaving him stateless. What had seemed to be a humanitarian gesture, permitting Han to seek treatment for his tuberculosis abroad, had become an enforced exile.

Journalist Liu Binyan once said that the main factor determining the success or otherwise of China's future development lies inside the minds of Chinese people. In contemporary China, to get rich is glorious, but social, intellectual and cultural development is of a lower priority, and not valued by the state in itself because it is associated with a loss of political control. Over the last forty years, the People's Republic has silenced millions of intellectuals and workers by sending them to the countryside or to forced labour camps. Today, the government is marginalizing 'dissident' thinkers like Han Dongfang by forcing them to leave the country. China's future will be poorer without those who could enrich the country and change the minds of Chinese from within.

Often dissidents who have just crossed the border into Hong Kong seek Han out for help. He gives them clear, pragmatic advice. 'It's a big change,' he says. 'You need money, you need food. Exiles coming here must change themselves, as I had to do. I always tell my friends when they come out of China not to immediately involve themselves in political work. Before you do anything, you need to make yourself strong, you need to feed yourself, you need to live by yourself. Sometimes they feel angry when they come here because it's so difficult. They think capitalism is bad, no one helps you, there's no justice in the world. But I tell them, please don't think about the world's injustices at first.'

Han Dongfang pauses for a minute, and adds his own view on the plight of the exile, whose footprints remain on the other side of the world: 'To put it simply, first you must eat, and then you can think.'

Notes

1. Zhang Xianliang, *Getting Used to Dying*.

2. Han's story is told in Robin Munro and George Black, *Black Hands of Beijing*, a clear and informative exposition of events and characters of the Tiananmen Square democracy movement in 1989. This chapter is based on an author interview, and draws on this book.

3. In *Black Hands of Beijing*, Robin Munro and George Black said that after interviewing him they were almost led to sympathize with the interrogators who were given the thankless task of attempting to break his indomitable spirit.

4. Artificial feeding of prisoners on hunger strike is also common in the Soviet gulag. In *The Gulag Archipelago*, Solzhenitsyn writes: 'The element of rape inheres in the violation of the victim's will: "It's not going to be the way you want it, but the way I want it; lie down and submit." They pry open the mouth with a flat disc, then broaden the crack between the jaws and insert a tube: "Swallow it." And if you don't swallow it, they shove it farther down anyway and then pour liquefied food right down the oesphagus. And then they massage the stomach to prevent the prisoner from resorting to vomiting. The sensation is one of being morally defiled, of sweetness in the mouth, and a jubilant stomach gratified to the point of delight . . . Science did not stand still, and other methods were developed for artificial feeding: an enema through the anus, drops through the nose' (vol. 1, p. 470).

5. The administrative system of the Public Security forces is complicated, as the Chinese term for department or section,

and sometimes for office, varies according to the administrative level. It has five levels: at the national level is the Gong An Bu, the Ministry of Public Security; at the province level is the Gong An Ting; at prefecture level the police are known as the Gong An Chu, and their offices are called *ke*; at the county level the police are known as the Gong An Ju and their offices called *gu*. In these cases the words *ting*, *chu* and *ju* are all equivalent to the English department or bureau, but indicate different levels of authority. At the District Office level, just above the *xiang* and neighbourhood offices, the police stations are called *paichusuo* or police sub-stations (Tibet Information Network report on security, 1995, p. 13).

6. Nicholas Kristof and Sheryl WuDunn, *China Wakes*.

7. The famous satirical writer Bo Yang analysed cultural differences like these and what they reveal about the unpleasant side of the Chinese psyche in *The Ugly Chinaman and the Crisis of Chinese Culture*. 'The most severe cultural shock most Chinese experience when they go to the United States is the variety and complexity of American etiquette,' writes Yang, who was jailed for ten years in Taiwan for translating into Chinese a Popeye cartoon that the Taiwan authorities found offensive. 'One admirable characteristic of Western civilisation is the way people acknowledge each other's existence, and treat each other with respect. This makes them conscientious about being polite to others all the time. If someone steps on your foot, it's "Sorry". If someone doesn't step on your foot but almost steps on your foot, it's still "Sorry." . . . If he has to take a piss in the middle of a conversation, naturally it's "Excuse me". And if a fire breaks out in his kitchen when you are

having dinner in his house, and he rushes away from the dining table in order to put it out, it's "Excuse me" once again . . . "Thank you" and "I'm sorry" are fixtures of daily life in democratic countries, and even children who are just learning to talk say "Thank you" to their mothers when they change their nappies.'

8. Available from PO Box 72465, Central Post Office, Kowloon, Hong Kong.

9. *Trade Union Rights in China*, prepared by *China Labour Bulletin* for the International Confederation of Free Trade Unions (ICFTU) seminar on trade union rights held in Brussels in June 1994.

10. The 'iron rice bowl' means a very secure job providing sufficient income for accommodation, food and daily living expenses. It generally includes welfare benefits and medical provisions for the family of the employee. The 'common rice bowl' (*daguo-fan*) refers to the socialist system, in which everyone is fed, in effect, from one big rice bowl, regardless of ability or level of work, which tends to reduce motivation.

11. China Labour Education and Information Centre, *The Unofficial Report: Women Workers in China*.

12. Quoted in *The Unofficial Report* and extracted from *Dapeng Bay* (March 1993).

13. Han Dongfang, quoted in *China Rights Forum* (fall 1994), p. 9.

14. 'Our Position towards the Relationship between the International Labour Movement and ACFTU', *The Eastern Express* (July 1994), quoted in *China Labour Bulletin*.

15. Mobo C. F. Gao in *China Rights Forum* (fall 1994), p. 28.

Afterword

Change the name, and the tale is about you.

Horace

To borrow a phrase from the Holocaust survivor and writer Primo Levi, this book is drenched in memory. It draws on the recollections of those who have suffered the direct consequences of inhumane policies and high-level power struggles. Sometimes, for those who have lived through them, retelling these stories is like crossing a field of barbed wire; the memory is snagged and held, and the pain is lived through again. For some, every detail of a particular trauma is unforgettable, while others will unconsciously block recollections of torture or shameful memories, and deny betrayals. Sometimes the memory itself betrays us by distorting the reality.

Primo Levi discovered that nearly all the survivors of concentration camps in Nazi Germany had experienced a similar nightmare during their imprisonment. They had returned home and were describing their suffering to a loved one. But as soon as they began to talk, the loved one turned and walked away. The horror of the dream lay in not being listened to.

As these nightmares show, there is a need in us to validate our experiences by seeking acceptance from others. We also tell our stories to create order from chaos, to transform the abysmal and the terrifying into normality, and to give structure to a broken and fragmented life. As expressions of humanity, the stories of individuals are all the more important when they emerge from an impersonal and autocratic state like China.

Memory links our past with our present and, ultimately, our future. The sight of thousands of students and citizens gathering in Tiananmen Square in 1989 may have awakened dark memories for senior statesman

Deng Xiaoping of another mass of rebellious young people – the hordes of Red Guards who surrounded him, screaming, during terrifying struggle sessions in the Cultural Revolution. Perhaps the key to the military crackdown on 4 June lay in the visceral fear of history repeating itself. Memories of millions starving to death during the Great Leap Forward may also have precipitated Deng's bullish enthusiasm for economic development, with the aim of immediate improvement in living standards.

Deng – who is dying and scarcely conscious as this book is written – has always encouraged the Chinese people to 'look forward, never backward'. Looking forward not backward means modernization at any cost. It means the destruction of elegant Ming Dynasty buildings to make way for soaring skyscrapers of dubious architectural significance and, in Tibet, tearing out the thirteenth-century heart of Lhasa to make room for a shopping complex and featureless concrete housing. 'Looking forward not backward' is also an unspoken warning; that it is impossible for the people to settle accounts with the Communist Party.

There is a heavy psychological price to pay for negating one's memories. It leaves people with no form of catharsis for their anger and feelings of retribution. In this system, men like John (whose story is told in Chapter Two) are 'compensated' for more than twenty years of imprisonment and the death of a father in the *laogai* with a mere couple of hundred *yuan*.

Today, those who tortured and killed during Mao's various political purges are friendly next-door neighbours, business entrepreneurs and ordinary-looking middle-aged men and women who take an active role in the community. China lives with an awareness of the darkness at its core.

'Only part of us is sane,' wrote Rebecca West. 'Only part of us loves pleasure and the longer day of happiness, wants to live to our nineties and die in peace, in a house that we built, that shall shelter those who come after us. The other half of us is nearly mad. It prefers the disagreeable to the agreeable, loves pain and its darker night despair, and wants to die in a catastrophe that will set back life to its beginnings and leave nothing of our house save its blackened foundations.'[1]

In the short term, perhaps this awareness of the 'darker half' in China can be forgotten in the new challenge of making money. But in the long term, rapid economic growth is not enough; there have to be accompanying cultural and moral values.

In the closing years of the twentieth century, the adulation of Mao and his aphorisms has been replaced by nihilism and a loss of faith. An escalating crime rate, increased levels of corruption, the aimlessness and desperation of the 'blind flow' of nearly 200 million unemployed, and the political instability in the transition to post-Deng China are manifestations of the moral vacuum and sense of insecurity under the surface of the economic success.

Western leaders have signalled their approval for China's economic reform without regard for its consequences. Although human rights have become an accepted part of the political agenda, concern for them is marginalized because world leaders know that China may well be the biggest economic player of the twenty-first century, and they don't want to lose out on their share of the riches. In Chinese eyes, US President Bill Clinton shaking hands with their premier has a symbolic importance that transcends any expression of concern for human rights by American statesmen.

Increasingly, governments are kowtowing to China in an extraordinary fashion, three centuries after Britain's trade representative Lord Macartney was sent packing by the Emperor Qianlong after refusing to prostrate himself. In May 1996, the cultural arm of the German government, the Goethe Institute, cancelled a debate on human rights after being warned by Beijing that there would be unspecified 'consequences' if the debate with 'enemies of the state' went ahead. In the same month, Deputy Prime Minister Michael Heseltine attended banquets in Beijing in the interests of Anglo-Chinese business deals while monks were being shot in occupied Tibet by Chinese troops.

There have even been guarded warnings from Beijing that drawing attention to human rights abuses could lead to discrimination against countries. The Chinese paper *Wen Wei Po* declared in May that: 'Britain wants both the fish and the bear's paw – to do lots of business with China but block China in Hong Kong. This can only result in Britain losing both the fish and the bear's paw.' At a time when competition among foreign companies to invest in China is intense, this is a potent threat. Yet human rights and trade with China are inextricably linked. Human rights issues in China can affect the welfare of employees of an investing company; they can damage its international reputation and threaten the security of its investment.

China describes criticism of its record of endemic torture, suppression of national and religious minorities, arbitrary arrest, imprisonment and forced labour as 'interference in its internal affairs'. Yet it has still signed the United Nations' Universal Declaration of Human Rights, which recognizes that these abuses transcend national boundaries. In 1993, China also put its name to the Vienna Declaration, which affirms that 'the promotion and protection of all human rights is a legitimate concern of the international community'.

The Chinese may agree in theory to these desirable aims, but the real situation in China proves that their official pronouncements have an uneasy relationship with the truth – bearing an uncanny resemblance to Lewis Carroll's intransigent character, Humpty Dumpty, when he declares: 'When I use a word, it means just what I choose it to mean – neither more nor less . . . Impenetrability! That's what I say!'

This use of official language by the Maoist bureaucracy, and later by Deng's politburo, created a dangerous gulf between appearance and reality. During the Great Leap Forward, the 'appearance' was represented by crowds of apparently happy peasants, who lined the streets whenever Mao toured the regions, and fields of healthy crops visible from the carriages of his official train. Disregarding the plight of hundreds of millions of peasants, leading cadres of the Party were ingratiating themselves with Mao by making preposterous claims of vastly increased production – such as one *mu* of land (0.16 of an acre) producing 200,000 pounds of rice. Because rural areas were taxed on a percentage of what they produced, some areas had to deliver all they had to the state to meet tax demands based on such faked, ridiculously high reports. As Mao's bandwagon rolled on, entertained by dancing girls and lavish banquets, millions were starving. With a few honourable exceptions, those with eyes to see did not report the reality, because they were terrified of being branded 'Rightists' and purged from the Party. The famine following the Great Leap Forward was a human disaster unrivalled this century, in which at least 30 million, perhaps even 43 million, people died of starvation.

If people had not been terrified of speaking out during those 'three lean years', public opinion could have been mobilized, and the authorities would have been forced to take action. Those who believe that China should have the freedom to develop economically and feed its people before the authorities consider 'other human rights' such as freedom of speech should remember the heavy price of this form of censorship.

In today's China, the authorities like to disguise the importance of cheap *laogai* labour to the state as concern for the people's 'spiritual welfare'. In February 1996, Prime Minister Li Peng told a group of former Red Guards that their 'spiritual standard had been elevated' through hard labour alongside the masses. He advised them to 'treat this part of our history with the correct perspective'. Although officials see forced labour as an integral part of the drive towards modernization, in reality cheap labour costs are only part of China's appeal for inward investment. The main attraction for foreign firms is market access to 1.2 billion people – more than four times the number of potential consumers in Europe.

Although China's economy has recently suffered a downturn (partly due to the increase in income inequality and partly due to market saturation of consumer durables and cheap goods in both urban China and overseas), all the signs are that it is developing a competitive mixed economy with perhaps the most extraordinary market share in the world. After the initial fervour of the Deng years, Chinese policy-makers have instigated a drive to cool down the economy and to restructure the inefficient and loss-making state-owned sector. The next century will be a testing time as China attempts to maintain growth while curbing inflation, but the economic miracle looks set to continue.

However, serious ruptures are likely to tear the social fabric of the country. One of the greatest challenges China has to face in the short term, if only in symbolic terms, is the death of Deng Xiaoping. Traditionally, a period of upheaval and power struggles has followed the death of a leader in China. In Beijing today, a Shanghai clique headed by Deng's anointed heir Jiang Zemin (who is President, party chief and chairman of the central military commission) is ready to assume power. Jiang will not want to remain in Deng's shadow for long; already he has travelled the country urging people to 'talk politics'. This may signify an emphasis on ideology and rhetoric in contrast to Deng's preference for tangible results, particularly in economic development. (As his infamous slogan runs, 'I don't care if it's a white cat or a black cat, it's a good cat as long as it catches mice.')

An upsurge in nationalism is already beginning to fill the psychological void created by disillusion with Maoism and the new nihilism in China. This resurgent nationalism shows every sign of developing into a wave of anti-foreign feeling and paranoia about the motives of the West. China's aggression towards Taiwan during the pre-election campaign in 1996 also sent shudders through policy-makers worldwide. The firing of missiles towards the island represented a serious threat to the stability of Asia which is unlikely to go away.

Over the next decade, unrest is likely to intensify in the vast Chinese-controlled territories of Tibet and Xinjiang. In May, a group of Tibetan monks were spotted in the Barkor market of Lhasa putting up an empty picture-frame. Passing worshippers bowed their heads in deference to this symbolic image of the Dalai Lama. It was a defiant act, expressing Tibetan opposition to a Chinese crackdown on religion, which in May 1996 involved a ban on all pictures and effigies of the exiled leader. To the north, in the vast desert region of Xinjiang, the Chinese instigated a sweeping campaign against Muslim activists. In the last week of April 1996, nearly 2000 'terrorists, separatists and criminals' were arrested, and on 2 May, nine alleged Muslim separatists were killed in a shoot-out with the police. The severity of the Chinese crackdowns in these 'minority areas' indicates a growing sense of panic over the violence involved in 'splittist' activities. It is unlikely that China will loosen its grip on these two strategically important regions, with their immense mineral and natural wealth; it has already begun to do the opposite by tightening control.

As the twenty-first century approaches, liberals co-exist with hard-liners within the Chinese politburo and among the people. China is more open than ever before, but it is still impossible for the Chinese to be free in a society which executes, imprisons and tortures those who stand against it. Even so, a growing number of dissidents are prepared to stay in the country and confront the hierarchy head-on.

The state in contemporary China uses a language of collective amnesia, a language which pays little attention to the reality of the past and present, and its painful legacy. To fully transform as a society, and to become as important culturally and politically as it is economically, China needs to listen to its dissident thinkers, to generate a spirit of openness and move towards a vision of democracy. Only then can the ghosts of the past be laid to rest. Otherwise, they will haunt China's future.

Notes

1. Rebecca West, *Black Lamb and Grey Falcon*, 1941.

Business and the *Laogai*
A Case Study

The 1897 Act forbidding importation of foreign prison-made goods into Britain was originally aimed at protecting British businesses from cheaper goods made by slaves and prisoners in the nineteenth century. However, it is still relevant in the twentieth century where China is concerned.

So far, UK Customs have held four investigations into goods thought to be imported into Britain from the Chinese *laogai* under the 1897 Act. None has so far been successful, generally because of a 'lack of evidence'. Research groups and human rights organizations believe there to be a political subtext behind the lack of prosecutions: an unwillingness on the part of the British government to be seen to be involved in pursuing cases against forced labour just before the handover of Hong Kong in July 1997.

Harry Hongda Wu and his Laogai Research Foundation have blazed a solitary trail with their research into goods from Chinese prisons. It is a trail with many twists and turns and a number of brick walls. The British-based Laogai Research Group, working with the LRF, gained an insight into the complexity of the process when they traced machinery on sale in British factories back to the largest light hoist factory in China, otherwise known as Zhejiang Province Number Four prison.

The trail began when group member Louise Fournier spotted a bright-orange chain-hoist (a mechanical lifting tool) and lever-lift in the industrial product list of a British factory. Two of the companies involved in selling the products confirmed that the goods were from China, and that they could be imported at prices well below those at which UK companies could manufacture similar hoists.

A representative of one company told Louise that some of their products were made in China, in a factory built by a US company. Harry Wu identified the goods from a picture in the brochure: they looked the same as those being made in a prison camp he had filmed during a clandestine trip to China. The chain-hoists and lever-lifts on sale in the UK bore a striking resemblance to those under seizure in the USA, which were made in a Chinese labour reform camp called Wulin.

Wulin is a large light-hoist factory nestling between a small mountain and the Sheng-tang river in the town of Linping, Yuhang county, some 30 kilometres north-east of the popular tourist city Hangzhou. It is also known as Zhejiang Province Number Four prison.[1] After Harry Wu named the factory in his book *Laogai: The Chinese Gulag* in 1992, the authorities changed its external name from Wulin to Hangzhou Superpower Hoist Works. A new office building was constructed, together with new phone and fax numbers.

According to an advertisement in an official Chinese government publication obtained by Harry Wu, Zhejiang Province Number Four was 'among the first 28 enterprises to trade with foreign customers'. Harry Wu traced the US agent of chain-hoists produced at Wulin, by doing business with a company in Hong Kong which was a subsidiary of the PRC government-owned Zhejiang Machinery and Equipment Import and Export Corporation. He had traced the Hong Kong agent by approaching the factory direct, posing as a businessman involved in importing machinery to the USA. The US agent was a company called Columbus McKinnon, a 118-year-old maker of chains and hoists in Buffalo, USA. It both makes hoists and imports them from China.

When Harry Wu presented US Customs with his evidence, they made a seizure of goods from Columbus McKinnon. The American legislation against *laogai* goods is USC 1307 (Section 307 of the Tariff Act of 1930, as amended). This reads as follows:

> *All goods, wares, articles, and merchandise mined, produced or manufactured wholly or in part in any foreign country by convict labour and/or forced labour and/or indentured labour under penal sanctions shall not be entitled to entry at any ports of the United States, and their importation is therefore prohibited.*

The Memorandum of Understanding (MOU) on Prison Labour agreed between the USA and China in August 1992 enables Customs to participate in investigations within China of suspected factories. However officials admit to difficulties in implementing the MOU, partly because the Chinese demand evidence *before* allowing US inspection of factories suspected to be *laogai* camps. When visits are made, considerable sanitization of the establishment concerned is undertaken by the Chinese, often to the extent of shifting prisoners into separate buildings, constructing new offices and so on.

A year before, directors of Columbus McKinnon had visited Wulin. They took photographs which, they claimed, showed their director among a happy, free group of workers. Former inmates of the *laogai* say that the shaven heads and grey uniforms indicate that the workers are in fact prisoners. While in China, Harry Wu had shot footage of prisoners with bowed heads and regulation uniform passing through the gates of the factory.

When the managing director of the UK company was told about the Laogai Research Group's research, he backtracked and said the goods in question came from 'Hangzhou'. The Wulin Machinery Plant is situated on the outskirts of Hangzhou, and is also known as the 'Hangzhou Wulin Machinery Works'.

The investigation that followed to confirm the initial evidence spanned the UK, Hong Kong, the USA and China. It involved interviews with all companies concerned, often dealing with contradictory information. However, it built up a solid body of evidence which was duly presented to UK Customs. Ultimately, no prosecution was made. The case had illuminated the lengths to which Chinese officials will go to hide the use of forced labour in the production of goods for export. It also highlighted the sensitivity of businesses in the UK and America to allegations of buying from Chinese prisons. Continued cases against suspected *laogai* goods being imported into the UK can only help to break down the lines of defence and hit the system in China and the wider business community where it hurts.

Note

1. Full details about this prison and the case against the US company Columbus McKinnon are given in the Laogai Research Foundation Report *Cruel Money*.

Forced Labour

There is nothing inherently wrong or exploitative with the concept of prison labour. In many countries, it is a humane feature of the penal system, providing relief from boredom and a release from the confinement of a cell. However, forced labour within the prison system is an entirely different matter.

The United Nations has to some extent steered clear of detailing the problem: international treaties adopted by the UN concerning human rights have been very careful not to prohibit 'forced labour' by some categories of prisoners. International standards adopted by the International Labour Organization (ILO) do not prohibit forced labour in all circumstances: they simply impose strict limitations on its use.

Anti-Slavery International, an independent organization based in London,[1] points out that 'forced labour' is not an alternative term for 'slavery', although confusion is sometimes created by implying that slavery is simply a category of forced labour. The practice of forced labour, however, does not carry with it the same notions of 'ownership' as slavery or slavery-like practices.

International standards recognize that the state is entitled to oblige people to undertake work of certain types and in some particular circumstances. These international standards also recognize that states may make convicted prisoners perform forced labour. However, these standards state that they should be remunerated, which they are not within the *laogai* system. Furthermore, forced labour should not be used to punish political dissidents. Again, China is guilty of contravening these standards.

China is a member of the UN Security Council, and so has a particular obligation to observe internationally approved standards. Declarations and other resolutions adopted by the UN, such as the Standard Minimum Rules for the Treatment of Prisoners, set an international standard to be observed by all states, even though they do not take the form of an actual treaty requiring ratification.

Some of these international standards are as follows:

ILO Convention (No. 29) concerning Forced Labour

This Convention, adopted in 1930, limits the use of forced labour very strictly and urges its total elimination. The Convention also prohibits government officials from imposing forced labour 'for the benefit of private individuals, companies or associations' (Article 4.2). The ILO's Committee of Experts on the Application of Conventions and Recommendations has urged governments only to allow prisoners to be placed at the disposal of private companies with the express consent of the prisoners concerned. China has not ratified this Convention.

ILO Convention (No. 105) Concerning the Abolition of Forced Labour

This prohibits the use of forced or compulsory labour in some specific circumstances; in particular 'as a means of political coercion or education or as a punishment for holding or expressing political views or views ideologically opposed to the established political, social or economic system' (Article 1.a). It also prohibits the use of forced labour to bring about economic development. One hundred and twelve states have ratified this Convention, but not China.

The UN Standard Minimum Rules for the Treatment of Prisoners

These rules, set in 1957 by the UN Economic and Social Council, state that prisoners who work should be remunmerated. Article 73 suggests that 'institutional industries and farms' where prisoners work should 'preferably' be 'operated directly by the [prison] administration and not by private contractors'.

China has a dismal record of keeping to these international standards. Both convicted and untried prisoners are forced to labour in conditions which clearly violate internationally approved standards. These prisoners are not remunerated for their work, and their labour benefits the state's economic development. China's failure in adhering to even minimum global standards should be noted by the rest of the international community when dealing with issues of trade with China.

Note

1. Anti-Slavery International can be contacted at Unit 4, Stableyard, Broom Grove Road, London SW9 9TL. I am indebted to their paper *Can Prisoners Be Subjected to Forced Labour?* for the content of this appendix.

Addresses of Organizations

China Labour Bulletin: Information on labour rights and the situation of workers in China. Contact PO Box 72465, Central Post Office, Kowloon, Hong Kong.

The Laogai Research Foundation: Up-to-date and detailed information on trade with the laogai, human rights campaigning and stories of laogai survivors. PO Box 361375, Milpitas, California, 95036/1375, USA.

The Laogai Research Group (UK), 9 Regency Lawns, Croftdown Road, London NW5 1HF. Works with the Laogai Research Foundation in campaigning for an end to Western trade with the laogai.

International Society for Human Rights, St George's House, Well Street, London. Tel: 0171–636 7468.

Human Rights Watch/Asia, Lancaster House, 33 Islington High Street, London N1 9LH. Tel: 0171–713 1995. Comprehensive reports on human rights abuses in China.

June 4th China Support (an organization set up after the Tiananmen Square democracy demonstrations), PO Box 190, London WC1X 9RL. Tel: 0171–403 6080.

Jubilee Campaign (information and campaigns regarding religious persecution in China), c/o Wilfred Wong, David Alton's office, The House of Commons, Westminster, London.

Index on Censorship, Lancaster House, 33 Islington High Street, London N1 9LH. Tel: 0171–278 2313. Informative magazine on censorship worldwide including China.

Anti–Slavery International, Unit Four, Stableyard, Broomgrove Road, London SW9 9TL. Tel: 0171–924 9555. Campaigning to end slavery worldwide; presented Harry Wu with an award for his work in 1995.

International PEN: Writers in Prison Committee, 9/10 Charterhouse Buildings, Goswell Road, London EC1M 7AT. Tel: 0171–253 3226.

Amnesty International, International Secretariat, 1 Easton Street, London WC1X 8DJ. Tel: 0171–413 5500.

Human Rights in China, 485 Fifth Avenue, 3rd Floor, New York, NY 10017. Tel: 212–661 2909

Tibet Support Group UK, 7–9 Islington Green, London N1 8XH. Tel: 0171–359 7573. An independent membership organization campaigning for the rights of the Tibetan people to freedom and independence.

Tibet Information Network, 7 Beck Road, London E8 4RE. Tel: 0181–533 5358. An independent news network supplying up-to-date reports and comprehensive background materials.

Bibliography

Anchee Min, *Red Azalea* (Gollancz, 1993).

Christopher Andrew and Oleg Gordievsky, *KGB: The Inside Story of Its Foreign Operations from Lenin to Gorbachev* (Sceptre, 1990).

Jules Archer, *China in the Twentieth Century* (Macmillan, 1974).

Asia Watch, *Detained in China and Tibet* (Human Rights Watch, 1994).

John F. Avedon, *Exile from the Land of the Snows* (Michael Joseph, 1984).

Bette Bao Lord, *Legacies: A Chinese Mosaic* (Chapmans, 1990).

Geremie Barmé and John Minford, *Seeds of Fire: Chinese Voices of Conscience* (Far Eastern Economic Review, 1986).

Robert Barnett and Shirin Akiner (eds), *Resistance and Reform in Tibet* (Hurst, 1994).

Bei Dao, *Waves: A Novella and Six Stories* (Sceptre, 1989).

George Black and Robin Munro, *Black Hands of Beijing: Lives of Defiance in China's Democracy Movement* (Wiley, 1993).

Bo Yang, *The Ugly Chinaman and the Crisis of Chinese Culture* (Allen & Unwin, New South Wales, 1992).

David Bonavia, *The Chinese: A Portrait* (Penguin, 1989).

Elinor J. Brecher, *Schindler's Legacy: True Stories of the List Survivors* (Hodder & Stoughton, 1994).

Fox Butterfield, *Alive in the Bitter Sea* (Coronet, 1982).

John Byron and Robert Pack, *The Claws of the Dragon: Kang Sheng – The Evil Genius Behind Mao – and His Legacy of Terror in People's China* (Simon and Schuster, New York, 1992).

Joseph Campbell, *The Hero with a Thousand Faces* (Sphere, 1975).

Commission Internationale Contre le Régime Concentrationnaire, *The White Book on Forced Labour in the People's Republic of China,* vol. 1: The Hearings and vol. 2: The Record (CICRC, 1957/8).

Percy Craddock, *Experiences of China* (John Murray, 1994).

Deng Xiaoping, *Selected Works of Deng Xiaoping and Fundamental Issues in Present Day China* (Beijing, 1987).

Jean-Luc Domenach, *Chine: L'archipel oublié* (Fayard, 1992).

Michael R. Dutton, *Policing and Punishment in China: From Patriarchy to 'the People'* (Cambridge University Press, 1992).

R. Randle Edwards, Louis Henkin and Andrew J. Nathan (eds), *Human Rights in Contemporary China: A Study of the East Asian Institute and the Centre for the Study of Human Rights* (Columbia University Press, 1986).

Erik Erikson, *Childhood and Society* (Vintage, 1995).

Michael Fathers and Andrew Higgins, *Tiananmen: The Rape of Peking 1989* (*The Independent,* in association with Doubleday, 1989).

Robert Ford, *Captured in Tibet* (Wisdom, 1993).

Victor Frankl, *Man's Search for Meaning* (Pocket, 1984).

John Fraser, *The Chinese: Portrait of a People* (Fontana, 1982).

Bob Geldof, *Is That It?* (Penguin, 1986) (for its account of a hamster beheading at a trial for 'bourgeois deviationism', p. 220).

John Gittings, *China Changes Face: The Road from Revolution 1949–89* (Oxford University Press, 1990).

Anthony Grey, *Hostage in Peking* (Michael Joseph, 1970).

James Henry Grey, *China: A History of the Laws, Manners and Customs of the People. Volume I* (Macmillan, 1878).

Gu Hua, *A Small Town Called Hisbiscus* (Panda, 1987).

George Hicks, (ed.), *The Broken Mirror: China after Tiananmen* (Longman, 1990).

Hong Kong Human Rights Commission, Hong Kong, *Human Rights Report 1991-2* The First Year Review of the Hong Kong Bill of Rights Ordinance.

W. J. F. Jenner, *The Tyranny of History: The Roots of China's Crisis* (Penguin, 1992).

Jung Chang, *Wild Swans* (Harper Collins, 1991).

Stanley Karnow, *Mao and China*, (Penguin, 1990).

Sam Keen, *Faces of the Enemy: Reflections of the Hostile Imagination* (Harper, 1986).

Brian Keenan, *An Evil Cradling* (Vintage, 1992).

Maxine Hong Kingston, *China Men* (Vintage, 1989).

Maxine Hong Kingston, *The Woman Warrior: Memoirs of a Girlhood among Ghosts* (Vintage, 1989).

Nicholas Kristof, and Sheryl WuDunn, *China Wakes* (Nicholas Brealey, 1994).

Milan Kundera, *The Art of the Novel*, (Faber, 1990).

Laogai Research Foundation, *The Laogai Handbook 1994 and 1995* (Laogai Research Foundation).

Leng Shaochuan and Chiu Hungdah, *Criminal Justice in Post-Mao China* (State University of New York Press, 1985).

Simon Leys, *Chinese Shadows* (Viking Penguin, 1977).

Simon Leys, *Broken Images* (Allison & Busby, 1979).

Simon Leys, *The Burning Forest* (Paladin, 1988).

Li Zhusui, *The Private Life of Chairman Mao* (Arrow, 1996).

Robert J. Lifton, *Revolutionary Immortality: Mao Tse-tung and the Chinese Cultural Revolution* (Weidenfeld & Nicolson, 1969).

Robert Jay Lifton, *Thought Reform and the Psychology of Totalism: A Study of Brainwashing in China* (Gollancz, 1961).

William Lindesay, *Marching with Mao: A Biographical Journey* (Hodder & Stoughton, 1991).

Liu Qing, 'Prison Memoirs', *Chinese Sociology and Anthropology*, vol. 5, nos 1-2 (fall/winter 1982-3).

Liu Shanqing, 'Encounter with Legalised Illegality: Liu Shanqing, the Democracy Movement, and Prison Reforms', *Chinese Sociology and Anthropology*, vol. 26, no. 4 (summer 1994).

Arnost Lustig, *Diamonds of the Night* (Quartet, 1989) (fiction).

Mao Zedong, *Chairman Mao Tse-Tung on People's War* (Foreign Languages Press, Beijing, 1967).

Mao Zedong, *Selected Readings of Mao Tse-Tung* (Foreign Languages Press, Beijing, 1971).

Anatoly Marchenko, *My Testimony* (Sceptre, 1987).

David McLellan, (ed.), *Marx: The First 100 Years* (Fontana, 1983).

Maurice Mesner, *Mao's China and After: A History of the People's Republic* (Free Press, 1977).

Samuel M. Meyers and Albert D. Biderman (eds), *Mass Behaviour in Battle and Captivity: The Communist Soldier in the*

Korean War, Research Studies directed by William C. Bradbury (University of Chicago Press, 1968).

Stanley Milgram, *Obedience to Authority* (Harper & Row, 1974).

Kate Millett, *The Politics of Cruelty: An Essay on the Literature of Political Imprisonment* (Viking, 1994).

Steven W. Mosher, *Made in the Chinese Laogai: China's Use of Prisoners to Produce Goods for Export* (Claremont Institute, 1990).

Mummy, Daddy and Me: Chinese Children Talk about Their Parents (New World Press, Beijing, 1986).

Andrew J. Nathan, *Chinese Democracy* (University of California Press, 1986).

Nien Cheng, *Life and Death in Shanghai* (HarperCollins, 1993).

Lynn Pan, *Tracing It Home* (Secker & Warburg, 1992).

Jean Pasqualini, (Bao Ruowang) and Rudolph Chelminsky, *Prisoner of Mao* (Penguin, 1976).

Brian Power, *The Puppet Emperor: The Life of Pu Yi, Last Emperor of China* (Corgi, 1986).

Lucian Pye, *China: An Introduction* (Little Brown, 1984).

Irina Ratushinskaya, *Grey Is the Colour of Hope* (Sceptre, 1989).

David Rice, *Conversations with Young Chinese* (Harper Collins, 1992).

Omar Rivabella, *Requiem for a Woman's Soul* (Penguin, 1986).

David Rosenberg (ed.), *Testimony: Contemporary Writers Make the Holocaust Personal* (Times, 1989).

Nawal el Sa'adawi, *Memoirs from the Women's Prison* (Women's Press, 1986).

Edward W. Said, *Orientalism: Western Conceptions of the Orient* (Penguin, 1991).

Harrison Salisbury, *Tiananmen Diary: Thirteen Days in June* (Unwin Hyman, 1989).

Harrison Salisbury, *The New Emperors: China in the Era of Mao and Deng* (Harper Collins, 1993).

Sansan, as told to Bette Bao Lord, *Eighth Moon: The Real-life Story of a Chinese Childhood, and Its Extraordinary Sequel* (Sphere, 1984).

Orville Schell, *Mandate of Heaven: A New Generation of Entrepreneurs, Dissidents, Bohemians and Technocrats Lays Claim to China's Future* (Warner, 1995).

S. Schram (ed.), *The Political Thought of Mao Tse-Tung* (Frederick A. Praeger, 1963).

Shao Daosheng, *Preliminary Study of China's Juvenile Delinquency* (Foreign Languages Press, Beijing, 1992).

Alexander Solzhenitsyn, *One Day in the Life of Ivan Denisovich* (Gollancz, 1963) (fiction).

Alexander Solzhenitsyn, *The First Circle* (Fontana, 1970) (fiction).

Alexander Solzhenitsyn, *The Gulag Archipelago,* vol. 1 (Collins/Harvill and Fontana, 1974).

Alexander Solzhenitsyn, *The Gulag Archipelago,* vol. 2 (Collins/Harvill, 1975).

Jonathan D. Spence, *The Search for Modern China* (Norton, 1991).

Tang Boqiao, for Asia Watch, *Anthems of Defeat: Crackdown in Hunan Province 1989–92* (Human Rights Watch, 1992).

Debbie Taylor, *My Children, My Gold: Meetings with Women of the Fourth World* (Virago, 1994).

Paul Theroux, *Riding the Iron Rooster: By Train through China* (Penguin, 1989).

Colin Thubron, *Behind the Wall* (Penguin, 1988).

Anne Thurston, *A Chinese Odyssey: The Life and Times of a Chinese Dissident* (Scribner, 1991).

Anne Thurston, *Enemies of the People* (Harvard University Press, 1988).

Paul Tillich, *The Courage to Be* (Fontana, 1962).

Tung Chiping and Humphrey Evans, *The Thought Revolution* (Coward-McCann, 1966).

Nora Wain, *The House of Exile* (Cresset, 1933).

Susan Whitfield (ed.), *After The Event: Human Rights and Their Future in China* (Wellsweep, 1993).

Susan Whitfield (ed.), *June Fourth Briefing Papers on China* (June 4th China Support, 1993).

Susan Whitfield (ed.) *Religious Persecution in the People's Republic of China* (Joint Report of Jubilee Campaign and June 4th China Support, 1994).

Harry Hongda Wu, *Laogai: The Chinese Gulag* (Westview, 1992).

Harry Hongda Wu, with Carolyn Wakeman, *Bitter Winds: A Memoir of My Years in China's Gulag* (Wiley, 1994).

Wu Ningkun and Li Yikai, *A Single Tear: A Family's Persecution, Suffering, Love and Endurance in Communist China* (Sceptre, 1994).

Yue Daiyan, with Carolyn Wakeman, *To the Storm* (University of California, 1985).

Zhang Jie, *As Long As Nothing Happens, Nothing Will* (Virago, 1988) (fiction).

Zhang Jie, *Love Must Not Be Forgotten* (Penguin, 1987) (fiction).

Zhang Xianliang, *Mimosa* (Panda, 1985) (fiction).

Zhang Xianliang, *Half of Man Is Woman* (Viking Penguin, 1988) (fiction).

Zhang Xianliang, *Getting Used to Dying* (Penguin, 1991) (fiction).

Zhang Xianliang, *Grass Soup* (Secker & Warburg, 1994) (autobiographical fiction).

Zhang Xinxin and Sang Ye, *Chinese Profiles* (Panda, 1986).

Y. H. Zhao and John Cayley (eds), *Under Sky under Ground: Chinese Writing Today: 1* (Wellsweep, 1994).

Index